EURIPIDES

Electra
Phoenician Women
Bacchae
Iphigenia at Aulis

EURIPIDES

Electra
Phoenician Women
Bacchae
Iphigenia at Aulis

Translated, with Notes, by
Cecelia Eaton Luschnig and Paul Woodruff

Introduction by
Cecelia Eaton Luschnig

Hackett Publishing Company, Inc.
Indianapolis/Cambridge

Printed in the United States of America

15 14 13 12 11   1 2 3 4 5 6 7

For further information, please address:
Hackett Publishing Company, Inc.
P.O. Box 44937
Indianapolis, IN 46244-0937

www.hackettpublishing.com

Cover design by Brian Rak and Abigail Coyle
Text design by Meera Dash
Map by William Nelson
Composition by Agnew's, Inc.
Printed at Sheridan Books, Inc.

The translation of *Electra* featured in this volume first appeared in *The Electra Plays* (Hackett 2009); the translation of *Bacchae* first appeared in *Bacchae* (Hackett 1998).

Library of Congress Cataloging-in-Publication Data

Euripides.
    [Selections. English. 2011]
    Electra, Phoenician women, Bacchae, Iphigenia at Aulis / translated, with notes, by Cecelia Eaton Luschnig and Paul Woodruff ; introduction by Cecelia Eaton Luschnig.
        p.   cm.
    Includes bibliographical references.
    ISBN 978-1-60384-460-4 (pbk.) — ISBN 978-1-60384-461-1 (cloth)
    1. Electra (Greek mythology)—Drama.   2. Seven against Thebes (Greek mythology)—Drama.   3. Bacchantes—Drama.   4. Iphigenia (Greek mythology)—Drama.   I. Luschnig, C. A. E.   II. Woodruff, Paul, 1943–   III. Title.
    PA3975.A2   2011b
    882'.01—dc22   2010044056

The paper used in this publication meets the minimum requirements of American National Standard for Information Sciences—Permanence of paper for Printed Library Materials, ANSI Z39.48–1984.

Contents

Introduction   vii

Map: Greece in the Mycenaean Era   xxxvii

On the Translations   xxxviii

Electra   1

Phoenician Women   65

Bacchae   143

     Bacchae: The Lost Speeches   204

Iphigenia at Aulis   209

Select Bibliography   279

Introduction

Euripides' Late Plays

The four plays in this volume all count as late Euripidean tragedies, beginning with *Electra,* written probably in the teens of the fifth century B.C.E., followed by *Phoenician Women,* produced around 410, and finally *Bacchae* and *Iphigenia at Aulis,* written around 406, the year of Euripides' death, but produced posthumously, with the latter left unfinished. All suffer textual problems: the incomplete condition of *Iphigenia at Aulis* was taken as a challenge, not only by Euripides' heir but by several later producers; major lacunae at the end of *Bacchae* have been filled in from various sources; the ending of *Phoenician Women* is somewhat chaotic; and *Electra,* the least battered, suffers from suspected interpolation and doubtful assignment of lines. *Phoenician Women* and *Bacchae* treat legends connected with the city of Thebes, and both are concerned with the city's religious life and the relations among Dionysus, Ares, and Apollo. The chorus of *Phoenician Women* is made up of captives dedicated to Apollo; that of *Bacchae,* of Dionysus' devotees. In both plays Thebes is a place people leave, in which the royal family ends up dead or dispersed. These two plays belong to the Euripidean canon, ten plays consciously preserved and anthologized for reading in schools. *Electra* and *Iphigenia at Aulis* are not part of the canon but were preserved fortuitously in a collection of the complete plays of Euripides arranged in alphabetical order by title that survives in two manuscripts covering the titles beginning with the letters eta through kappa. The latter two plays deal with events at either end of the Trojan War and concern the fates of the children of Agamemnon and Clytemnestra. All of the plays in this volume treat troubled parent-child relationships. In each, sacrifice is a striking feature. Of the four, only *Bacchae* is generally considered a well-made play, universally accepted (along with *Hippolytus, Medea,* and *Alcestis*) as one of Euripides' best plays.

In these four plays Euripides gives special attention to issues that interested him throughout his career, especially the blurring of polar opposites such as slave–free, freedom–compulsion, male–female,

Greek–foreigner, human–god, human–beast, friend–enemy, and victim–agent. For example, in *Phoenician Women* the enemy at the city's gates is the much-loved son and brother of the women whose lives he risks. In *Iphigenia at Aulis* the commander in chief of the Greek forces perceives himself as a slave to the Greek army. His daughter, who really has no freedom, asserts a choice that is not hers in order to die freely. In *Bacchae* the women who have broken free of the confinement of a society that kept women secluded have done so under compulsion and god-imposed madness. In *Electra* the woman takes on the manly role by planning the matricide and even helping with the actual deed when her brother's hand falters.

The playwright also makes his audience look anew at assumptions by calling the heroic and literary tradition into doubt. In *Electra* the heroic tale of Orestes' revenge looks quite different when removed from the Mycenaean palace to a poor rural farmstead and performed by people from everyday life. In *Iphigenia at Aulis* Euripides teases us with the possibility that the Trojan War did not have to take place. *Phoenician Women* rings so many changes on the story as it was known from Aeschylus and Sophocles that it must have left the audience gaping. Euripides creates a hospitable Aegisthus, a regretful Clytemnestra, a Polynices with right on his side, a Menelaus who is ready to remarry and call the whole thing off, and a Pentheus who, after all his threats of violence against the women of the city and his family, turns out to be a sweet and caring grandson ever protective of his grandfather's dignity. In all four of the plays Euripides' interest in the intellectual innovations of the Sophists is evident: in Orestes' pretentious musings on the nature of nobility; in Eteocles' immoralist views on power; in Tiresias' rationalistic explanation of Dionysus' birth and nature; in Agamemnon's sophistic opportunism and ability to argue both sides of the question.

All in all, these four very different plays offer their readers an adventure in late fifth-century Greek thought and theater practice. Most of all they warn us against seeing the world in terms of black and white, good and evil, through some stunningly beautiful poetry and breathtaking human action and suffering. And they remind us of the value not only of great works but also of not-so-great works of great writers.

Electra

The Electra Plays

Electra has a special place among Euripides' tragedies in being his
only extant play that follows the same basic plot as surviving plays
by both Aeschylus and Sophocles: the revenge taken by Orestes on
his father's killers. Aeschylus' *Libation Bearers* and the *Electra*s of
Sophocles and Euripides all treat the return of Orestes to Argos
unannounced and incognito, the recognition of Orestes and his reunion with Electra, and the killing of Aegisthus and Clytemnestra
(with the order reversed in Sophocles). Both *Electra*s are full of references to Aeschylus' version and clearly respond to it: the variations on the tokens by which Orestes is identified, on the use of
vessels (pitchers for libations, an urn of ashes, or a water jug), and
on the role of Apollo's oracle in motivating Orestes are examples
of intentional allusion to the older playwright's masterpiece. Both,
furthermore, move Electra from the sidelines to the center of the
action. In Aeschylus she participates with Orestes and the chorus
in the long lyric exchange (*kommos*) that attempts to summon the
aid of their dead father's spirit, but she is dismissed before Orestes
turns to the deed. While Sophocles' Electra suffers in a grander, more
operatic way, Euripides' protagonist is the only one of the three to
be present at and participate in the matricide. In Euripides she holds
the sword when Orestes recoils from the deed. In Sophocles she
remains outside egging him on: her only weapons are words, however potent. Presentation of the matricide and its aftermath is a
crucial area of difference in the treatments. In both Aeschylus and
Euripides the fact that Orestes must kill his mother in order to
avenge his father is central and leads him to question the deed mo-
ments before he perpetrates it. Not so in Sophocles: neither Orestes
nor Electra feels any qualms before or after the matricide. Nor do
Furies (Erinyes) explicitly come to haunt Orestes as they do in both
Euripides and Aeschylus.

   Although cogent arguments have been made on both sides, the
jury is still out on the important question of which of the two later
treatments was earlier. Neither can be firmly dated by external evidence. Metrical evidence is inconclusive: Sophocles' *Electra* is placed
between 420 and 410 B.C.E.; Euripides' between 422 and 417 or
415 and 413. The argument for the earlier date relies almost solely
on metrical evidence, and that in favor of a later date uses both
perceived references to contemporary events in Euripides' version

(especially a reference to the Sicilian expedition of 415 B.C.E., 1347–48) and a possible announcement of Euripides' *Helen* of 412 B.C.E. (1280–83). The plot and characters of Euripides' *Orestes*, in many ways a sequel to his *Electra*, have led some critics to the conclusion that Sophocles' *Electra* is a response to Euripides' *Electra*, while his *Orestes* brings the story back down to earth. This shows a rather unsophisticated conception of the relation of playwrights to their work and their motives for producing a new play.

#

See Gregory 2009, pp. xxi–xxxii; Hartigan 1991, pp. 85–88; Roisman and Luschnig 2011, esp. pp. 6–11, 28–32; Ronnet 1970; Schlegel 1833 (tr. 1946), pp. 122–33; Segal 1985; Solmsen 1982, pp. 38–47; Webster 1968, pp. 38–43; Zuntz 1955, pp. 64–71.

Questions of Genre

Euripides' *Electra* is full of everyday objects: household utensils, agricultural tools, implements for sacrifice. Food, domestic animals, and clothing—from the rags of Electra and the Old Man to the dazzling royal garb of Clytemnestra and her slaves—receive more attention than in most tragedies. The rustic setting is more suggestive of folktale than tragedy, which usually takes place in front of a royal palace, as is the marriage of the royal Electra to a poor farmer. Such quotidian details have led some critics to describe the play as somehow less than or other than tragic. The poverty and simplicity of the setting as well as the recognition of Orestes (after what seems to many an untragic parody of Aeschylus' recognition scene) by means of a scar are reminiscent of scenes from Homer's *Odyssey* (14; 19.390–475). To Aristotle, however, both the *Iliad* and the *Odyssey* were prototypes for tragedy (*Poetics* 1449a1), a fact that encourages us to accept a broad definition of the tragic genre, even when Euripides plays with his audience's expectations of what tragedy is.

The displacement of the setting and the conversion of the royal and heroic into the mundane, whether of objects or of persons, is at the heart of Euripides' version. In Aeschylus and Sophocles the palace and the tomb of Agamemnon are central to the scene and the action. In all three plays Orestes returns to his native Argos to reclaim his palace, which is part of his birthright. He prays at his father's tomb, whether it is part of the set, imagined just offstage, or farther away; and in both Sophocles and Aeschylus he enters his palace to perform the matricide. Euripides has removed both palace and tomb, making the attainment of Orestes' goal more elusive and illusionary. He never even sets foot inside his native city, either before or after the matricide. The tomb of Agamemnon, which is the focus of Electra's feelings in the other plays, is off in the distance. The theme of hospitality is present in all three plays. In order to carry out his revenge, Orestes must enter the scene building. In Sophocles and Aeschylus he uses the ruse that he brings news of Orestes' death and is welcomed into the palace. In Euripides his news is that Orestes is alive but that he is not present. With an irony befitting her reduced circumstances, Electra finds herself in the position of browbeating her husband for inviting well-born guests into their poor and squalid hovel. This is, in any case, not the house in which the victims of their revenge are to be found: Aegisthus must be killed at his country estate and their mother summoned to the scene, with the ruse that a child has been born to Electra, the very event Clytemnestra most feared.

The change in setting and the constant reference to the everyday world of work and childbearing make us rethink this heroic story. When performed by characters from real life (a housewifely Electra, an Orestes testing his Sophistic education) upon less villainous victims (a welcoming, cordial Aegisthus and a Clytemnestra who is concerned with her daughter's well-being and repentant of her past deeds), it loses its glamour, but in the suffering, loss, and separation of the characters and in their recognition of their wrongdoing and failure, it remains tragic. The solution by the dei ex machina with their criticism of Apollo only adds another jarring note to the feeling of displacement and the realization that these obsessed characters do not belong in the world of ordinary mortals and perhaps, also, that this is not a story to be used as a guide for proper behavior as it was by Homer in the *Odyssey*.

#

See de Jong 1990; Foley 1985, pp. 43–45; Gellie 1981, pp. 1–12; Goff 1991, pp. 259–67; Gregory 1999–2000, pp. 59–74; Hammond 1984, pp. 373–87; Jones 1962, pp. 239–60; Knox 1979; Lloyd 1986; Luschnig 1995, pp. 87–120; Marshall 1999–2000; Michelini 1987, pp. 182–230; Roisman and Luschnig 2011, esp. pp. 241–46.

Inorganic Odes

As early as Aristotle, Euripides was criticized for not making his choruses as integral to the play as a whole as Sophocles did (*Poetics* 1456a19). Though the chorus participates in the plot and interacts with the characters, *Electra* is a good example of this perceived fault.

Electra has an unusual distribution of spoken and sung parts. There are only three stasima (formal choral odes): first 432–86; second 699–746; third 1147–71, interrupted by Clytemnestra's death cries. But there are many sung parts: Electra's mournful monody (solo) before the entrance of the chorus; two short choral celebrations, one right after the recognition of Orestes (585–95) and another after the Messenger's speech announcing the death of Aegisthus (859–65, 873–79); a formal and perhaps ominous greeting to Clytemnestra (988–97); the *kommos* (lyric exchange between actors and chorus, 1177–1237); and, finally, the chanted anapestic ending (1292–1359). Except for the two mythological odes, the chorus is well integrated and functions like another actor in the play and a good parallel and contrast to Electra: they bring news, offer sympathy and encouragement, and by their normalcy provide contrast to Electra's single-mindedness while at the same time taking her side against her mother, and they join in both the joy and the remorse.

While it is a recognized function of the chorus to fill in background and extend the story in time and space, the first and second stasima could almost stand as poems in their own right. The first ode takes us back to a beginning, just before the sailing to Troy. The second looks to an even more remote past but draws a close parallel to what is taking place offstage during the choral song.

The Achilles Ode (as the first stasimon, 432–86, is called) immediately follows the domestic episode that ends with Electra scolding her husband and sending him off to summon Agamemnon's old slave from the fields. One could hardly ask for a greater contrast between that rude scene and the sparkling, lively picture of ships and dolphins dancing together as the hero goes off to the war in which he will win glory and be killed. It is as if Orestes and Electra are only playing at being heroes. The ode becomes increasingly darker and more in tune with the second half of the play with the slaying of the Gorgon (458–62, a scene added to Achilles' armor), which is to be enacted in the play, not against a frightening monster but against a mortal woman (1221–23, in which Orestes averts his eyes when he slays his mother). The ode ends with a sword to be thrust through Clytemnestra's neck (481–86) when, in the epode, the chorus mentions Achilles' sword and uses this reference to bring the song back to the plot. The death of Agamemnon (478–79) and the unmentioned deaths of Achilles and so many heroes and ordinary people are the war's outcome. The ode is followed by another domestic scene with Agamemnon's old attendant bringing food. This episode also turns dark as the siblings, with the Old Man's help, plot the murders of their kin.

The ode on Thyestes and the Golden Lamb (699–746) follows the departure of Orestes and his entourage to kill Thyestes' son Aegisthus. During this song the murder of Aegisthus is imagined as taking place. After beginning with a bucolic setting, once more the ode turns dark as the chorus sings of secret and shameful doings in the palace. The parallel between the adultery of Thyestes with Atreus' wife and that of Aegisthus and Clytemnestra is clear enough. The horrors (the slaughter of Thyestes' children and cannibalism) that follow the first are left unspoken; those that accompany the second are the subject of *Electra*.

Whether or not readers experience these odes as integral to the play, the correlation between the images in the odes and what happens on stage cannot be denied: the sword of Achilles and the sword of Orestes; slaying the Gorgon and the slaying of Clytemnestra; the lamb chosen from the flocks by the old slave and the lamb brought by Pan; the astronomical details of the decoration on Achilles' shield (464–68), the reversal of the sun's course (726–36), and the arrival of the Dioscuri through the sky in the exodos to close this chapter in the saga of the house of Atreus.

#

See King 1980; Kubo 1966; Morwood 1981; O'Brien 1964; Roisman and Luschnig 2011, pp. 14–16, 153–60, 181–86; Rosivach 1978; Walsh 1977; Zeitlin 1970.

The Principal Characters

—   Electra: a monomaniacal harridan, a victim of sexual jealousy toward her mother, who feels more sorry for herself than for her father or her brother, bullying her reluctant brother to commit matricide.

—   Orestes: a snobbish youth, uncertain of his identity, undecided about his mission, too cowardly to enter the city and face his father's killers, in need of his sister's help and stronger personality.

Do these characters reach the heroic stature of their counterparts in other tragedies? At least since Aristophanes, Euripides was known for deflating his characters and making them more like living human beings than heroes from the distant past. Even so, Aristotle called him the "most tragic of poets" (*Poetics* 1460a11; 1453a10). In defense of the two principals, Electra is a young woman whose expectations have been deceived. She is deprived of her home and her family, and because her mother's lover inadvertently married her off to a poor but good man, she is even denied the chance to have children. She is left to mourn without even the satisfaction of being seen by her mother or Aegisthus (something Sophocles' Electra glories in). The little generosity of spirit that she has left she shows to her husband, in sincerely desiring to make his life better by helping around the house (72–76, even if her motives are mixed) and in defending his honor (253, 261). Orestes, on the other hand, though now on the road, was brought up to a life of privilege in the home of his uncle Strophius. From his first speech in the play we know that his decision to take vengeance on his father's murderers has been made (89), and it does not change. Unlike other Oresteses, he has come to the Argolid without a plan on how to take his revenge (614) and in fact he is looking for his sister (98) as a helper and coconspirator (100). That he remains incognito for so long may be understood as a sign of reluctance to do the deed and take up the identity that must be his as soon as he is recognized. In forming a plan he needs the help of others, as he said at the beginning, but once the plan to kill Aegisthus is made, he does not hesitate but sets out at once (669). Before killing his mother he shows the same reluctance as Aeschylus' Orestes (*Libation Bearers* 899–902) and in fact questions the oracle (*Electra* 962–81), something Pylades dissuades him from in *Libation Bearers*.

The characters in Euripides' *Electra* are presented in new roles and new settings that take away some of the heroic-age respectability from the story. In addition, their enemies are given certain positive characteristics. Clytemnestra prevented Aegisthus from killing Electra (28); she seems genuinely concerned for her daughter's sorry state (1107–8) and even shows some contrition for her past misdeeds (1105–6, 1109–10). Aegisthus, for all the paranoia attributed to him by the Farmer and Electra, is a generous host, so unwary that he provides his killer with the murder weapon (779, 784–87; 817, 836–37). Finally, Euripides has not neglected the Farmer but provided him with his own parallel tragedy, that of a man whose life is disrupted, first by being given a royal wife he feels he cannot touch and then by being taken from the land his family has worked for generations (35–36, 1286–87). His translation to the mythical realm is one of the folktale elements in the play, but, as often, it has a darker side: unlike characters in folktales, this man never wished for wealth or a life with the rich and famous.

#

See Arnott 1981; Denniston 1939, pp. xxvi–xxxiii; Halporn 1983; Hartigan 1991, p. 113; Luschnig 1995, pp. 151–56; Roisman and Luschnig 2011, esp. pp. 246–59; Tarkow 1981; Thury 1985.

Phoenician Women

An Overstuffed Play

Phoenician Women (*Phoenissae*) is Euripides' version of the end of the story of Oedipus, Jocasta, and their children. It is not one of the well-made plays to be found in anthologies of ten or twelve famous Greek dramas. In antiquity and the Middle Ages, however, it was among the most popular of Euripides' tragedies: it has the fullest scholia (ancient commentaries) of any Euripidean play and more surviving pieces of ancient manuscripts than any other tragedy. In part because it fills in gaps in the legend not covered by the other playwrights, *Phoenician Women* was part of the ancient canon, clear testimony to the facts that tastes change and the canon even of classical works is not eternal. Despite the neglect *Phoenician Women* has experienced in recent years, there is something especially Euripidean about the play: it is intellectually and aesthetically challenging, and it makes compelling reading in our ongoing search for answers or approaches to fundamental questions. How can people or families bear up under a life of ceaseless suffering? How can we face wrongs done not only to us but by us? Why is war so alluring to human beings and rational alternatives so unattractive?

An ancient Hypothesis (the blurb attached to some of the manuscripts) supplies our earliest criticism of the play. The first paragraph outlines the plot, but the second and third offer some cogent ancient opinions about the play.

(2) *Phoenician Women* is full of pathos in its treatment of the tragedy. Creon's son met his end, dying on behalf of the city [by throwing himself] from the wall; the two brothers died as well, at each other's hands; Jocasta also killed herself over her sons, and the Argives who made war on Thebes perished. Besides this, Polynices lies unburied, and Oedipus is driven from his homeland and his daughter Antigone along with him. The drama has many characters and is full of many excellent maxims.

(3) The theatrical effects are spectacular, but the play is overstuffed. Antigone watching from the walls is not part of the drama and Polynices enters under truce to no effect; in addition to everything else, Oedipus going into exile singing inanely is patched on out of the whole cloth.

#

See Burian and Swann 1981, p. 4; Craik 1988, pp. 58–59; Cribiore 2001; Kitto 1939, pp. 104–6; Luschnig 1995, pp. 160–63; Mastronarde 1994, pp. 3–11; Michelini 1987, p. 98; Webster 1966, pp. 94–95.

Phoenician Women and Other Theban Dramas

The stories from the Theban cycle were second only in popularity to those about the Trojan War as subjects for tragedy. Because little is known of the content of the Theban epics, the tragedies are our best source for the legend. While the ending of *Phoenician Women* covers some of the material treated in Sophocles' *Antigone*, the main event, the war, had been treated by Aeschylus in *Seven against Thebes* (467 B.C.E.), a single-minded play, in which it is clear from the beginning that Eteocles is the protagonist. *Phoenician Women*, on the other hand, goes off in a number of directions, and it is unclear who, if anyone, in its unusually large cast (of eleven characters in speaking roles) is the main character. Aeschylus' *Seven* was the last in his Theban trilogy (three plays written for performance together at the same festival) of which the first two, *Laius* and *Oedipus*, are now lost. What is sometimes referred to as the Theban trilogy of Sophocles is in fact three plays produced at widely different times: *Antigone* (about 442 B.C.E.), *Oedipus Tyrannus* (likely 428–425), and *Oedipus at Colonus* (Sophocles' last play, written around 406, but produced posthumously in 401). *Antigone* treats the day after the battle of the Seven against Thebes and is concerned with Creon's refusal to bury Polynices; *Oedipus Tyrannus* is about Oedipus' finding

out that he has already killed his father and married his mother,
background referred to again and again in *Phoenician Women*;
Oedipus at Colonus covers the exile and death of Oedipus, events
announced at the end of our play.

The Oracle Given to Laius   All three playwrights treat an oracle from Apollo at Delphi to Laius, Oedipus' father. Laius is childless. Jocasta fills in this detail in *Phoenician Women*, quoting the
oracle that tells Laius not to have a son because if he does, his son
will kill him (17–20). In Aeschylus' *Seven against Thebes* we hear
that three times Laius was told to "die without issue and save the
city" (746–49). In Sophocles' *Oedipus Tyrannus*, Jocasta reports the
oracle as saying that it is fated that Laius "die at the hands of a son /
That would be born to him and me" (713–14, tr. Meineck, not con-
ditional, as in Euripides and Aeschylus). In the same play Oedipus
himself has received an oracle that he repeats (791–93), not realiz-
ing what it has in common with his wife's. In Aeschylus the oracle
to Laius is political, referring as it does to the city's preservation; in
Sophocles it is only personal (though the play is political from its
opening scene of petition to the king and gradually turns personal
as Oedipus looks into himself); in Euripides it is personal and ex-
tends to the whole family, but it does not refer to the city, although
in the next generation the city is at stake because of the warring
brothers. The oracle to Laius says nothing about the incest in any
of these versions. In Aeschylus (*Seven against Thebes* 745–46, 750)
and Euripides (*Phoenician Women* 21–22), Laius is said to disobey
the oracle through lust.

Laius, naturally, tries to escape the oracle by getting rid of the
baby. As often happens, this effort to outrun the oracle—the simultaneous belief and disbelief in its finality—leads to its inevitable ful-
fillment. Of Aeschylus' *Laius*, which is believed to have treated the
death of Laius, there are no fragments of which scholars can be certain. In both *Phoenician Women* (26) and *Oedipus Tyrannus* (717–
22), Laius first pierces his son's ankles. Then the infant is given to
herdsmen to dispose of. He is then passed on to another herdsman
and taken to Corinth, to King Polybus and his wife (*Oedipus Tyrannus* 1022–40; *Phoenician Women* 28–31).

Oedipus at the Crossroads   Oedipus spends his childhood safe
in Corinth with parents who are not his blood kin. Ignorance, of
course, is the necessary condition for his committing the terrible
deeds of killing his father and marrying his mother. The Euripidean

Jocasta is unable to fully explain why her son left the safety of his home in Corinth, whether he heard something or had a vague suspicion about his origins (*Phoenician Women* 32–34). Sophocles' Oedipus is very explicit (779–93): at a banquet a man who had drunk too much wine "blurted out that I was not my father's son" (*Oedipus Tyrannus* 780, tr. Meineck). The slander grew, and he went away in secret to consult the oracle. Apollo sent him away dishonored (789), he says, with respect to what he had come for, but the god uttered terrible prophecies, saying:

> I would
> mate with my mother and reveal a race
> too vile to stand in the sight of a man.
> He said I would kill my father.
> (*Oedipus Tyrannus* 790–93, tr. Meineck)

At this, Oedipus flees, avoiding Corinth, and reaches the place where the king was slain, where three roads meet. A herald and an old man in a wagon try to cut him off and Oedipus strikes the charioteer, at which the old man hits him on the head with the goad (794–812). "And," says Oedipus, "I killed every last one of them" (813; tr. Meineck). In all the versions Laius and Oedipus meet at a crossroads: a fragment from Aeschylus' *Oedipus* says, "We were coming to a place where three highways branch off." Again Euripides is vague about the actual killing, but he makes some significant changes (*Phoenician Women* 35–45). Jocasta fills in the detail that Laius was going to the oracle to assure himself that the child was dead, but in this version neither reaches the oracle. Oedipus never hears that he was destined to kill his father and marry his mother. The cruelty of Laius resurfaces and the old wounds are reopened. Oedipus kills Laius and in an act of filial piety takes the spoils back to his father Polybus.

#

See Baldry 1956, esp. pp. 24, 36; Craik 1988, commentary; Luschnig 1995, pp. 171–82; Mastronarde 1994, pp. 17–30 and commentary; Meineck and Woodruff 2003.

Surprise in *Phoenician Women*

Because the myths on which Greek tragedies were built were so well known, the audience knew what the end would be and, it is sometimes said, Greek tragedy offers little or no surprise. Euripides' *Phoenician Women* makes us rethink this truism. It is a play full of surprises, making it exciting to imagine the reactions of its first audience. We have to have expectations of some kind in order to be surprised when watching a traditional story. Famous scenes in earlier Theban plays are reactivated and changed and even quite deliberately distorted in *Phoenician Women*. Some of the surprises are a product of the play's disjointedness, of things seeming to happen out of control or to no purpose, an unusual feature for a Greek tragedy. Others are founded on the scholarship of the author, as if Euripides wanted to fill in details left out by his predecessors.

Even the title is a surprise. It is not obvious that a play called *Phoenician Women* would be concerned with the Theban legend. Phrynichus (an early tragedian, contemporary of Aeschylus) had written a *Phoenissae*, but it was about events from the Persian War. *Phoenician Women*'s rooftop scene of the young pretragic Antigone and her servant is unique in extant tragedy. The chorus is no longer the citizen chorus of Aeschylus' *Seven against Thebes* or Sophocles' *Antigone* or *Oedipus Tyrannus*. The audience would wonder at first sight what a crowd of foreign women (conspicuous by their exotic dress) was doing in a city under siege. And yet their part is to give a survey of the history of Thebes, connecting the foundation of the city with the present war. The justice of Polynices' cause and the sympathy he receives must have come as a surprise. *Seven against Thebes* had emphasized the city, people, and land of Thebes and the violence and impiety of those attacking her. In *Antigone* Polynices had been called the screaming eagle swooping down to devour the city (110–16). That the two estranged brothers should meet would have been a delightful surprise to the Athenian audience, fond as they were of discussing everything in open debate. Eteocles' speech in the *agōn* (debate scene) is full of alarming political views. Besides this, Euripides breaks the convention that usually calls for a pair of matched harangues by adding a third speech, expounding democratic ideology from Jocasta herself. It is surprising that the brothers are still alive at the end of the first battle and that Jocasta and Antigone go off to witness their duel. In the exodos, the final battle is won by the Thebans because they keep their armor on and surprise the Argives, creating a plain of death (1470–72) and carrying off a victory (1478–79) that is democratic, if of dubious morality. The chaos of the final scene is also surprising, but much of it may not be genuine.

Perhaps the biggest surprise is the role of Jocasta. Everybody in the palace is related, but only Jocasta has a close, primary relationship to all the royal characters. Creon is her brother. Antigone (and Ismene, mentioned at 57), Polynices, Eteocles, and Oedipus are her children. She refers to Polynices and Eteocles by the relationship they bear to her (son to son, at 82–83), rather than to each other. Menoeceus is her nephew, but the relationship is closer to that of mother and son because she nursed him. In *Antigone* Creon's wife kills herself in despair over the loss of her last son Haemon. In *Phoenician Women* this role is taken by Jocasta, who reared Creon's children and dies in despair over her own. Her influence is felt in every scene, even when she is not present. Jocasta provides an emotional and rational center, holding together, at least loosely, the complex plot with its many characters. At the end, without her, even the plot falls apart. Creon turns cruel and stubborn, reverting to the roles of other Creons in other plays. Oedipus and Antigone, both long confined inside the palace, break out into a chaos of mourning and too many choices. Jocasta can be seen as a unifying element, though the randomness of events is a counterforce that militates against unity of action. The known end of the story also weighs against her efforts, as if, try as she and her author might, they cannot overcome the forces of death, destruction, and tradition.

Euripides has used familiar material to create a drama that is different from those of his predecessors. He has put Jocasta in charge of her own life and made her, for a brief moment, no longer dependent on the men in her family, and he has given her the chance to live out her life after the discovery of her marriage to her son. Polynices is the much-loved brother and son, and justice is attributed to his cause. Though his brother is shown to be a foolish strategist, in the actual battle his actions and ultimate sacrifice put him on a par with Aeschylus' brave and doomed Eteocles. Antigone's growth from girl to woman and the subdued but eerily dignified Oedipus add to the wonder. The story of Menoeceus at the center of the play is another novelty. The fact that these events seem random is deliberate. Sophoclean connectedness and the feeling that a divine pattern (not necessarily benign) is directing everything is replaced by primitive violence and superstition. But equally there are acts of social responsibility, altruism, goodness, and love—Jocasta's attempt to reconcile her sons; Creon's love for his son; Menoeceus' self-sacrifice; Antigone's devotion to her brother and father—again disconnected, but still balancing the brutality. At the end of this day in the life of

Thebes, the city is saved. The chorus, alien once more, can sing of victory because it is made up of foreigners, separated by many degrees from the royal family and even from the citizens. In spite of the brothers the city is not sacked. Many lives are lost and the regime is changed from the line of Cadmus to that of the *Spartoi* or Sown Men. Even epic glory is not won by the fratricidal warriors. Menoeceus, by offering another road to glory, through civilian heroism, earns a story, but it fills very few lines of the play and is soon overshadowed by events. Since Euripides probably invented Menoeceus and his sacrifice, his story faded after *Phoenician Women* went out of fashion.

\#

See Altena 1999–2000, pp. 313–14; Arthur 1977; Barlow 1986, pp. 57–60; Burgess 1978, pp. 107–8; Conacher 1967, pp. 92–101; Craik 1988, p. 41 and commentary; Foley 1985, pp. 106–46; Goff 1988; Loraux 1987, pp. 14–15, 26, 144; Luschnig 1995, pp. 161–98; Mastronarde 1994, pp. 28–30; Meltzer 2006, pp. 1–27; Meredith 1937; O'Connor-Visser 1987, pp. 73–98; Papadopoulou 2008, pp. 27–48; Podlecki 1962; Rawson 1970; Verrall 1895, pp. 231–33.

Three Actors Play Eleven Characters

Various suggestions have been made regarding the distribution of roles among the three actors available to each playwright. Because there are so many characters and none of them clearly the central figure, it seems a worthy subject of speculation to try to come up with a scheme that adds to the coherence of the piece. This is my suggestion:

Protagonist: Jocasta and Creon

Deuteragonist: Paidagogos, Eteocles, Tiresias, Messengers 1 and 2, Oedipus

Tritagonist: Antigone, Polynices, Menoeceus

This scheme gives the two major mature roles to the protagonist, who is on stage in every scene (except the rooftop dialogue) and plays to all the other characters. It also explains why neither set of brother-sister siblings meets on the scene. That the same actor would play Jocasta and Creon, both elderly, both statesmen trying to save their city and their sons, adds to both ethos and pathos. The deuteragonist plays all the functional roles as well as Eteocles and Oedipus, in my opinion an appropriately professional range for one actor. The three young people then are played by the tritagonist, also an accomplished actor. That Antigone and the brother she most loves would be played by the same actor adds pathos to the sad fact that the two never meet again. Menoeceus, who dies because of the selfishness of Polynices and shares the idealism of Antigone, is an appropriate third role. This division assumes a highly skilled professional troupe of actors and implies a desire by the author to show an ethical connection among the characters represented by the same actor, which, though it is by no means universally accepted, is still worth considering.

#

For other role assignments, see Craik 1988, p. 46; Mastronarde 1994, p. 16.

Bacchae

The Subject Is Dionysus

The ancient Greek tragedies were performed at festivals in honor of the god Dionysus, but, though tragedy may have originally been concerned with Bacchic themes, Euripides' *Bacchae* is the only surviving play about Dionysus. Dionysus is well known as the god of wine and intoxication, but he is more than that: "[Dionysus'] domain is . . . the whole of *hugra phusis*, not only the liquid fire of the grape, but the sap thrusting in a young tree, the blood pounding in the veins of a young animal, all the mysterious and uncontrollable tides that ebb and flow in the life of nature" (Dodds 1960, p. xii). He is the god of mystery cult and communion with the divine and of theater and dance. What all these have in common is that they allow humans to stand outside their narrow confines of identity. Seaford (2006, p. 11) speaks of "the power of Dionysos to transform individual identity": this is what ecstasy is (from Greek *ek-stasis,* "standing outside").

The basic pattern of the play is a familiar one. A human being resists a god. The god shows the difference between mortals and gods by destroying the defiant human with no regard for what we would call justice or fairness. In this case the god, Dionysus, is son of Zeus by the mortal woman Semélē, one of the daughters of Cadmus, Thebes' founding father. Semélē, according to some versions, because of her desire to see Zeus in all his glory, was consumed by lightning and died before the child was born, but he was rescued and was, in the popular story, born from Zeus' thigh (*Bacchae*, 286–95). The royal family of Thebes—Pentheus, the king, and his mother and her sisters, who are, respectively, the cousin and aunts of the god—refuse to accept the divinity of Dionysus. Before the play begins, the royal women, along with the ordinary women of the city, are taken over by the god, driven into Bacchic frenzy and forced to participate in his rites.

The heart of the play is a play within a play: the beginning and end are Dionysus' appearance *in propria persona* to announce first his presence and then his victory. At the beginning he tells us he is wearing the mask of a man, his own priest. At the end he appears as himself, that is, wearing the mask of Dionysus. In between, in what comprises the body of the play, he demonstrates who he is and what his rites are. Inside the play within a play is another play, the infatuation of Pentheus. All this might be thought of as metatheatrical: the play is about drama. The actor playing Dionysus puts on a mask and becomes his priest. The actor playing Pentheus puts on a costume and a wig and becomes a Bacchant. Once in costume each ceases to be himself and to be seen as himself. Like a god, an actor does not reveal himself, or in the case of Dionysus, the immortal most present to mortals; he reveals himself only to his initiates. Dionysus demonstrates his power; Euripides demonstrates the power of drama.

#

See Dodds 1960, pp. xi–l; Foley 1980, pp. 109–16, 126–33; Foley 1985, pp. 218–34; Seaford 2006, pp. 87–104; Woodruff 1998, pp. ix–xii.

Dionysus' Cult in the *Bacchae*

The play has often been taken as representing an actual historical event, the reception of the cult of Dionysus into Greece (Dodds 1960). Dionysus was a Greek god whose name appears in Linear B tablets from the thirteenth century B.C.E. from Pylos and Kea (Ceos), but he and his cult are treated as foreign and as newcomers to Greece. Though the play takes place in Thebes, it brings what Woodruff (1998, p. xii) calls "an Athenian sensibility" to the foundation of the cult. The Athenians were hostile to foreign cults, and Seaford suggests that "the aetiological sequence of rejection, crisis, acceptance may have provided for the Athenian polis a mythical model for the resolution of this tension between dislike of new cult and the need to accept it" (1996, p. 52). However we react to what happens on the stage, we also must understand that the cult exists to benefit the whole community and "was part of an orderly civic life" (Woodruff 1998, p. xvi). The democratic nature of Dionysus and his gift of wine makes him an especially appropriate god to bring about political cohesion in Athens, where there were in fact numerous celebrations of Dionysus, including the two major dramatic festivals. He has his own mysteries and also plays a part in the Eleusinian mysteries, Athens' own unique mystery cult.

The play is also about participating in the cult of Dionysus and is often seen to reflect initiation practice. Unfortunately, our knowledge of actual cult practices is imprecise, so that we cannot use the play as dogma. Greek literature tends to rely on myth more than actual cult practices. Still, as Seaford points out, "myth often merely expresses in an extreme form (too extreme to be actually enacted in the ritual) the symbolic significance of the ritual, so that even if maenads did not tear apart animals (as at *Ba.* 735–47) and eat them raw, such mythical savagery might be a valid means of interpreting the lesser wildness of actual maenadism" (1996, p. 37). Because he resists so strenuously, Pentheus experiences conversion as a violent process, too violent, of course, to parallel religious rituals. Initiation into the mysteries brought the initiate into direct contact with the god and promised a more fulfilling and happy life and a better life after death. Initiates into a mystery cult go from ignorance to knowledge, from darkness into the light; they pass through a symbolic death to full enlightenment. These are the characteristics of any initiation. They are perverted in Pentheus' personal initiation.

The play includes, whether in action, song, or narration, a considerable amount about the Dionysiac experience as well. Dionysus was accompanied by female worshipers, represented by the chorus. The lyrics of the parodos, sung by the chorus of initiates, have the characteristics of a cult hymn to Dionysus, giving his many names, the story of his birth, and the nature of his worship. The god was worshiped by bands (*thiasoi*) of women, Maenads, who danced ecstatically for the god in the mountains apart from men (like the women on Mount Kithairōn). Though intoxication is one of Dionysus' gifts to humankind, in *Bacchae* it is not present in the worshipers, either on the mountain or in the orchestra, but only in Pentheus' mind. Perhaps it is hinted at in the diplopia the king experiences after he comes under the god's spell (918–19). The divine madness of the enthusiasts (those who are *entheos*, that is, have the god in them) brings intensified mental power, but "Dionysian ecstasy is not something achieved by an individual on his own; it is a mass phenomenon and spreads almost infectiously" (Burkert, p. 162), a happening that is anathema to Pentheus as ruler. Some of what the play includes is fantastical: reason tells us milk does not flow from the ground, for example. But the peaceful picture of the Maenads at rest conveys their perfect freedom, which the tyrant Pentheus cannot abide. The god has paradoxically compelled the women to be free, driving them from the confines of their closed female chambers, even so far as to leave their children, sleep in the mountains, and suckle gazelles. It is, however, the potential violence of the spying men that turns them violent (728–64).

The cult is real, a fact of Hellenic religious practice, and therefore must prevail: "In bringing women from every Theban household to the mountainside, Dionysos disrupts every household for the sake of communal cult" (Seaford 1996, p. 49). As in other tragedies (*Hippolytus*, *Heracles*), the destruction of the royal family leads to a cult for the whole polis, conflating the god's mystery cult and the hero cult that worships the dead hero (Seaford 2006, pp. 86, 95).

#

See Burkert 1985, pp. 161–67; Dodds 1960, pp. xi–xxv and commentary; Foley 1980; Foley 1985, pp. 254–58; Seaford 1996, pp. 35–44 and commentary; Seaford 2006, pp. 27–48; Woodruff 1998, pp. xii–xvii, xl–xlii.

Blurring Distinctions and the Ambiguity of Tragedy

Throughout his career, Euripides blurs the polar distinctions of which Greek language and literature are so fond: free and slave; human and god; animal and human; male and female; Greek and non-Greek (in Greek, "barbarian"); young and old; inside and outside; city and wilderness; hunter and hunted; victim and agent. In no play are such distinctions more conspicuously blurred than in *Bacchae*. The conversion scene and its aftermath bring many of these together. Pentheus sees the beast in the god (920–22); he had seen him as a bull earlier (in the reported prison scene, 618), but there he had thought the bull was something other than the man/god. The violent, threatening Pentheus becomes docile as he is readied for being

led through the main thoroughfares of Thebes, but the beast inside
him is all that is seen by the Theban Maenads on Mount Kithairōn.
He meets his destruction as a beast but is finally recognized as a
man and as her once-loved child by his mother after she has led her
sisters in tearing him to pieces. The distinction between male and
female is blurred when the virile King Pentheus lets himself be
dressed in women's clothes and wig and paraded through the streets
of Thebes. From his former confidence and peculiar self-knowledge,
this exhibition is at once tragic and trivial: he asks to be conducted
through the middle of Thebes, still boasting of his machismo, in his
mother's dress, with crimped hair, worrying about the state of his
curls. The Maenads on Kithairōn overpower men. In the Dionysiac
experience, human and god fade into one. Dionysus is the god most
felt to be present among his worshipers. In the play, the god paradoxically appears as a man to reveal his divinity to his human devotees, who then become one with their god and receive his miraculous
powers. In appearance Pentheus becomes like his divine cousin,
whom he has taunted for effeminacy, when he becomes his wor-
shiper and his victim.

Part of the experience of drama is the blurring of the separation
between illusion and reality. The play presents us with one set of
Bacchae, the chorus of Asiatic women, the god's devotees; in the
play they are tamed, never ecstatic, but often—like their god—cruel
and vengeful. Another set of Maenads, the women of Thebes, do
not appear on stage except when they have ceased to be a community, and one of their number, their leader Agavē, represents them.
Yet the audience is constantly aware of their presence beyond the
scene. Their actions are twice described by messengers. Pentheus'
reaction to the first messenger is skeptical. What are we to believe?
We know such things do not happen, and the messenger describes
things he cannot have seen with his own eyes (765–68). Pentheus
will have to see for himself. Like it or not he will become our witness. Nobody makes a better witness than a doubter. When he goes
off to see for himself, his addled state of mind spoils even *his* cred-
ibility, though we are told that he comes out of it before the final
horror. Part of the irony is that in order to see for himself, Pentheus
has to pretend not to be himself. What he sees and what he suffers
are only narrated, but we do know how he was killed because the
result is manifested in the final scene. And we know that he was
seen as a wild animal because we see Agavē believing it. What we
see is the head of Pentheus fixed to her thyrsus, or more accurately,

we see the mask the actor wore, carried by the actor who played him, now in the role of his mother.

Can we say that the Maenads see clearly, that their god has given them the ability to see the essence under the costume, that they recognize the beast that is in Pentheus, in his violent nature and crude prurience? He was ready to slaughter the women, the wives and mothers of his fellow citizens, including his own mother. But that was not the whole of him. He had a gentler side that Euripides forces on our attention through Cadmus' farewell to his dead grandson (1308–22). Unlike Dionysus, the man-god-beast, there was only one Pentheus: "I am Pentheus, son of Agavē. My father was Echion." This is how he defines himself to Dionysus (507), perhaps too narrowly. He does not recognize that this new god, Semélē's unborn child, could make him more than himself, could liberate him from society's and even nature's laws. In his death we see the other side as well: that the Dionysiac experience makes a man less than himself, robbing him of the dignity of age and competence, of his freedom to make reasoned choices.

The name Pentheus means "man of pain or grief"; his mother Agavē is "Glory," his father Echion, the "Snake." Pentheus may not realize what he is saying, but his self-definition speaks of the aspirations of humanity and its limitations, what it means to be human, where we human beings are in the world. There's always another hand when one is talking about Greek tragedy. In Dionysus' realm, as Segal says, "fusion replaces boundary, and the mutually exclusive opposites of our everyday logic disturbingly coexist" (1986, pp. 284–85). This is part of mystic initiation, which "must abolish the fundamental categories that constitute personal identity" and "may . . . enact a controlled confusion of male with female, human with animal, living with dead, mortal with immortal" (Seaford 2006, p. 75).

#

See Foley 1980, pp. 122–26 passim; Rosenmeyer 1963, pp. 132–49; Seaford 1996, pp. 31–32; Seaford 2006, pp. 75, 96; Segal 1986, pp. 284–85; Segal 1997, pp. 27–54, 214–71; Woodruff 1998, pp. xii–xvii.

Interpretations

The literature on *Bacchae* reveals an array of interpretations worthy of Polonius' "tragical-comical-historical-pastoral" (*Hamlet,* Act II, scene ii) from mythistorical to tragicomical, psychopolitical, and socioreligious as well as the more mundane, such as structuralist, metatheatrical, psychoanalytical, and on and on. The play's most famous critic (though not held in much favor by classicists) is the German philosopher Friedrich Nietzsche, who in his *Birth of Tragedy* (1870) posited the theory of the development of tragedy through the tension between the Apollonian and the Dionysiac. To Nietzsche, the overrationalism of Euripides brought on the death of tragedy, even though the source of much of the philosopher's knowledge of Dionysus was *Bacchae* itself. The purpose and place of *Bacchae* in the Euripidean corpus has given rise to an impressive, if not to say obsessive, array of theses, among them:

— Recantation theory: Euripides recants his former atheism or agnosticism and returns to the religion of his fellow citizens. This notion, popular through the nineteenth century but subsequently discredited, presupposes that Euripides had been consistently attacking the gods.

— Rationalist theory: Euripides is still debunking the gods and religion. Dionysus is an impostor, a conjurer, a charlatan; his miracles are illusions; and the story is a pretense (Verrall 1910), an opinion that, like the recantation theory, misses the play's subtlety and complexity.

— Abstract issues: *Bacchae* is an indictment of the amorality and seductiveness of the myth (Winnington-Ingram). The play asks the fundamental questions "What is man?" and "What is knowledge?" (Rosenmeyer). Or it is a great "critique of culture" in the Euripidean theater of ideas (Arrowsmith 1963, p. 47). In the words of Philip Vellacott, "*The Bacchae* . . . is a play about freedom," which, to his mind, relates it to *Iphigenia at Aulis*, produced in the same year (pp. 223–24).

— Psychological interpretations: Because of Pentheus' obsessions and exclusions, the play lends itself to a psychoanalytic approach (Sale and others); Segal complements "a psychological by a structural approach" (1986, p. 285).

— Political interpretations: *Bacchae* confirms or questions Athenian civic ideology.

"Euripides' *Bacchae* demands interpretation on many levels." With these words, Helene Foley begins her brilliant essay (1985,

p. 205) on the play as drama about drama (see also Foley 1980; Segal 1997, esp. pp. 215–71 on *Bacchae* as metatragedy). The more the better: all these ideas add richness to our reading. We have no reason to believe or hope that the proliferation of interpretations will stop with us. For a reasonable and readable summary of interpretations, see Woodruff's introduction (1998, pp. xxix–xlii) and, more fully, Segal 1997.

#

See Dodds 1960, pp. xxxix–l; Foley 1985, pp. 205–58; Rosenmeyer 1963, pp. 127–28, 150; Sale 1977, pp. 80–123; Segal 1986, pp. 282–93; Segal 1997, pp. 349–93; Vellacott 1975; Verrall 1910, pp. 1–161; Winnington-Ingram 1998; Woodruff 1998, pp. xxix–xlii.

Iphigenia at Aulis

The State of the Text

Iphigenia at Aulis was produced posthumously by Euripides Minor ("the Younger"), identified by the sources as the playwright's son or nephew. Whether the play was left unfinished by its author or had not been edited for the stage, the textual problems are thought to begin with that first production and to have continued in subsequent revisions in the fourth century and thereafter. Every reader of a play must be a virtual director. This is true even when there are full stage directions. Ancient Greek plays are entirely without stage directions except those that are made clear in the actors' words, demanding that the reader block the action, pace it, choreograph the dances, compose the music, and direct the actors' voice, gait, and bearing, in addition to determining masks, scenery, props, and all that comes after those optimistic words, "Let's put on a play." For *Iphigenia at Aulis,* so corrupt is the text that every reader must also be a playwright, called upon to put together from a multiplicity of possibilities a drama that is coherent in character and plot and that makes sense as a piece of theater. James Diggle, editor and creator of volume 3 of the 1981 Oxford Classical Text (OCT) of Euripides, felt the need to invent a new set of sigla ranging from "not by Euripides" to "perhaps by Euripides." It being futile to arrive at "what Euripides wrote," we are blessed or cursed with many Iphigenias at Aulis (as Sean Gurd wisely and whimsically titles his 2002 book on the philological history of the play).

Of 1629 lines in the received text, Diggle accepts as *fortasse Euripidei* ("possibly Euripidean"), the most positive of his terms, the following [the lines in brackets are less certain]:

164–230
303–403 [366–75]
442–535 [465–70, 508–10, 520–21]
631–738 [635–37, 652, 665, 674–75, 681–94, 720–26]
819–918 [899, 900–916]
1036–1079
1120–1275 [1124–26, 1130–33, 1170–72, 1185, 1241–52, 1270]
1336–1402
1421–74 [1424–25, 1430–32, 1435–39, 1448–49, 1458–61]

Left out are the prologue (both parts), the ending (or epilogue), and most of the lyric sections: the parodos after the first strophic pair and epode, the first and second stasima, Iphigenia's lament, and her exit song. What remains is a series of scenes but not a coherent, performable play.

David Kovacs (2003) offers a more creative solution. Instead of trying to establish what Euripides wrote, he aims to determine what the audience saw at the first performance (*FP*). This alleviates the need to reject all that is not by Euripides since it is understood that Euripides Minor is responsible for some of the material. Instead, noting that there are two incompatible treatments of Calchas' prophecy—one that it was delivered publicly, the other that it was kept secret and therefore known to only a small circle of Agamemnon's fellow officers—Kovacs identifies the parts that make for a coherent plot around what he considers the genuine treatment of the prophecy: that it was known throughout the Greek camp. By using this criterion he is able to eliminate much from the text that is troubling on various grounds. Kovacs' *FP* text is as follows:

49–105 (Prologue, which must introduce the Old Man with the letter)
164–230 (First three stanzas of the parodos)
303–34, 442–64, 467–68, 538–42 (First Episode, omitting the brothers' *agōn*, the Messenger, Menelaus' change of heart, and the baby Orestes)
543–89 (First Stasimon)

631–748 (Second Episode, with major deletions at 633–37, 681–94)

751–800 (Second Stasimon, omitting the first half of the epode, the sorrows of the Trojan Women)

801–1035 (Third Episode, with major omissions at 919–43, 995–69, 973–1007, 1017–21)

1036–97 (Third Stasimon)

1098–1337 Exodos Part 1 (or Fourth Episode, with several shorter deletions and a major deletion at 1148–84)

1338–1474 and 1510–31 Exodos Part 2 (or Fifth Episode, with major omissions at 1407–30: Iphigenia's farewell song is omitted)

Although I find Kovacs' solution admirable, I have not followed it in the translation, in part because it leaves out some passages I am committed to and because custom frowns on the translator who overuses the scalpel. Instead I have included the work not only of the two members of the Euripides family but also that of the fourth-century producer called by Kovacs "the Reviser," who, in my opinion, was not altogether dramaturgically inept. The translation offers readers a rendering of the whole of the received text, with numerous passages bracketed (and explained in the notes), so that directors, whether virtual or theatrical, may choose what version to produce.

The prologue has long caused consternation. Although a few critics accept the received text in the order given, many choose between the parts of the prologue; others reverse their order. In his OCT of 1913, the standard text for several generations of readers, Gilbert Murray printed Agamemnon's iambic monologue (49–114) before the anapestic dialogue between Agamemnon and the Old Man (1–48), followed by lines 115–63. Willink (1971) argues for the variation 49–96, 1–48, 97–163 (the order I have chosen for my translation) because Euripides almost always begins with an expository monologue, and breaking up the dialogue for so long a speech (49–114) seems too awkward. Needed information is given in both parts. The play obviously had a prologue, so that deleting it altogether is not an option.

It is almost universally agreed that the "epilogue" (the section of the exodos after the departure of Iphigenia) as it stands cannot have been written by either Euripides, for reasons of style, metrics, language, taste, and theatrics. Diggle marks as *non Euripidei* ("not

Euripidean") 1578–1629 (and 1510–77 as *vix Euripidei,* "unlikely Euripidean"); Kovacs rejects from 1532 to the end. Taking 1531 as the end of the play does the most justice to Iphigenia's integrity as a young victim of sacrifice and her acceptance of it and to Clytemnestra's decision to hate her husband. It is likely that the epilogue was added by a later producer to bring the play into line with Euripides' earlier *Iphigenia among the Taurians* (c. 414–412 B.C.E., in which Iphigenia lives on after the sacrifice as a priestess of Artemis), in the same way that Aeschylus' *Seven against Thebes* was expanded so it would conform to the popular Sophoclean *Antigone.* Among the most contested passages between the prologue and epilogue are the scene in which the messenger announces the arrival of Clytemnestra and her children in camp (413–41); most of Achilles' indignant speech (919–43); and Clytemnestra's tale of her first husband and early life with Agamemnon (1148–84)—that is, all the passages that might surprise a reader or viewer.

In spite of the uncertainty of the text, interpretations of *Iphigenia at Aulis* show the variations common in the criticism of Euripides. Two areas are approached in particular: the meaning of the war and inconsistencies in characterization. Interpretations of the former range from seeing the play as a clarion call to Panhellenic unity against a common foreign foe to an antiwar drama in the vein of Euripides' *Trojan Women.* The latter focuses on the bridging of the *aporia* (impasse) that separates the mythical world of heroic virtues from Euripides' contemporary reality of cynicism, ambition, and deceit through an irrational and improbable anomaly of character.

\#

See Diggle 1981, p. 358; England 1891/1979); Foley 1985, pp. 102–5; Gurd 2005; Knox 1972; Kovacs 2003; Luschnig 1988, pp. 126–27; Michelakis 2006, pp. 105–14; Murray 1913; Page 1934; Willink 1971.

Anomaly of Character

At 1252 Iphigenia, pleading for her life, makes the unheroic statement, "To live badly is better than honorably to die." At 1318 she sings of the "the godless sacrifice of a godless father." Less than one hundred lines later she is ready to give herself for Greece and insists upon the sacrifice (1375–1401, 1474–75). Aristotle comments on this anomaly of characterization by saying, "The suppliant Iphigenia is nothing like the later one" (*Poetics* 1454a32). The contradiction could hardly be more obvious.

Iphigenia's change of mind, though unexpected, comes at the end of a long series of sudden about-faces. When we meet Agamemnon in the prologue, he has already made a decision (not to sacrifice his daughter, 94–96), reversed that decision (under pressure from his brother Menelaus, 99), and dispatched a letter to his wife telling her to send their daughter Iphigenia to the camp, and he is in the process of making up his mind for a third time (in the second letter countermanding the first, 115–20). Before he has a chance to reverse the last decision, Menelaus, who was previously hell-bent on the war and the sacrifice, suddenly reverses himself and renounces the war (477–503). At this, Agamemnon reverses his position of opposition to the sacrifice and declares it necessary (511–12), a decision that never changes, though its implementation is delayed for a thousand lines. Other characters are also shown in transition: Clytemnestra, a perfect wife, loyal and concerned with the social conventions, before our eyes turns into the woman likely to be obsessed with revenge whom we know from Aeschylus; Achilles, a young man almost indifferent to Iphigenia but determined to maintain his honor and integrity, becomes an ardent defender of the woman he never wooed.

Aside from Iphigenia herself, these are characters we know from other sources, from epic and early tragedy: Achilles and Agamemnon, bitter rivals at Troy because of the theft of Achilles' bride by his commander; Clytemnestra, the image of the powerful single-minded avenger burned into our minds by Aeschylus; Menelaus, husband of Helen in Homer's *Iliad* and *Odyssey* and Euripides' *Trojan Women*. In the course of the play the characters are seen through their own or others' decisions to take up the roles that will be theirs forever, dismissing alternatives, as Agamemnon decides once and for all that he will be the commander of the army at the expense of his family. Iphigenia never had such a role. She is absent from Homer. Traditionally she is (as in the parodos of Aeschylus' *Agamemnon*) a passive victim, sacrificed like an animal with a gag in her mouth to keep her from cursing her father and the expedition. Euripides allows her to choose a different role, not that of victim but as director of the action. She calls herself *heleptolis* (1476, "sacker of the city" or "city-destroyer"), a pun on Helen's name coined by Aeschylus (*Agamemnon* 689), usurping not only Helen's role as cause of the war but her father's as commander of the forces and destroyer of the city. To capture the pun in English, translators sometimes have used "Hell" to translate the first syllable of *heleptolis,* as in "Hell at the gates," Fagles; "Hell to the city," Meineck. The element *hel-* in *heleptolis* means "capture" or "destroy" and is not etymologically related to the name Helen, which, though of uncertain origin, is often associated with roots referring to light.

#

See Fagles 1975; Luschnig 1988, pp. 91–92, 126–27; Meineck 1998; Michelakis 2006, pp. 78–81; Michelini 1999–2000; Rabinowitz 1983, pp. 21–26; Sansone 1991, pp. 162–65; Siegel 1980.

Panhellenism and the Meaning of the War

A fight over a woman, war madness, a patriotic undertaking against foreign aggression, Panhellenism: which of these is the cause of the Trojan War that is presented in the play? By beginning with the courting of Helen and the oath of Tyndareos (51–65, described by no fewer than four expressions for oath-taking, 58–60), Agamemnon makes clear that Helen's marriage is at the heart of the conflict. The erotic side is also there from the beginning, in the desire for Helen accompanied by the suitors' violence (53–54), in Helen's choice (69), in the description of the foreign lover and Helen's second choice (73–75), and in Menelaus' passion for war (77–79). A second motive for the war comes in with Menelaus' petulant response to Agamemnon's decision not to sacrifice his daughter; the Greeks, he claims, are being thwarted from doing a great deed against the "barbarians" (370–72). Even before this Menelaus had called up the oath of Tyndareos (78), which is also fraught with Panhellenic associations (51–52), except that its wording applies to Greek and foreigner alike (65). It was by chance that the man who seduced Helen away from her rightful husband was foreign (and not one of her original suitors and, therefore, not one of the signatories to the Tyndarean oath). In his opening monologue Agamemnon is careful to stress the frivolous side of both the oath and the mustering of troops and to make sure that everyone knew that as an already married man (50), he was above it all. On the other hand, Eros, which in this situation signifies an irrational passion for war and a desire to die gloriously, is needed to inspire armies to fight and face death against all reason and self-interest. This is true even when the Eros involved is called a "fierce passion" (808, *deinos Erōs*), sickness (411), and madness (1264).

Menelaus, being the most interested party, makes the least credible witness for the argument that the war is not for him but for the glory of Greece. He is dismissed by his brother as merely wanting to hold his beautiful wife in his arms (385–86). The patriotic argument is further deflated when Menelaus renounces his claim and suggests that he could remarry (485–86) and the army be dismissed (495). What is most astounding is that for a short period of time (from Menelaus' change of heart until 510) there is no longer a reason for the war or the sacrifice. There is no one, at least of the participants in the drama, who favors it. At this point Agamemnon speaks up out of the blue to assert that the sacrifice is necessary. The girl has arrived in camp—whether the plan to sacrifice her is already generally known or has only been shared with a few, news will soon spread. The army will rise up. As so often in tragedy, the "facts" are ambiguous. The army at rest as described by the chorus was far from mutiny. Odysseus is charged with ambition by Agamemnon, but ambition is not restricted to him (as Menelaus makes clear in his description of Agamemnon's campaign for office, 337–42). When Achilles comes onstage to complain, it is to report not rebellion but boredom. His men are ready to deploy or to go home. In any case Agamemnon's new motivation is not so much Panhellenic patriotism as fear of the mob (514–35).

When next the motivation for the war and sacrifice comes up, it is in Clytemnestra's denunciation of Agamemnon, especially at 1168: "to recover Helen for Menelaus." This refrain is taken up by the suppliant Iphigenia (1236–37) and the chorus (1253–54). In his answer Agamemnon works himself up to the Panhellenic fervor that will be necessary for the execution of the war and its first sacrifice: he starts with the size of the army (1259–60), then turns to its passion (1264), and, as if he is feeling his way, rounds off with, "It is not Menelaus . . . [but] Greece for whom I must sacrifice you" (1269–71). His turning his fear of the army into a war to end the rape of Greek women is part of the irrational Eros that makes it possible to persuade young men to leave their land and families to become warriors.

The theme of Panhellenism is not overlooked: its most eloquent expression is from the mouth of Agamemnon's loving and innocent daughter, who (instead of Helen) becomes the symbol under which the men will fight and die. Her death unites the factions in the army. Euripides plays to the Panhellenic zeal of his day ambiguously at best. A Panhellenic adventure against a foreign foe for the glory of Greece is patched onto shabbier motivations. We know the tragic outcomes—the deaths of Achilles and the young warriors described by the chorus, the destruction of Troy and the mourning of the Trojan women (of which the chorus reminds us, 751–800), the success of Agamemnon and his fatal homecoming, the killing of Clytemnestra by Orestes (in the play still a baby). To many readers the words of Iphigenia, when she takes up the cause of Penhellenic patriotism, ring hollow but all the more tragic because she has been tricked. The foreign enemy is trivialized as worthless and slavish. The great tradition of the Trojan War passed on from Homer to the present day is on the verge of breaking down into a war of Greek against Greek (seen in the story of the oath, Menelaus' threats to go to other friends, Agamemnon's fear of the army, and the rebellion of Achilles' men). Tragedy is often a debate with the past. The possibility is presented that the Trojan War will not take place. In the end, however, the tradition prevails as it always does.

#

See Foley 1985, pp. 78–84, 92–102; Luschnig 1988, pp. 6–55; Mellert-Hoffmann 1969, pp. 9–31, 89–90; Michelakis 2006, pp. 52–53, 76–81; Michelini 1999–2000.

Greece in the Mycenaean Era

On the Translations

Electra, Phoenician Women, and Iphigenia at Aulis

My aim in turning my hand to translation has been to offer a text close enough to the Greek to be usable in class for teachers and students to talk about the play, yet not so foreign to the English language that it would embarrass actors if they had to speak the lines in front of an audience, whether in a theater or classroom. I was moved to think about making translations fifteen or so years ago by the experience of a young director—now a playwright—who at fifteen fell in love with Sophocles' *Antigone* and managed to stage it for a weekend's worth of performances in Moscow, Idaho. It was a remarkable achievement. Because he was limited to staging a version that was already in the public domain, the translation was more remote than the lively performance deserved.

A translator, like a director, has to make decisions that preclude other possibilities. I have included stage directions even though the Greek texts have none. I chose to have line numbers more or less match the Greek. As a teacher of Greek tragedy I always found it annoying not to know what line something was or to have to give the students two sets of line numbers. Some choices were easy—using "heart" instead of "liver" (*Electra* 688) because liver would be too distracting—and others less so, like that between Hades and hell (*Electra* 662); keeping (most of the time) the various names for Apollo (Loxias, Phoebus) and for the Argives (Mycenaeans, Pelasgians, and Danaans) in *Phoenician Women;* retaining Cypris for Aphrodite, both for its sound and the geographical memories; using "in the musings of poets" for "the Pierian tablets" of the Greek (*Iphigenia at Aulis* 798). Sometimes I impose my interpretation on the reader: that Electra has no slave, for example. For most of these I have tried to indicate in the notes that there is room for other readings (for example, at *Electra* 1110, I suggest different possibilities for the reader to consider, and for *Iphigenia at Aulis* the reader or director has more than enough to choose from). Tragedy is full of untranslatable noises, some of which I have kept rather than translate them as "ah," "alas," or "woe," because they sound so sad that they seem the only way of imitating the tragic devastation expressed in the lines (see especially *Phoenician Women,* fourth stasimon).

The translations are based on the Murray (1913) and Diggle (1981/1994) Oxford Classical Texts. The commentaries I used most are those of Denniston and Cropp (*Electra*), Mastronarde and Craik (*Phoenician Women*), and England (*Iphigenia at Aulis*).

I would like to thank Diane Arnson Svarlien and the late John Quinn, anthology editors at Diotima, for their help with my earlier translations, Hackett's readers for their helpful and humane advice, my husband, Lance Luschnig, who read the translations aloud with me and saved them from some unspeakable lines, and Hannah Etherton, Interlibrary Loan librarian at the University of Idaho, always welcoming, kind, and efficient.

My part of this collection is dedicated to the memory of my brothers, Jim and John Eaton. χαίρετε, σύγγονοι φίλτατοι.

C. E. L. (adapted from Meineck, Luschnig, and Woodruff 2009)

Bacchae

This translation is intended primarily for classroom use. I have aimed first of all at being clear and true to the basic meaning of the text. After that, I have tried to bring across some of the beauty of poetry given the chorus as well as the rhetorical power and cleverness of the dialogue and speeches. And I have tried to give the characters the different voices I hear in the Greek, so that the translation can be produced on stage with minimal changes.

The transmission of this play through manuscripts is unusually troublesome; many lines seem to have fallen out during copying and storage over the centuries and many errors have been introduced. Although I have supplied a few lines to fill small gaps where the meaning is obvious, I have not devised speeches to make up for the lost passages at the end; instead, I have included a section with the main evidence we have that pertains to them. In a stage production, I would have the messenger declare that the speeches are lost and summarize their content.

In the cult songs and other lyric passages given to the chorus, I have tried to preserve their concision, their striking use of compound formations, and their ambiguities. I have avoided the repetitions with which some translators have tried to render poetic and religious elements.

The translation is almost exactly line-for-line, with marginal numbers referring to the Oxford text. My version is not word-for-word, however, or syntax-for-syntax. I have often chosen to be faithful to the rhetorical emphasis of Euripides' word order at the expense of other sorts of accuracy.

Most footnotes give information that will be helpful to readers with no classical background, though some deal with major questions of interpretation or scholarship. Following the lead of previous editors, I have supplied a small number of stage directions.

The text I have translated rarely departs from Diggle's. I have everywhere used the classic commentary by Dodds and the new one by Seaford, with its novel and interesting interpretation.

I am grateful for advice to the publisher's anonymous reader and to my colleagues Barbara Goff and Paula Perlman. I am grateful to Tom Palaima for encouragement and advice. Special thanks are due also to Philip Bobbitt, whose poetry group encouraged me to carry on translating verse into verse.

P.W. (adapted from Woodruff 1998)

EURIPIDES

Electra

Translated, with Notes, by Cecelia Eaton Luschnig

Cast of Characters

FARMER (unnamed)   Electra's husband
ELECTRA
ORESTES
CHORUS   of young Mycenaean women
OLD MAN   former personal slave of Agamemnon
MESSENGER   slave of Orestes
CLYTEMNESTRA
DIOSCURI   Castor [and Polydeuces, nonspeaking]
                   ex machina

                   Nonspeaking Roles
PYLADES   Orestes' companion

Several extras serve as Orestes' entourage and as male and female attendants to Clytemnestra.

Euripides' *Electra* was first produced for the Greater Dionysia between 422 and 413, possibly around 415 B.C.E.

Electra

SCENE: *The Mycenaean countryside in front of the poor farmhouse of Electra's husband. The time is just before dawn. It is about seven years after the end of the Trojan War. The two side entrances represent routes to the country (stage right) and the highway (stage left).*

Prologue

(Enter Farmer through the central doors.)

FARMER:
Earth's timeless soil, Inachus' streams,
here once King Agamemnon deployed the forces of war
and with a thousand ships sailed to the land of Troy.
On Trojan ground he killed old Priam, their king,
sacked the famous city Dardanus built,   5
and came home to Argos. On the high temples
he dedicated the lion's share of foreign spoils.
Over there he had success, but at home
he was killed by the treachery of his wife Clytemnestra

1: Inachus—the main river of the land of Argos. Like most rivers, he is a god.

5: Dardanus—the son of Zeus and Atlas' daughter Electra. He built the citadel of Troy and ruled over the Troad (Troy and the area around it). He was the ancestor of the kings of Troy down to Priam. Line 5 sets together the first and last of the kings of Troy. This is a favorite device in Greek poetry: at the end of a story, the poet takes us back to the beginning.

6: Argos and Mycenae are used interchangeably.

6–7: Spoils, in particular, refers to the armor stripped from dead enemies (see also 1000). Returning warriors nailed the armor to the temples. See Homer, *Iliad* 7.81–84; Herodotus, *The Histories* 5.95.1; Aeschylus, *Agamemnon* 577–79.

9: Clytemnestra—The original spelling was "Clytæmestra" (without the "n"). The name means "renowned schemer" rather than "famously courted," which applies more aptly to her sister Helen.

3

10   and the hand of Thyestes' son Aegisthus.
      He left behind the age-old scepter of Tantalus
      when he died. Aegisthus is now king of the country
      and keeps for himself Tyndareos' daughter, the late king's wife.
      But *he* left his children at home when he sailed to Troy,
15   his son Orestes and a young daughter Electra—
      the father's aged minder absconded with the boy
      after Aegisthus resolved to kill him,
      and gave him to Strophius to raise in the land of the Phocians.
      But the girl Electra stayed behind in her father's halls,
20   until she ripened into a young woman, and suitors,
      prominent men from all over Greece, came to court her.
      In terror that she would marry well and bear a child
      to avenge Agamemnon, Aegisthus kept her
      in the house and would not let her marry any of them.
25   When even that strategy failed to ease his fear

11: "Age-old scepter"—The long history of Agamemnon's scepter is told in Homer's *Iliad* 2.102–9: it was made by Hephaestus and given by him to Zeus, who passed it on to Hermes, who gave it to Pelops. From Pelops it passed to his sons, first Atreus and then Thyestes, and finally to Atreus' son Agamemnon. Tantalus was Pelops' father, but the Homeric scepter was never in his hands and is projected backward here. Agamemnon's scepter figures in Clytemnestra's dream in Sophocles' *Electra* (420). The Farmer takes a long view, showing interest in the generations of the people he mentions.

12: According to Homer, Aegisthus ruled for seven years until Orestes came back and slew his father's murderer (*Odyssey* 3.305–8). Exactly how Clytemnestra died is unclear in the *Odyssey*.

18: Strophius was married to Agamemnon's sister Anaxibia. He was king of Phocis (in central Greece; see map), where the Delphic sanctuary was located. Pylades was Strophius' son and Orestes' cousin. The two grew up together and were inseparable. Pylades is a presence in all three of the *Electra* plays, but has a speaking part (of three lines) only in Aeschylus' *Libation Bearers* (900–902). He has speaking parts in Euripides' *Orestes* and *Iphigenia among the Taurians*.

22–24: Aegisthus acted as Electra's *kurios* (guardian): Women, as a rule, did not act on their own in contractual matters (though Clytemnestra and Helen made second marital choices for themselves). Aegisthus clearly does not have Electra's best interest—nor that of her side of the family—at heart, and the farmer who receives Electra as his wife does not view Aegisthus as having the authority to give her in marriage.

that she might have children by a secret liaison with some noble,
he planned to kill her, but her mother, bloodthirsty
as she was, saved her from Aegisthus' hands.
For her husband's death she made an excuse, but she was afraid
the murder of her own child would cause an outcry.   30
Aegisthus had a brainstorm then—he put a price on the head
of Agamemnon's son, already in exile,
and *to me* he gave Electra to be my lawful
wedded wife. My people are Mycenaean;   35
there's no fault to be found on that score—
we are respectable but poor—
so much for good breeding! By giving her
to a poor man, he hoped to quell his fears.
If a man of rank had married her,   40
he would rouse the sleeping murder of Agamemnon
and at last Aegisthus would have gotten his just deserts.
I have never touched her—Aphrodite be my witness—
I could not shame her. Yes, Electra is still a virgin.
I was ashamed to lay rough hands on the daughter   45
of a wealthy family, being a working man myself.
I feel for poor Orestes, in name my kinsman,
if he ever comes home to Argos and sees
the miserable marriage they made for his sister.
And if anyone says I'm a fool to take a young   50
virgin into my home and not touch her,
he should know that he is measuring
right and wrong by false standards. He's the fool.

> *(Enter Electra through the central doors, carrying a
> hydria [water vessel].)*

ELECTRA:
Black night, nurse of golden stars,
I go now to the running stream

33: "He gave Electra"—Up to this point the audience would be wondering
who the Farmer is. He is not a mythological figure, not part of the traditional story, but an outsider, a person from contemporary society. This is
an absolutely extraordinary fact.

Enter Electra: The characters are introduced in successive scenes of the
prologue. Fetching water from the stream or springhouse is a traditional
task for women.

55 with this jug balanced on my head,
not that I need to do such menial tasks,
but I want to show before the gods Aegisthus' insult
and let my laments for Father fly to heaven.
60 Tyndareos' daughter, my mother, damn her to hell,
threw me out of my home to please her husband.
Now she bears Aegisthus a new brood
and makes Orestes and me unwanted stepchildren.

FARMER:
Poor thing, why are you slaving away for my sake
65 and taking on chores, unsuited to the life you used to live,
and why don't you stop, even when I ask you to?

ELECTRA:
You are my true friend. I put you on a par with the gods
for not adding abuse to my troubles.
It's a great stroke of good fortune to find
70 relief from bad luck as I have found in you.
I must then, with whatever strength I can muster, without your
　　asking,
try to lighten your load, so you can handle it more easily,
and to share your toils with you. You have enough work
outside. The household chores should be mine
75 to take care of. When a working man comes home
it is nice to find things inside in good order.

(Exit Electra, as she concludes this speech, stage right to
the country.)

FARMER:
Go on, then, if you want to. It's not so far
from the house to the spring. But with the break of day
I must drive my oxen to my lands and sow my fields.
80 A lazy lout with the gods on his lips
cannot eke out a living except by working hard.

(Exit Farmer stage right to the country.)

————————————

75–76: This is the traditional division of labor in Greek society: women
work mainly inside the house, men outside.
78: This line (see also 102) gives the time of day (daybreak) for the play's
opening.

*(Enter Orestes stage left from the highway with Pylades;
two servants carry their baggage. Orestes is dressed in a
fine traveler's cloak and a broad-brimmed hat.)*

ORESTES:
Pylades, in my eyes you are first and foremost
my dearest, most loyal friend and host.
You alone of friends continue to respect Orestes
in my current situation, horrors brought on by Aegisthus   85
who killed my father with the help of that damnable woman,
my mother. I have come from the god's sacred rites
here to Argive land, in secret
to repay my father's murderers with death.
During the night just past I went to Father's grave,   90
shed tears, made an offering of my hair,
and slaughtered a sheep on the altar
in secret from the masters of this country.
I will not set foot inside the city-walls,
but have come to the country's borders   95
with two possibilities in mind: to leave
for another place if their spies get wind of me
and to look for my sister. I hear that she has been joined
in marriage and is no longer a virgin.
My plan is to find her and make her my accomplice in   100
  revenge
and thus gain knowledge about affairs inside the city.
Now that dawn is raising its white face,
let's get out of the road
in case some farmer or serving woman
shows up, so we can find out   105
if my sister lives anywhere nearby.
Look, I see a slave woman coming this way

(Electra comes into view and is heard singing.)

87: "The god's sacred rites"—The oracle at Delphi is central to Orestes'
revenge plot, but in this play Apollo seems less involved. In Aeschylus' *Libation Bearers* (269–96), Apollo is most graphic in his pronouncements of
what will happen to Orestes if he fails to avenge his father: physical tor-
ments, social ostracism, and visitation by the Furies. In Sophocles' *Electra*,
Apollo's part is full but not clear. Orestes is told by the oracle to use deceit.
Euripides' *Orestes* is vague about the content of the oracle.

carrying a heavy water jug on her shaved
head. Let's crouch down and listen
110 to this servant in case we can learn anything
about what we have come here for, Pylades.

(They hide behind the altar in the center of the orchestra.)

Electra's Monody

*(Enter Electra stage right from the country, alone with the
water jug on her head, singing.)*

ELECTRA:
Hurry along—the time has come—
go on, go on in tears. Ah, ah me.
115 I am Agamemnon's child,
and Tyndareos' loathsome daughter Clytemnestra
gave birth to me.
Down in the city, people
call me unhappy Electra.
120 Ah, ah for my never-ending toils
and hated life.
Father, you lie dead and gone,
slaughtered by your wife
and Aegisthus, O Agamemnon, my father.

125 Move on, waken the same refrain of sorrow,
raise high the pleasure that comes with mourning.

Hurry along—the time has come—
go on, go on in tears.
Ah, ah me.
130 In what city, in what house,
my poor brother, do you wander
leaving your sister
to the bitterest sorrows
in Father's chambers, mourning?
135 Come, release me from my life of misery,

108–9: "Shaved head"—See note on 147–50.

131: "Do you wander"—"Are you a slave?" is another reading for this
question.

from these toils.
Zeus, Zeus, bring ashore to Argos
the wanderer, the avenger
of Father's hideous bloodshed.

Take this vessel from my head and put it   140
on the ground. O Father, I cry out
in nightly keening.
A shrill wail, a song of death,
Father, I call to you, a song of death
down deep in the earth
with cries of grief I pass my days   145
forever, tearing at my neck,
dragging down my nails,
and beating my hands on
my head close-cropped for your death.

Aiai. Tear the head,   150
like a droning swan
beside running streams
that calls its own dear father
killed by the cunning snares
of nets, so I cry for you,   155
poor Father.

The last bath, your deathbed
bathed in blood—

140: "Take this vessel"—Does Electra have a slave, as some scholars believe, to whom she addresses these second-person imperatives, or does she
speak to herself? In either case, she needs to have her hands free for the
gestures of mourning.

147–50: Electra catalogs the rituals of mourning: her hair is shorn, she
strikes her head, and she tears her skin with her nails.

151: "Like a droning swan"—Birds, especially swans, were admired by
the Greeks for their filial piety. The swan was thought to sing in mourning
and even in sorrow for its own impending death. Electra thinks of her father as snared by his wife, caught in deadly cloths (see Aeschylus, *Agamemnon* 1382–83).

157: "The last bath, your deathbed"—In Homer (*Odyssey* 4.534–35;
11.410–11) and Sophocles (*Electra* 203–7, 269), Agamemnon is killed at a

160   ah me, ah me,
        the bitter axe blow,
        the bitter plot
        you came home from Troy
        your wife welcomed you
        not with wreaths, not with crowns
        but with merciless outrage she handed you over
165   to Aegisthus, his two-edged sword
        and took the traitor as her lover.

        *(Enter the chorus along the side entrances, from both
        directions.)*

Parodos

CHORUS:
        Daughter of Agamemnon, Electra, I have come
        to your rustic farmyard.
        A stranger is here; a milk-drinking

---

banquet. Euripides' *Electra* (1148–49) follows Aeschylus' *Agamemnon* (1107–35).

160, 165: The axe is associated with Clytemnestra (in Aeschylus' *Libation Bearers* she calls for one when she realizes Orestes has returned, 889). In Homer, Agamemnon dies by the sword of Aegisthus (*Odyssey* 11.424). What weapon Clytemnestra used is not so clear in *Agamemnon*. In art, Aegisthus is usually depicted wielding a sword; Clytemnestra sometimes is shown with a sword and sometimes with an axe (Prag, Pl. 11c). In Sophocles, the instrument used by both Clytemnestra and Aegisthus is an axe (*Electra* 98–100, 193–96, 485). In Euripides, Clytemnestra uses an axe (160, 279, 1160), but Aegisthus wields a sword (165). It is possible that Clytemnestra killed him with an axe and Aegisthus mutilated him with the sword. The use of the axe, an instrument for killing an animal or felling a tree, dehumanizes the victim more than the sword, a weapon of war. On the mutilation, see Aeschylus, *Libation Bearers* (439); Sophocles, *Electra* (445–46); Euripides, *Electra* (164, *lōban,* "outrage").

167–212: Parodos—the entrance-song of the chorus.

169: "A stranger is here"—The man who brings the news of the festival is a herdsman, drinker of milk rather than wine. His life is so remote and he so poor that he lives off what his flock produces. Wine is the drink of the civilized. In Homer's *Odyssey,* the Cyclops is so uncivilized that Odysseus is able to overcome him with wine. (See Euripides, *Bacchae* 272–85 on the gifts of grain and grape.)

mountain-roaming man has come from Mycenae.   170
He brings news that two days from now
the Argives will proclaim a public sacrifice
and all the girls will march
in a procession of honor for Hera.

ELECTRA:
No, not for parties, my dear friends,   175
and not for golden rings
does my poor heart
take wing and I will not lead dances
with the Argive brides
or beat my whirling feet.   180
I spend the night in tears,
and mourning becomes me
in my daytime misery.
Look at my matted hair
and my dress in rags.   185
Are they fit for Agamemnon's
royal daughter
and for Troy, the city that can never forget
it was laid waste by my father?

CHORUS:
Hera is a great god. Come, now,   190
and borrow from me a fancy
dress to put on
and golden ornaments to grace its beauty.
Do you think if you do not honor the gods
you will defeat your enemies with your tears?
No, it's not with laments   195
but with prayers revering the gods
that you will reach your happy day, dear girl.

ELECTRA:
None of the gods hears the voice
of the unlucky, none cares about the ancient
butchery done to my father.   200
I cry for the one dead and gone

174: The *Heraia* (festival to Hera), which celebrates Hera's marriage to
Zeus, was a major festival in Argos. The procession the chorus mentions is
for unmarried girls.

and for the living, the vagabond,
who lives somewhere in another land,
unhappy wanderer
205   at the drudges' hearth,
son of a proud father.
And here in a poor man's hovel
I live, wasting away my life
banished from my father's house,
210   along these mountain crags,
while my mother lives in criminal marriage
with another husband.

First Episode

CHORUS:
So many troubles for all Greeks and for your own house
were brought on by your mother's sister Helen.

*(Orestes and Pylades and their attendants get up from
behind the altar.)*

ELECTRA:
215   Oh my god! Women, I must break off these laments.
Some strangers are here near the house, lurking
behind the altar, and now they are getting up from their
ambush;
run—you go back along the road and I'll head for the house—
we must try to escape from these outlaws.

ORESTES:
220   Wait, poor woman. Don't be afraid of me.

ELECTRA:
Phoebus Apollo, I beg you for my life.

ORESTES:
There are others I might kill, more my enemies than you.

ELECTRA:
Go away. Do not touch what you should not.

214: The reference to Helen may seem irrelevant, but the end of the play
will reveal that assumptions about her guilt have been made for a purpose.

ORESTES:
  There is no one I have more right to touch.

ELECTRA:
  Why are you hiding there with a sword in your hand?   225

ORESTES:
  Stay and listen. You'll be glad you did.

ELECTRA:
  I'll stay. I'm in your power. You're stronger than me.

ORESTES:
  I have come here with news from your brother.

ELECTRA:
  My dear friend. Is he alive or dead?

ORESTES:
  Alive. I'm happy to give the good news first.   230

ELECTRA:
  Bless you. Thank you for this most welcome message.

ORESTES:
  It is something we both share.

ELECTRA:
  Where in the world is he living his dreary life of exile?

ORESTES:
  He doesn't keep to one place but moves from city to city.

ELECTRA:
  Does he have enough for his daily needs?   235

ORESTES:
  That much he has, but a homeless man carries no weight.

ELECTRA:
  What word of him do you bring?

ORESTES:
  He wants to know if you are alive and if so in what
    condition.

ELECTRA:
  First of all, do you see how drawn my skin is?

ORESTES:

240   Worn by your cares—it makes me want to cry.

ELECTRA:

And my head with the hair shaved off.

ORESTES:

You must miss your brother and your dead father.

ELECTRA:

Ah me, there is no one dearer to me than they.

ORESTES:

Ah! And your brother: don't you think he feels the same?

ELECTRA:

245   But he is away and not here with us.

ORESTES:

Why do you live out here so far from town?

ELECTRA:

I am married, stranger, a lethal match.

ORESTES:

I am sorry for your brother. Who is your husband?

ELECTRA:

Not a man my father expected to choose for me.

ORESTES:

250   Tell me so I can report it to your brother.

ELECTRA:

This is where I live, here at the border, in his house.

241: "With the hair shaved off"—in Greek, *eskythismenon,* "scalped with a razor" (like a victim of the Scythians; see Herodotus, *The Histories* 4.64.2–3).

244: "Ah!"—In Greek, *pheu* is a cry of dismay or surprise, amounting almost to a gasp. Orestes utters exometric *pheu* after 261, 281, 366, and 968.

247: The word for "stranger" (*xenos*) means "friend in a foreign country, guest, host," so that Electra's term of address to her brother could also be translated as "my friend," but the irony of her having to call her brother "stranger" is maintained in the translation. At 83 Orestes calls Pylades both "friend" (*philos,* "loved one, family member") and "host" or "stranger" (*xenos*).

ORESTES:
Some dirt farmer or cowhand would live here.

ELECTRA:
My husband is poor but decent and respectful to me.

ORESTES:
What form does your husband's respect take?

ELECTRA:
He has never taken advantage of me. 255

ORESTES:
Is it some sort of religious abstention or doesn't he care for
you?

ELECTRA:
He did not think it right to insult my parents.

ORESTES:
And why didn't he count his blessings in making such a match?

ELECTRA:
He didn't think the man who gave me to him had authority,
stranger.

ORESTES:
I understand. So he would not suffer Orestes' retribution. 260

ELECTRA:
He is aware of that, but he is also a decent man.

ORESTES:
Well, then, he must be one of nature's gentlemen. He deserves a
good turn.

ELECTRA:
Yes, of course, if my missing brother ever comes home.

ORESTES:
Your own mother: did she put up with this?

ELECTRA:
Women's affections belong to their husbands, not their children, 265
stranger.

262: "Well, then"—This is another of Orestes' *pheus*; see note on 244.

ORESTES:

Why has Aegisthus insulted you in this way?

ELECTRA:

By marrying me to such a man, he hoped I would have power-
less children.

ORESTES:

So your children would not be able to take vengeance?

ELECTRA:

That was his ploy. I pray he will pay for it.

ORESTES:

270   Does your mother's husband know you are still a virgin?

ELECTRA:

No, he doesn't. We are keeping it a secret from him.

ORESTES:

And these women who are listening, are they friends?

ELECTRA:

Yes. They will keep their lips sealed.

ORESTES:

What, then, is Orestes' part in this if he comes to Argos?

ELECTRA:

275   You ask that! Shame on you. Isn't now the time for action?

ORESTES:

Then suppose he does come: how can he kill your father's
murderers?

ELECTRA:

By doing to his enemies what they did to Father.

ORESTES:

Would you really have the heart to help him kill your
mother?

ELECTRA:

With the same axe that killed my father.

ORESTES:

280   Should I tell him this, and that he can count on you?

ELECTRA:
Let me die once I have shed my mother's blood.

ORESTES:
Ah, if only Orestes were nearby to hear this.

ELECTRA:
But, you know, I wouldn't recognize him if I saw him.

ORESTES:
I'm not surprised. You were both very young when you were
    separated.

ELECTRA:
Only one person I know would recognize him.   285

ORESTES:
The one they say saved him from being murdered?

ELECTRA:
Yes: my father's old childhood slave.

ORESTES:
Did your father get a decent burial when he died?

ELECTRA:
He got what he got, flung out as he was from the house.

ORESTES:
What a story! Even strangers' troubles   290
can actually make a person feel pain.
Go on with your tale so I can tell your brother
the news, unwelcome, but he needs to hear it.
Pity is not found in boorish ignorance,
but in men of finer feelings; and even for the sensitive,
too much sensitivity has to have its price.   295

CHORUS:
I have the same longing in my heart too.
We live far from town and do not know
the troubles in the city, but want to learn them now.

ELECTRA:
I'll tell—or should I?—yes, you are a friend so I must tell   300
the heavy fortune that has struck me and my father.

Since you press me to tell the tale, stranger, I beg you,
bring news to Orestes of my troubles and his own.
First, look at the rags I am kept in, here in this stable,
305   how much grime I am weighed down with, under what roof
I live after my home in the royal palace.
I have to toil at weaving my own clothes
or else go naked and do without
and I carry water from the spring myself.
310   I live in privation, without sacred festivals and dances,
and shrink from the company of women because I'm still a
      virgin,
and I am ashamed to face Castor, my kinsman
to whom I was betrothed before he went up to the gods.
But my mother, decked out with the spoils of Phrygia,
315   sits on her throne, and beside her are stationed
slave women, my father's captives,
in Trojan gowns fastened with golden pins.
While in my home Father's blood is still
putrefied to black and his murderer
320   goes driving in the same chariot Father used,
and the scepter with which Father commanded the Greek
      armies,
he swaggers around holding it in his blood-drenched hands.
And Agamemnon's burial mound lies dishonored
and never received libations or boughs of myrtle
325   and his altar stands neglected, without offerings.
Meanwhile the rumor is that mother's splendid husband

312–13: The betrothal of Electra to her uncle (a degree of consanguinity allowed by Athenian marriage practice) may be an invention of Euripides. Castor and Polydeuces (Pollux) were the twin sons of Zeus and Leda (Dioscuri; in Latin, *Gemini*), one mortal, one divine. When Castor died, they were allowed to share immortality as stars and protectors of sailors.

314–17: Phrygia and Phrygians are metonymies for Troy and Trojans, respectively.

324: Myrtle is an aromatic evergreen shrub (genus *Myrtus*), native to the Mediterranean region, and is a favorite plant for various kinds of ceremonial decoration.

326–31: Electra's description of Aegisthus at the tomb mocking her father is based on rumor, as she admits (327 lit., "so they say"), and contrasts strongly with the gracious Aegisthus we meet in the reported scene.

gets drunk, leaps on his grave, and throws rocks at Father's
   headstone
and has the gall to utter these words to mock us:
"Where is your boy Orestes? Is he here to protect your tomb   330
like a good son?" This is how he is insulted because he's not
   here.
But, stranger, please, bring him this report.
Its senders are many and I speak for them,
my hands, my lips, my broken heart;
my shorn head and his own father.   335
It is a disgrace if Father wiped out the Trojans,
but *he,* one on one, cannot kill this man,
though he is young and born of a nobler father.

CHORUS:
   I see him, your husband, I mean.
   He has left his work and is heading home.   340

     (Enter Farmer stage right from the country.)

FARMER:
   What's this? Who are these strangers I see in front of my door?
   Why have they come out here to my house in the country?
   Are they looking for me? It's not proper, you know,
   for a woman to be in the company of young men.

ELECTRA:
   Oh no, dear, do not be suspicious of me.   345
   Let me tell you what their story is. These strangers
   have come from Orestes to bring me news of him.

     (To Orestes and Pylades.)

   Please, excuse what he just said.

FARMER:
   What do they have to say? Is he alive?

341–400: The Farmer and Orestes do not engage with each other. The
Farmer addresses Orestes, but Orestes does not answer him directly, showing a class distinction.

344: In Athenian society, women were secluded. It was the man's job to
negotiate with strangers. The social norms are defied in tragic action, which
takes place at the gates of the scene building and thus requires that the female characters be outside.

ELECTRA:
350   Yes, at least that's what they say and I have no reason to
            distrust them.

FARMER:
        And does he keep in mind what was done to his father and
            you?

ELECTRA:
        That's what I hope. But a man in exile is powerless.

FARMER:
        What news have they brought of Orestes?

ELECTRA:
        He sent them to observe my troubles.

FARMER:
355   Well, some they can see. The rest, I imagine, you told them.

ELECTRA:
        Yes, they know. They have no deficiency on that score.

FARMER:
        Why haven't we opened our doors to them by now?
        Please, go into the house. For your welcome news
        you will receive whatever hospitality my house can offer.

            (To Orestes' attendants.)

360   Go on and take the baggage inside my house.

            (To Orestes.)

        And don't say no. You come as friends
        from a friend. Even if I am a poor man,
        I will not show a mean spirit.

ORESTES:
        My god, is this the man who helps you mask
365   your marriage, to spare Orestes' good name?

ELECTRA:
        He is called unhappy Electra's husband.

ORESTES:
        Ah, there are no easy answers in the matter of a man's worth.
        Human nature is beyond comprehension.

In the past I've seen the son of a noble father
amount to nothing and outstanding children born of worthless   370
  men.
I've seen the poverty of a rich man's mind
and a keen intellect in a poor man's body.
[How is anyone to make a correct distinction?
According to wealth? Then he'll be relying on a corrupt judge.
By lack, then? But poverty carries its own disease: 375
it leads a man to crime because of need.
But should I use military prowess? Can anyone face a spear
and bear witness to another's valor?
No, it's best to leave these things to fall as they may.]
This man is nobody of importance in Argos;   380
he can claim no distinction of family.
He may be common as dirt, but he's a man of quality.
Why not be sensible, instead of deceiving ourselves
with empty speculations, and judge people
by associating with them and knowing their character?   385
[This is the kind of man who could manage a city or home
well. But empty muscle men without a brain
are only good for statues in the public square. The strong arm
does not hold out against the spear any better than the weak
but it is a matter of a man's nature and his mettle.]   390
The son of Agamemnon who sent us
is worthy, whether he is here or not,
so let us enjoy the hospitality of this house.

        (To his servants.)

You may go
into the house. I'll take a poor but considerate man   395
as my host over a rich one.

        (Exit servants into the house with baggage.)

I accept the invitation into this man's house,
but I would prefer to have your brother
receive me into a prosperous home in happier circumstances.

373–79: Brackets [ ] around lines in the translation indicate sections of
doubtful authenticity, especially those scholars suspect of being interpolations made for later productions, as this one is (see Page 1934, pp. 74–75),
or editors' notes that crept into the text from the margins.

Maybe he will come. The oracles of Loxias
400   are certain. Though for human fortune-telling I have no use.

(Exit Orestes and Pylades through the central doors into
the house.)

CHORUS:
Now more than before, Electra, my heart is warming
with joy. Maybe now at last
your fortune is looking up and will turn out well.

ELECTRA: (To her husband.)
You fool, you know how poor we are. How could you invite
405   these guests who are so much better off than you?

FARMER:
What's this? If they are as well-bred as they seem,
won't they be just as content with the meager as the plentiful?

ELECTRA:
Meager is what you have! But since you have made this
    blunder,
go to my father's dear old childhood slave
410   who was cast out of the city and keeps sheep for company
near the Tanaus River where it forms the border
between Argive and Spartan territory.
Tell him that guests have come and he should bring
something for the strangers' dinner.

(Farmer starts to object.)

415   Oh, he'll be glad, I assure you, and he'll thank the gods
when he hears the infant he saved all those years ago is still
    alive.
We would get nothing out of our ancestral home
from Mother. It's bitter news we would bring her
if that awful woman learned that Orestes is alive.

FARMER:
420   Well, if you think so, I'll take the news
to the old man. But hurry on in
and get things ready inside.

399: Loxias—Apollo in his role as prophet.

(Exit Electra into the house.)

If she wants to, a woman
can find plenty to serve for a meal.
There is still enough in my house
to fill their bellies for a day.   425
When my mind falls to thinking this way
I consider what great power money has—
to give to strangers and when you fall ill
to pay for medicines. To sustain yourself
day to day doesn't cost a lot. Everybody,   430
rich or poor, can only hold so much.

(Exit Farmer stage left to the highway.)

First Stasimon

CHORUS:

[Strophe 1]

Famous ships that sailed once to Troy
with oars too many to count,
escorting the chorus of Nereid nymphs.
To the music of the pipe a dolphin leapt alongside them   435
whirling around the dark prows
bringing the son of Thetis,
swift Achilles, nimble of foot,
to accompany Agamemnon   440
to the banks of Simois in Troy.

[Antistrophe 1]

Nereids leaving Euboean headlands
carried the armorers' toils from the anvils
of Hephaestus—golden armor

434: Nereids are sea nymphs, daughters of Nereus, sisters of Achilles'
mother Thetis.

444: In Homer, the set of body armor made by Hephaestus (*Iliad* 18) is
very different from that described here and is brought to Achilles in Troy
by his mother after his first set was worn into battle by Patroclus and
stripped from his fallen body.

445   up Pelion's slopes, up through the woodlands of Ossa
       searching for high lookouts of nymphs
       where the Centaur Chiron like a father
       raised a bright light for Hellas,
450   the sea goddess Thetis' swift-footed
       son, for the sons of Atreus.

[Strophe 2]

       I heard from someone in the port, back from Troy
       who had come to Nauplia,
       how in the circle of your famous shield,
455   son of Thetis,
       these icons were forged,
       terrors for the Phrygians:
       around the surface of the rim
       Perseus above the sea on winged sandals
460   holds the Gorgon's severed head
       in the company of Hermes, Zeus' messenger,
       the rustic son of Maia.

[Antistrophe 2]

       Shining in the middle of the shield there glinted
465   the sun's orb
       mounted on heavenly horses
       and the ethereal choreographies of stars:
       Pleiades and Hyades, causing
       Hector to turn away his eyes;
470   and on the helmet made of gold
       Sphinxes bearing in their talons
       their deadly song's prey

445: Pelion—the site of the wedding of Achilles' parents, Peleus and Thetis, and the home of Chiron, the Centaur who reared and educated Achilles
and other heroes.

460–63: A direct look at the Gorgon, Medusa, turned people into stone.
Perseus used mirrors to see her face, slew her, and carried her head around.
Later he gave the head to Athena.

471–75: A Sphinx is a bird-woman who brings death. The Theban Sphinx
sang a riddle and seized and devoured men who could not solve it, until
Oedipus guessed it right.

and on the breastplate's rounded form, breathing fire
the Chimera raced on her lion's claws
peering up at Pegasus, the flying colt of Peirene.   475

[Epode]

On the stabbing sword galloped
four-footed horses, black dust swirling over their backs.
The king of those great men in arms
your marriage killed,
evil-minded daughter of Tyndareos.   480
For that, one day, the gods in heaven
will dispatch you to death. Truly one day
to come I will see the blood of murder
pouring out beneath your neck   485
gashed by the sword.

Second Episode

*(Enter Old Man, pulling a sheep and carrying provisions,
stage left from the highway.)*

OLD MAN:
Where is she? Where is my young lady, my mistress,
daughter of Agamemnon, him that I brought up myself?
What a steep climb she has up to her house
for a shriveled old man like me to get to on foot.   490
Still, she is dear to me and on my wobbly knees
I must drag along this hunched back.
Hello, daughter, now I see you there in front of the house.
I'm here to bring you a young lamb
from my flock—here it is, the one I picked   495
and wreaths and some cheese from the press
and this precious vintage wine full of aroma,
just a drop, but something sweet to add,
a cup or so, to a weaker drink.
Someone go and bring this to the guests inside.   500

474: Chimera is a compound female monster made up of lioness, goat,
and snake who breathes fire. She was killed by Bellerophon with the help
of Pegasus, the colt of Peirene, the winged horse that sprang from the Gorgon (Medusa) when Perseus beheaded her.

I have to lift my ragged cloak and wipe
my eyes that are drenched with tears.

ELECTRA:

Why are your eyes dripping with tears, old man?
Does my situation remind you of your troubles after all this
    time?
505   Or do you weep over Orestes' hard exile
and my father you once held in your arms
and cared for, in vain for yourself and those you love?

OLD MAN:

In vain, that's right. Still I did not hold back.
I took a detour to visit his tomb,
510   and I knelt down and wept at seeing it deserted;
then I opened the wineskin I'm carrying for your guests
and poured a libation and I covered his mound with myrtle.
There on the altar I saw a sacrificed sheep,
a black one for the dead, and blood spilled not long ago.
515   There were locks of hair cut in mourning.
I was amazed, my girl, to think who in the world dared
to visit the tomb. No Argive would have, that's for sure.
Look here, maybe your brother has come in secret
and paid respect to his father's neglected grave.
520   Go look at the hair. Put it next to your own
to see if the color is the same as yours.
It often happens that people with the same father
have many physical traits in common.

ELECTRA:

What you are saying makes you sound stupid, old man,
525   if you think my brave brother has come
to the country in secret out of fear of Aegisthus.
Will two locks of hair be alike,
one from the head of a noble youth raised in the wrestling
    schools,
the other a woman's and well-combed? It's absurd.
530   Besides, many people have hair the same color
who do not share the same blood, old man.

515–46: The cut lock of hair, the footprint, and the weaving are the tokens
of recognition in Aeschylus' *Libation Bearers* (167–234).

OLD MAN:

    Well then, why don't you go to where I saw his footprint
    and see if it's the same size as your own, child?

ELECTRA:

    How could his feet leave an impression
    in the rocky ground? And even if there is,   535
    the feet of brother and sister, a man and a woman,
    would not be alike. The man's are bigger.

OLD MAN:

    If your brother has entered the country, is there any way
    you could recognize him by some weaving from your loom
    in which once long ago I stole him away from imminent   540
      death?

ELECTRA:

    Don't you know that I was a child when Orestes
    went into exile? And even if I was already weaving cloth,
    he was only a baby then. How could he still be wearing
    the same clothes, unless they grew to keep up with him?
    But either some stranger took pity on the grave   545
    and cut his hair or they were sent to spy out the land.

OLD MAN:

    Where are the strangers? I want to see them
    and ask them about your brother.

ELECTRA:

    Here they are, coming out of the house with quick steps.

OLD MAN:

    They look well-born, but there's no telling from looks.   550
    Many well-born men are worthless.
    Still, I bid the visitors good day.

ORESTES:

    Greetings, old man. Really, Electra, this antique relic
    of a man, who in the world is he?

ELECTRA:

    This, stranger, is the man who tended my father.   555

546: Textual problems make it uncertain what Euripides wrote here or
what exactly "they" refers to.

ORESTES:
What? Is he the one who spirited away your brother?

ELECTRA:
Yes, he is the one who saved him, if he is still alive.

ORESTES:
Ah, why is he staring at me as if he is examining
the shiny imprint on a coin? Do I remind him of someone?

ELECTRA:
560   Maybe he is happy to see someone Orestes' age.

ORESTES:
Well, Orestes is a friend of mine. Why is he walking around me?

ELECTRA:
I'm wondering about that, too, stranger.

OLD MAN:
My lady, dear daughter, Electra, praise the gods.

ELECTRA:
Why? What for, of all that is possible in the world?

OLD MAN:
565   For the thing you most desire, which god is revealing.

ELECTRA: *(Electra gestures, raises arms in prayer.)*
There, I call on the gods. Or what do you mean, old man?

OLD MAN:
Look at this man, my child, the man closest to you.

ELECTRA:
I have been looking at him for quite a while. Are you all right?

OLD MAN:
Of course I'm all right. I am looking at your brother.

ELECTRA:
570   What do you mean, old man, by this astonishing statement?

OLD MAN:
That I see Orestes right here: Agamemnon's son.

ELECTRA:
What sign do you see that I can trust?

OLD MAN:
See the scar over his eyebrow? He got that in your father's
   house
one day when he fell and bloodied it, while you two were
   chasing a deer.

ELECTRA:
What are you saying? Yes, I do see a scar from an accident.   575

OLD MAN:
Do you hesitate to embrace your dearest brother?

ELECTRA:
Not any more, old man. I am convinced in my heart
by your token of recognition. *(Embracing Orestes.)* I hold you
at last, against all hope.

ORESTES:
                    And at last you are in my arms.

ELECTRA:
Never expected.

ORESTES:
                    I dared not hope.   580

ELECTRA:
Are you he?

ORESTES:
                    Yes, your only ally.
If I pull in the catch I am going after . . . and I am confident.
Or else we should stop believing in the gods,
if wrong triumphs over right in the end.

Choral Interlude

CHORUS:
You have come, you have come, long-awaited day,   585
you have shone down, you have revealed to the city
a beacon in blazing light, who in long exile

573–74: In Homer's *Odyssey* (19.390–475), Odysseus' old nurse recognizes him because of a scar. Odysseus in turn uses it to identify himself to his herdsmen (21.217–19).

from his father's house
was wandering in misery.
590 Now some god, yes, a god brings us
victory, my dear.
Raise up your hands, raise your voice in prayers
lifted to the gods that your brother
595 will enter the city in good fortune.

Second Episode: Continued

ORESTES:
Well. I have enjoyed the sweet pleasure
of your embraces and in time we will share them again.
But, you, old man, you have arrived in good time.
Tell me, what should I do to take revenge on Father's murderer
600 and my mother, his partner in unholy marriage?
Are there any in Argos kindly disposed toward me,
or, like my luck, am I completely bankrupt?
Who are my allies? Should I act at night or in the daylight?
What road can we take against our enemies?

OLD MAN:
605 Son, you have no friends when your luck runs out.
It is a rare find, you know, if you have someone
to share in common both good times and bad.
In the eyes of your friends you are totally ruined
and have left them no hope. But listen to me:
610 you hold in your own hands and in fortune everything
you need to recover your estate and your city.

ORESTES:
What must I do to reach this goal?

OLD MAN:
Kill Thyestes' son and your mother.

ORESTES:
This is the crown I have come here for, but how do I get it?

OLD MAN:
615 Even if you wanted to, *not* by going inside the city walls.

ORESTES:
Is he surrounded by a garrison and bodyguards?

OLD MAN:
That's right. He lives in fear and does not sleep soundly.

ORESTES:
Good. Old man, you plan the next step.

OLD MAN:
Wait. Listen. I just remembered something.

ORESTES:
Tell me some good news. I would be happy to hear it.   620

OLD MAN:
I saw Aegisthus on my way here.

ORESTES:
I'm very glad to hear this. Where was he?

OLD MAN:
Where he pastures his horses, not far from this farm.

ORESTES:
What was he doing? I see hope coming out of my helplessness.

OLD MAN:
I think he was preparing a festival to the Nymphs.   625

ORESTES:
For bringing up a child or a coming birth?

OLD MAN:
I don't know, but he came prepared to slaughter a bull.

ORESTES:
How big was their party or did he just have his household
    slaves?

OLD MAN:
No Argive citizens were there, just a bunch of his slaves.

ORESTES:
I don't suppose there's anybody who will recognize me, old man.   630

625: Mountain Nymphs are divinities of springs and are worshiped at specific locations. They are associated with fertility, childbirth, and good health ("nymph" means "bride"). Line 626 hints that Clytemnestra might be pregnant.

OLD MAN:
They are slaves who've never seen you.

ORESTES:
Would they be disposed toward us if we succeed?

OLD MAN:
That's the character of slaves, and a bonus for you.

ORESTES:
So how can I get close to him?

OLD MAN:
635   Go where he'll see you as he is sacrificing.

ORESTES:
It looks like he has his lands right off the road?

OLD MAN:
Yes, and when he sees you there, he'll invite you to join the
    feast.

ORESTES:
A distasteful dinner guest, god willing.

OLD MAN:
From there you must look to the throw of the dice.

ORESTES:
640   Good. Thank you. But my mother—where is she?

OLD MAN:
In Argos; but she will join her husband for the sacrifice.

ORESTES:
Why didn't she set out with Aegisthus?

OLD MAN:
She stayed behind out of fear of public censure.

ORESTES:
Of course. She must know she is an object of suspicion in town.

OLD MAN:
645   That's so. Everybody detests an immoral woman.

ORESTES:
How will I kill her and him with one blow?

ELECTRA:
I will take care of the murder of my mother.

ORESTES:
With him so close, luck is surely on my side.

ELECTRA: *(Pointing to Old Man.)*
Let him be assistant to both of us.

OLD MAN:
I'll do that. What manner of death do you have in mind for   650
your mother?

ELECTRA:
Old man, go tell this story to Clytemnestra:
bring her news that I have just given birth to a baby boy.

OLD MAN:
Was the birth a while ago or just now?

ELECTRA:
Ten days ago, the time it takes for a new mother to be purified.

OLD MAN:
And how exactly does this bring about your mother's death?   655

ELECTRA:
She will come when she hears I am indisposed from the birth.

OLD MAN:
Why do you think she cares about you, dear child?

ELECTRA:
She does. And she will shed real tears over the baby's status.

OLD MAN:
Maybe so, but bring your story back to the goal.

ELECTRA:
When she gets here, obviously, she dies.   660

OLD MAN:
She will come right to the doors of your house.

654: A woman was considered ritually unclean through the labor, during the birth, and for ten days after the birth. On the tenth day, the baby was named and acknowledged as a member of the family.

ELECTRA:
And from there it is just a small step to Hell.

OLD MAN:
Once I have seen this I'll die a happy man.

ELECTRA:
First, old man, show him the way.

OLD MAN:
665   Where Aegisthus is sacrificing to the gods?

ELECTRA:
Yes—then go find my mother and tell her my news.

OLD MAN:
She will think she is hearing it from your own lips.

ELECTRA: *(To Orestes.)*
It's your work now. You have drawn the first killing.

ORESTES:
I'm off, if he will guide me there.

OLD MAN:
670   Yes, I am happy to show you the way.

ORESTES:
Zeus of my ancestors, defend me against my enemies.

ELECTRA:
Pity us; our suffering makes us worthy of your pity.

OLD MAN:
Pity your descendants.

ELECTRA:
And Hera, you have power over Mycenae's altars.

ORESTES:
675   Grant us victory, if what we ask is right.

OLD MAN:
Grant justice in requital for their father's death.

ORESTES:
And you, Father, foully murdered, living down below in the earth . . .

ELECTRA:
And Earth, queen of all, I strike with my hands.

OLD MAN:
Defend these dear, dear children, defend them.

ORESTES:
Come now, bring armies of the dead as our allies. 680

ELECTRA:
Those who with you annihilated the Phrygians in war.

OLD MAN:
All who abhor the unholy polluters.

ORESTES:
Do you hear, Father, you who suffered outrage from Mother?

OLD MAN:
Your father hears all this. Time now to go.

ELECTRA:
And so I declare to you: Aegisthus must die. 685
Since if you go down, pinned in a fatal fall,
I'm dead, too; don't speak of me as being alive,
for I shall stab myself in the heart with a two-edged sword.
I am going inside to get ready
so that if good news of you comes the whole house 690
will lift its voice in songs of thanksgiving, but if it is news
of your death, the opposite. This is what I had to say to you.

ORESTES:
I know all I need to know.

ELECTRA:
For this, you must be a man.

686: "Pinned in a fatal fall"—a metaphor from wrestling. See Aeschylus, *Agamemnon* 171–72.

688: For "heart" the manuscripts have "head," which has been emended to either "liver" or "heart." This is a masculine manner of suicide, but women sometimes threaten to use it; in ancient Greek literature, a woman's favored method of suicide was hanging (see Loraux 1987, pp. 14, 54).

689–93: Some scholars suspect that these lines, seen as bathetic rather than pathetic, are interpolations by actors or producers (Page 1934, pp. 75–76).

(Exit Orestes with Old Man, accompanied by Pylades and the servants, stage left.)

But you, women, kindle a torch to shout
695   the outcome of this contest, and I will stand watch,
holding a sword ready in my hand,
and never, if I am overwhelmed by my enemies,
I will *never* allow them the satisfaction of abusing me while I'm
alive.

(Exit Electra through the central doors into the house.)

Second Stasimon

CHORUS:

[Strophe 1]

This myth is told in shadowy rumors
that once in the Argive
700   mountains Pan, steward of fields,
blowing sweet music
on well-pitched pipes,
brought a lamb with
705   gorgeous golden fleece from its tender mother.
And standing on the stone steps
the herald cried,
"To the square, to the square,
Mycenaeans, come all, to see
710   the marvel, the blessed kings'
portent." With dances they celebrated
the houses of the sons of Atreus.

[Antistrophe 1]

Fire-pans worked with gold were spread
up and down the town—fires gleamed
715   on the altars of the Argives.
The lotus reed, servant of the Muses,
piped in melodious voice.

700–706: Pan—the god of fields and forests who pipes to his flocks on the panpipes, a rustic instrument of graduated reeds.

Sweet songs swelled
celebrating the golden lamb. A new ending
for Thyestes' story: in a secret liaison
he had seduced the dear wife   720
of Atreus and brought the marvel
home. Walking then
among the assembled people he proclaims
that he has in his house
the horned sheep with golden wool.   725

[Strophe 2]

Then, it was then that Zeus changed
the shining orbits of the stars
and the fire of the sun
and the pale face of dawn,   730
and he harried the western expanses
with hot god-fanned flame;
in the north, rain-filled clouds,
but the arid ground of Ammon Ra
withers without moisture,   735
deprived of beautiful rains from Zeus.

[Antistrophe 2]

So it is told, but in my eyes
it carries little credence
that the golden-faced sun   740
reversed course and moved
the torrid zone
to afflict the mortal race
for the sake of human justice.

718–19: "A new ending for Thyestes' story"—The meaning of the word *epilogoi* in the manuscripts is doubtful. Emendations include "then came Thyestes' trick"; "in praise of the golden lamb"; "Thyestes had the luck." *726–36:* The sun used to set in the east, but Zeus changed its course in outrage at Thyestes' crime. See Plato, *Statesman (Politicus)* 268e–269a. *734:* Ammon Ra—the oracle of Ammon (Amun) at the oasis of Siwa in the desert of Libya.

Frightening myths are a blessing
for mankind and advance the gods' service.
745   Forgetful of them, you killed
your husband, sister of celebrated brothers.

Third Episode

(Loud shouting is heard in the distance.)

CHORUS:
What's that?
Friends, did you hear a shout—or has some vain impulse
come over me? Like Zeus' rumbling from under the
    ground.
Listen, these rising winds must mean something.
750   Electra, come out of the house, dear lady.

ELECTRA:
Friends, what is it? How have we come out in the contest?

CHORUS:
All I know is that I just heard a scream of murder.

ELECTRA:
I heard it too, but from far away.

CHORUS:
The sound comes a long way, but still it is sharp.

ELECTRA:
755   Is the cry Argive or from those I love?

CHORUS:
I cannot tell. It's just noise. The words are all mixed up.

ELECTRA:
You announce my death. Why delay?

CHORUS:
Wait until you learn your fate more clearly.

746: "Sister of celebrated brothers"—this probably refers to Clytemnestra
as sister of the Dioscuri (Castor and Polydeuces).

748: "Zeus' rumbling"—Earthquakes are caused by Poseidon, but here
the sound of an earthquake (subterranean or seismic rumblings) is compared to thunder, which comes from Zeus.

ELECTRA:
No. We are defeated. Where are the messengers?

CHORUS:
They will be here. It's no trivial matter to kill a king.   760

(Enter Messenger stage left.)

MESSENGER:
Women of Mycenae, happy in victory,
I bring news of Orestes' triumph to all who love him:
Agamemnon's murderer, Aegisthus, lies dead
on the ground. Let us praise the gods.

ELECTRA:
Who are you? Why should I believe what you are telling me?   765

MESSENGER:
Don't you recognize your brother's servant when you see him?

ELECTRA:
Dear, dear man. I was so terrified that I could not recognize
your face. Now I know who you are. What are you saying?
Is he really and truly dead, the hated murderer of my father?

MESSENGER:
He is dead. A second time I tell you what you want to hear.   770

ELECTRA:
O gods and Justice that sees all, at last you have come!
Tell me the manner and order of events
in which he killed Thyestes' son. I want to hear it.

MESSENGER:
When we left this house
we walked along a rutted wagon trail   775
to where the "illustrious" king of the Mycenaeans was.

759: The choral ode covers an indeterminate passage of time during which
Aegisthus is killed while the chorus sings of the crime of his father Thyestes
that started the interfilial feud. Messengers often seem to arrive at the end
of an ode, too soon after an event. This question may be a metatheatrical
allusion to the stage convention or an indication of Electra's impatience or
anxiety.

765: Of the twenty-six messengers in Greek tragedy, this is the only one
whose truthfulness is questioned.

In fact he had gone into a well-watered garden
and was cutting sprays of young myrtle for his head.
When he saw us, he called out, "Hello, strangers, who are you?
780   Where are you traveling from? What country do you call
      home?"
And Orestes answered, "We are Thessalians. We are going
to the Alpheus River to sacrifice to Olympian Zeus."
When he heard that, Aegisthus continued,
"Now you must join us here at our hearth
785   and share the sacrifice with me. I am slaughtering a bullock
to the Nymphs. At dawn after a good night's sleep
you can start out from here refreshed. Come, let's go in."
And just as he was saying this, he took us by the hand
and led us off the road with the words, "You cannot say no."
790   When we were inside, he went on, saying to his servants,
"Hurry, one of you, and bring water for the strangers' hands
so they can stand at the altar beside the lustral bowl."
But Orestes broke in, "We washed just now
in pure water from a flowing river.
795   If strangers are permitted to join in sacrifice with citizens,
King Aegisthus, we are ready and will not say no."
This conversation took place in the midst of the company.
Setting aside their spears, their master's defense,
all the servants set their hands to the task:
800   some brought bowls for the blood, others lifted the baskets,
others lit the fire, and around the sacrificial altars
some were setting up basins. The whole building was abuzz.
Then your mother's husband took the barley cakes
and threw them on the altars with these words,
805   "Nymphs of the rocks, I pray that with my wife,
the daughter of Tyndareos, I may continue to sacrifice,
in prosperity as I do now, but for my enemies nothing of the
      sort,"

791–837: This is a fairly complete documentation of the ritual of sacrifice:
the ritual washing, the carrying in of the implements for sacrifice, the
throwing of barley from the basket onto the altar, the cutting of hair from
the victim, the raising of the animal (if it is small enough) and the cutting
of its throat, the butchering, the inspection of the liver (at this point, the
sacrifice is cut short) for omens, roasting, libations of wine, and the sharing
of the meat (see Burkert 1985, pp. 56–59, 112–13).

meaning Orestes and you. My master, of course,
without speaking the words out loud, prayed the opposite,
to recover his father's house. Aegisthus took a straight-bladed   810
    knife
out of the basket and cut a tuft of the calf's hair
and placed it on the fire with his right hand,
and he cut its throat while servants hoisted the beast up
on their shoulders. Then he said to your brother,
"The Thessalians boast that it is a sign   815
of merit, if anyone excels at butchering a bull
or at breaking in horses. Here, stranger, take the sword
and show us that the legend about Thessaly's men is true."
Orestes took the well-made Dorian sword,
threw off his fine traveling cloak,   820
and, taking Pylades as his assistant in the work,
he made the servants stand aside. Grabbing hold of the calf's
    hoof,
he reached out, bared the white flesh,
and skinned off the hide quicker
than a racer on horseback completes a double track.   825
Then he loosened the flanks. Aegisthus took the sacred parts
in his hands and examined them. The lobe of the liver
was missing. The portal vein and gallbladder next to it
revealed to him ordeals of ill omen.
His face clouded over, and my master asked him,   830
"Is something troubling you?" "Stranger, I am in terror
of some treachery from outside. Agamemnon's son
is my worst enemy, and he is at war with my house."
To this Orestes said, "Do you really fear the treachery of an
    exile,
and you king of the city? Let's get ready for the feast—   835
will somebody bring us a Phthian cleaver
instead of this Dorian so I can break open the breastbone?"
He took it in his hands and struck. Aegisthus was still holding
    the guts,
scrutinizing them, trying to sort them out. As he was nodding

---

836: "Phthian cleaver"—a butcher knife.

839: "As he was nodding"—At a sacrifice the victim is made to nod as if
assenting to its death by being given a bowl of water to drink or having its
head pushed down so that it seems to be bowed.

840   over them, your brother, standing on tiptoe,
         struck his vertebrae and smashed the joints
         of his back. His whole body convulsed up and down
         and he bellowed in the throes of a horrific death.
         When they saw what was happening, the slaves rushed to arms,
845   a lot of them for two to fight against. With a show of courage
         Pylades and Orestes took their stand, brandishing weapons
         in the face of the mob. And he said, "I have not come
         as an enemy to the city or my former comrades.
         I have avenged myself on my father's killer.
850   I am the misused Orestes. Do not kill me.
         You were my father's servants in days past." Hearing his
              words,
         they stayed their spears. And he was recognized
         by an old man from the household.
         They started at once to crown your brother's head,
855   rejoicing and raising a happy cry. He is coming now,
         bringing not the Gorgon's head to show you,
         but Aegisthus whom you hate. Blood has now been shed
         in bitter repayment for the blood of the dead man.

Choral Dance

CHORUS:

[Strophe]

         Set your feet to dancing, dear,
860   like a fawn skipping up
         in a joyful leap high in the air.
         Your brother wins the crown,
         a victory surpassing those on the banks
         of Alpheus. But sing
865   a song of victory while I dance.

ELECTRA:
         Daylight, gleam of the sun's chariot,
         Earth and Night, which I saw before,
         now my eyes are free to open wide
         since Father's killer Aegisthus has fallen.

864: The site of the ancient Olympics.

Come, let me bring whatever I have,   870
whatever is stored in the house
to adorn his hair, friends,
so I may crown the head of my victorious brother.

CHORUS:

[Antistrophe]

Bring garlands for his head
while our dance, the Muses' joy,
goes on and on,   875
now that the kings we loved in times gone by
have overthrown the usurpers
and will rule the land in justice.
Now raise the shout in gladness to the music of the pipe.

(Enter Orestes, Pylades, and servants stage left from the
highway, carrying the body of Aegisthus.)

Fourth Episode

ELECTRA: (To Orestes, as she puts garlands on his head.)
Glorious in victory, born of a father   880
victorious in the war at Troy, Orestes,
take this garland for your curls.
You have come home, not after running
a useless footrace, but from killing our enemy
Aegisthus, who killed your father and mine.   885
And you, too, his companion in arms, son of a most loyal man,
Pylades, take this crown from my hand.
You shared equally with him in the contest.
I wish you happiness and prosperity.

ORESTES:

First, Electra, believe the gods are authors   890
of this good fortune and then praise me
as a servant of the gods and of luck.
Yes, I have come back from killing Aegisthus
not in word, but in deed; to add
to your certain knowledge of this, I bring you his dead body,   895
and if you so desire, make him prey for wild beasts
or fix him on a stake for birds to scavenge,

children of the sky. Now he is your slave,
who before was called your master.

ELECTRA:

900   I am ashamed, though I do want to speak.

ORESTES:

What is it? Go ahead and speak. You have nothing to fear.

ELECTRA:

I'm reluctant to insult the dead for fear of animosity.

ORESTES:

There is nobody who would find fault with you.

ELECTRA:

Our city is hard to please and quick to blame.

ORESTES:

905   Have your say, sister, if you desire. We were engaged
with him in a hatred that could make no truce.

ELECTRA:

Very well. Where start the tale of woes
and where end it? What words go in the middle?
Every day before dawn I never left off
910   rehearsing what I wished I could say to your face
if ever I could be free of the old fears.
Now at last I am free. I can even the score,
abusing you as I wanted to when you were alive.
You ruined my life. You made me and my brother
915   fatherless orphans when we had done you no wrong.
You entered an illicit union with Mother after you killed her
        husband,
commander of the Greeks, when you never even went to Troy.
And you reached such a depth of lunacy that you expected
you would not get an evil wife when you married my mother,
920   even after the two of you had fouled my father's bed.
You can be sure of this: when a man corrupts another's wife
in a secret liaison and then has the chance to marry her,
he is a fool if he thinks that when she was
unfaithful to the first she will be faithful to him.
925   You didn't see it, but your life was miserable.
You knew you had made a sinful marriage, and in you

my mother knew she had acquired a godless husband.
United in evil you shared each other's fate,
you her depravity and she yours.
This is what everybody in Argos was saying about you: 930
"He belongs to his wife, not she to her husband."
It's a disgrace, for the woman, not the man,
to be head of the household. And the children—
not called after their father's name
but their mother's—I have no respect for them.   935
When a man marries his better,
he loses his reputation; it's all about the woman.
And this is what deceived you most—though you were
    oblivious—
you prided yourself in *being* somebody because of your wealth,
which is nothing but a passing acquaintance.   940
It is nature, not property, that is steady.
Nature stays with you forever and relieves your troubles.
But wealth is unjust and keeps fools for company,
and after blossoming a day or two it is gone in the wind.
Your relations with women—not a proper topic for a   945
    virgin—
I will not speak of it, but will put it as a riddle.
You had your way because you ruled the royal roost
and were endowed with good looks. I hope I never have a
    husband
with a face like a girl, but one with a manly character:
their children grow up to be like Ares;   950
but the handsome ones only adorn the dance floor.
To hell with you. Time has found you out; you have paid up
but never learned—here is a lesson for a criminal:
even if he runs the first lap without a misstep
he should not think he has overtaken justice until he reaches   955
the finish line and rounds the final goal of life.

CHORUS:
  He has done awful things and paid an awful price
  to you and your brother. Justice has proved stronger.

ELECTRA:
  So far so good. Now we must carry his body inside
  and consign it to darkness, so when Mother   960
  arrives she will not see him dead before her throat is cut.

ORESTES:
Wait. Let's turn to a different story.

ELECTRA: *(Looking off down the road.)*
What's this? Do I see a rescue party from Mycenae?

ORESTES:
No, but my mother who gave me life.

ELECTRA:
965   Perfect timing then. She is coming straight into the
           snare.
       She really is magnificent in her carriage with all the
           trappings.

ORESTES:
What do we do about Mother? Are we going to kill her?

ELECTRA:
Has pity come over you because you see your mother in
     person?

ORESTES:
Woe!
How can I kill her? She gave me life and brought me up.

ELECTRA:
970   The same way she killed your father and mine.

ORESTES:
Phoebus! Your prophecy shows a total lack of wisdom.

ELECTRA:
If Apollo is a fool, who are the wise?

ORESTES:
Who decreed that I kill my mother, which I must not do.

ELECTRA:
How can you be tainted if you avenge your father?

ORESTES:
975   I will have to stand trial for matricide. Before this, I was free of
           guilt.

968: "Woe!"—another use of *pheu*. See note on 244.

ELECTRA:
> And yet if you do not vindicate your father you are guilty of
> impiety.

ORESTES:
> But my mother—how will I atone?

ELECTRA:
> And what if you fail to appease your father?

ORESTES:
> Did an avenging demon speak in the guise of the god?

ELECTRA:
> Sitting on Apollo's sacred tripod? I don't think so.   980

ORESTES:
> I cannot believe that was a true prophecy.

ELECTRA:
> You must not lose heart and turn into a coward.

ORESTES:
> Will I treat her with the same treachery?

ELECTRA:
> Yes, the same as when you killed Aegisthus.

ORESTES:
> I will go in. I am about to begin a terrible business,   985
> and I will do terrible things. If it is the gods' will
> so be it, but the ordeal is at once bitter and sweet.

> *(Exit Orestes into the house.)*

CHORUS: *(Addressing Clytemnestra as she arrives stage left from*
>   *the highway in a carriage attended by two or more*
>   *Trojan women and driven or led by male attendants.)*
> Hail!
> Royal lady of the Argive country,
> Tyndareos' daughter,

976: See Aeschylus' *Libation Bearers* 269–96 for what happens to a man
who does not avenge his father's murder.
980: "Apollo's sacred tripod"—The priestess of Apollo (the Pythia) delivered her prophecies seated on a tripod, a three-legged stand or altar.

990   sister of the two noble sons of Zeus,
       who live among the stars
       in the bright fire of the sky and hold the privilege
       of rescuing mortals on heavy seas.
       Greetings. I bow to you as to the blessed ones
995   for your vast wealth and happiness.
       Now is the time to look
       to your fortunes. Hail, my queen.

CLYTEMNESTRA:
       Climb down from the carriage, Trojan women.
       Take my hand to help me step down.
1000   The houses of the gods are decked out with Phrygian spoils,
       and these women chosen from the Trojan land are my share
       in place of my daughter who was taken from me,
       a small trophy, but they add to the grace of my house.

ELECTRA:
       Am I not a slave, too, cast out of my father's house
1005   to dwell here in poverty—Mother,
       may I not take your blessed hand?

CLYTEMNESTRA:
       My slaves are here. Do not trouble yourself.

ELECTRA:
       You sent me like a captive slave from my home,
       and with my home captured I am captured
1010   like these women, left without a father.

CLYTEMNESTRA:
       That was your father's doing when he made
       the decision to harm those dearest to him.
       I will have my say, and yet when a bad reputation
       possesses a woman, there is bitterness in her mouth,
1015   not a good thing. I speak from experience. If you understand
       the facts, you have the right to hate her, if she is
       deserving of hatred. Otherwise, why the hostility?
       Tyndareos gave me in marriage to your father
       not so that I or the children I bore him would be killed.
1020   Then Agamemnon, after enticing my daughter

1015–17: Compare to Euripides, Medea 219–21, 292–305.

with a promise of marriage to Achilles, took her away
to Aulis where the ships were drawn up. And there
he hoisted her over the altar
and cut through Iphigone's white cheek.
If it had been to avert the capture of the city or to benefit his   1025
    house
or to save our other children that he had to kill one
for the good of many, there might have been an excuse.
But, in fact, because Helen was a wild thing and her
    husband
didn't know how to control his straying wife—
for that he killed my daughter.
I was aggrieved over losing her, but still   1030
I did not turn savage and kill my husband at once.
But he came home with that god-possessed madwoman
and introduced her into our bed and we were installed
together, two brides in the same house.
We women are giddy creatures, I can't deny it,   1035
but—that being the case—when the husband strays
and pushes away his wife, the woman is likely
to imitate her husband and take on another "friend."
Then blame puts the spotlight on us,
but the responsible party keeps his sterling reputation.   1040
If Menelaus had been carried off from his house in secret,
would I have had to kill Orestes to rescue
my sister's husband? How would your father
have put up with that? Was it right that I suffer
at his hands but he not die for killing my child?   1045
Yes, I killed him. I turned, where I found a way,
to his enemies. Do you think any of your father's friends
would have abetted me in his murder?
It's your turn to speak if you wish and respond freely.
Tell me, if you can, how your father's death was undeserved.   1050

CHORUS:
    What you say is just, but it's a disgraceful kind of justice.
    A woman must go along with her husband in everything

1024: Iphigone—alternate form of Iphigenia.
1032: "That god-possessed madwoman"—Cassandra, the captive priestess and prophetess.

if she is sensible. Whoever does not agree with this
does not count in my book.

ELECTRA:

1055   Remember, Mother, that your last words
gave me the right to speak freely.

CLYTEMNESTRA:
Yes, and I say it again and I won't take it back.

ELECTRA:
When you hear what I have to say, will you hurt me?

CLYTEMNESTRA:
No. I promise not to. Set your mind at rest.

ELECTRA:

1060   I can speak, then. This is what I have to say first.
Mother, if only you had better sense.
Your good looks do you credit,
Helen's and yours both, but you were born alike,
both vain and unworthy of Castor.

1065   She was "raped" of her own free will and ruined herself,
and you destroyed the best man in all Greece,
holding out the pretext that it was because of your daughter
that you killed your husband. They don't know you as well as
        I do.
Before your daughter's sacrifice was authorized,

1070   as soon as your husband was out the door
you started arranging your hair in the mirror.
When the man is away from home, if a woman starts
making herself pretty, write her off as a whore.
She has no reason to show her beautiful face

1075   outside the house unless she is looking for trouble.
I'm the only one in all Greece who knows what you are:
if the Trojan side was doing well, you were all smiles
and if it went badly, then your face clouded over
because you did not want Agamemnon to come home from Troy.

1080   And yet you had every opportunity to be virtuous:
you had a husband no worse than Aegisthus,
chosen by all of Greece to be commander in chief;
and when your sister Helen did what she did,
it was possible for you to attain an excellent reputation.

Badness provides an example to do the right thing for all to see. 1085
But if, as you claim, my father killed your daughter,
what harm did my brother or I do you?
How is it that after you killed your husband you did not
    attach us
more closely to our father's house, but instead brought to your
    marriage
what didn't belong to you, adding our inheritance to your 1090
    dowry?
And why is your husband not in exile for your son
or why is he not dead for me, since he killed me twice
as much as my sister even if I am still alive? And if in
    repayment
for murder there will be more murder, am I to kill you
with the help of your son Orestes, to avenge our father? 1095
If what you did is right, that is right, too.
[Anyone who marries a bad woman for money
instead of nobility is a fool. Poor but virtuous
marriages are better for the home than great ones.]

CHORUS:
[Women's marriages are a matter of luck; 1100
I have seen some turn out well, others badly.]

CLYTEMNESTRA:
My dear girl, naturally you love your father.
This happens. Some children favor the male parent
and others love their mothers more than their fathers.
I understand. And I'm not really 1105
very happy with what I did, dear child.
But why are you so unwashed and ill-clothed
when you have just given birth?

1097–99: These lines seem to be added to make sense of the chorus' two
lines that follow, and are probably an editor's interpolation.

1100–1101: The chorus usually speaks between the speeches in an *agōn*
(debate scene) to mark off the different speakers. Choruses like to make
general remarks that are not necessarily very significant—or even relevant—
to what the actors are saying.

1107–8: Some editors move 1107–8 to open the speech that begins at
1132 because these lines interrupt the flow of Clytemnestra's remarks. In
defense of keeping them here, she has just called Electra *teknon* ("my

I regret some of my decisions, especially that
1110   I drove my husband to anger more than I needed to.

ELECTRA:

It's too late for regret when there is no remedy.
Father is dead, but why don't you bring home
your son from his life of exile far from his homeland?

CLYTEMNESTRA:

I'm afraid. I have to look out for my own welfare, not his.
1115   They say he is angry over the murder of his father.

ELECTRA:

Why do you keep your husband so savage against us?

CLYTEMNESTRA:

That's his nature, but you are stubborn, too.

ELECTRA:

I am grieving, but I'll put an end to my rage.

CLYTEMNESTRA:

Then he will not be so hard on you.

ELECTRA:

1120   He has proud thoughts. He is in my house.

---

child"), and now takes a real look at her. The sight of Electra's sorry state makes Clytemnestra feel regret more poignantly.

1110: This is a difficult line: the manuscripts have *posin* (accusative of the Greek word for "husband"), which in this context would refer to Aegisthus. With this reading, Clytemnestra regrets egging him on and encouraging his mistreatment of her children from her first marriage (see 1107–8 and 1116). An objection to this is that earlier, the Farmer said she protected them (27–28). Clytemnestra might also refer to her urging Aegisthus' participation in the murder of Agamemnon. The dative *posei,* referring to Agamemnon, has been suggested, and is accepted in many editions and translations. It would mean something like: "that I whipped up my anger excessively against my husband" or "I drove [myself] into anger at my husband." A degree of ambiguity could be maintained by translating "I whipped up anger against my husband more than I should." Clytemnestra regrets nursing and goading anger (her own and Aegisthus') against Agamemnon. This would suggest that she almost cannot remember why she killed him. What is interesting is that the two arguments begin to blend together, as do the two husbands.

CLYTEMNESTRA:
There you go. You are igniting new rancor.

ELECTRA:
I'll be silent. I fear him as I fear him.

CLYTEMNESTRA:
Let's stop this talk. Why did you summon me, daughter?

ELECTRA:
You have heard of my miserable childbearing:
help me sacrifice for it—I don't know how— 1125
at the tenth moon, as is customary for a birth.
I have no experience, since this is my first child.

CLYTEMNESTRA:
That's not my job, but the woman who delivered you.

ELECTRA:
I delivered myself and gave birth all alone.

CLYTEMNESTRA:
Is your house so remote and far from friends? 1130

ELECTRA:
No one wants to be friends with the poor.

CLYTEMNESTRA:
Very well. I will go in and sacrifice to the gods
for the completion of the infant's term, and after I do this for you
I must go to the farm where my husband is sacrificing
to the Nymphs. You, servants, take the beasts 1135
and put them to their mangers. Be ready when you think
I have finished this sacrifice to the gods.

(Servants lead away the animals and carriage stage right.)

I have to be there for my husband, too.

(Exit Clytemnestra through the central doors.)

ELECTRA:
Go now inside my impoverished home. But, please, watch out
not to soil your dress on my sooty walls. 1140

1140: "My sooty walls"—an allusion to Aeschylus' *Agamemnon* 773–74,
"Justice shines her light on humble, smoke-filled homes." Not even there,

You will sacrifice as you must to the gods.
The basket is ready for beginning the ritual and the knife is
      sharpened
which took down the bull. You will fall, struck down
beside him, and be his bride in Hades' halls,
1145   the man you slept with in life. That favor
I will give you. And you will pay for Father's death.

(Exit Electra through the central doors.)

Third Stasimon

CHORUS:

[Strophe]

Requital of evils—breezes blow
in reverse on the house. Then, in the bath
our leader fell dead:
1150   a loud scream from the house and from the stone copings
when he cried out, "Hard woman, why do you kill me
when I come back to my homeland in the tenth seed time?"

   . . . . . .

   . . . . . .

[Antistrophe]

1155   Time turning back brings her to justice
for her illicit bed; with her own hand
she killed her husband coming home at last
to the high Cyclopean walls
1160   with the sharp blade, taking the axe in her hands. O suffering
husband, what evil took hold of the wretched woman?
A mountain lioness dwelling in the woods
by the meadowlands brought this about.

---

as the displacement of the setting tells us: any hut or hovel can serve as the
scene building and become the scene of brutal, unseen murder.

1154: Two lines are missing here, the metrical match for 1163–64.

1158: "High Cyclopean walls"—The massive stone architecture in and
around Mycenae was attributed to the Cyclopes, one-eyed giants, sons of
Uranus and Gaia.

CLYTEMNESTRA: *(From within.)*
  Children, in the name of the gods, do not kill your mother.   1165
CHORUS:
  Do you hear her cry from inside?
CLYTEMNESTRA:
  Oh my god!
CHORUS:
  I cry out for her, too, as she is overpowered by her children.
  A god, you know, metes out justice, whenever it happens.
  You suffered harshly. You committed atrocities,   1170
  wretched woman, against your husband.

  *(Enter Electra and Orestes with the dead bodies through
  the central doors on the* ekkyklēma.)*

Exodos

Kommos

CHORUS:
  Look, here they are, coming out, soaked
  in the fresh blood of their mother,
  evidence of her defeat, the meaning of her miserable cries.
  There is no house more unhappy than that
  of Tantalus' descendants, and there never has been.   1175
ORESTES:
  Earth and Zeus, who see all
  of mortals' affairs, look on these deeds, murderous
  and foul, the two bodies lying
  together on the ground, struck   1180
  by my own hand in vengeance for my loss.
ELECTRA:
  So sad, so sad, and I am the cause.
  Through fire I plunged against my mother, in my misery,
  my mother who gave me life, her daughter.

Ekkyklēma: The *ekkyklēma* (thing rolled out) was a revolve or platform
on wheels, used to display the result of interior action.
Kommos: A lament sung by chorus and actors.

CHORUS:
Bad luck, it was your bad luck,
1185   mother who bore unforgettable
miseries, unforgettable and worse,
suffering at the hands of your children,
justly you paid for their father's death.

ORESTES:
1190   Phoebus, you intoned your justice
obscurely, but clear are the sorrows
you caused and you bestowed on me,
the murderer's sentence of exile from the land of Hellas.
What other city can I go to?
1195   What stranger, what decent man
will look me in the face,
the man who killed his mother?

ELECTRA:
Woe, woe. Where will I go,
to what choral rites, what marriage?
1200   What husband will take me into his bridal bed?

CHORUS:
Again, your thinking
has shifted again with the wind.
Now your mind is right, but then
it was not, and you did terrible things,
1205   dear girl, to your brother against his will.

ORESTES:
You saw how the poor woman opened
her gown, bared her breast as she was being murdered.
Woe. She let the limbs that gave me birth
fall to the ground, and her hair—I—

1208–9: "She let the limbs . . . and her hair"—Orestes cannot finish the
line (an example of *aposiopesis,* an abrupt breaking off in the midst of a
phrase). During the murder, when Clytemnestra dropped to the floor, he
would have taken hold of her hair—the only part of her he would have had
to touch—as he pulled her head back to slit her throat. He would have
leaned over her and she reached up to touch his cheek (1216). According
to another reading of 1209, Orestes says, "I felt faint."

CHORUS:
  I see clearly how you passed through torment   1210
  when you heard the heart-rending moan
  of the mother who gave you life.

ORESTES:
  These words she screamed as she stretched out her hand
  to my face: "My child, I beg you."   1215
  She hung from my cheek
  so the weapon fell from my hand.

CHORUS:
  The unhappy one, how did you dare to look
  with your own eyes on the murder of your mother
  as she breathed her last?   1220

ORESTES:
  I held my cloak over my eyes
  and began the sacrifice, letting the knife
  go into my mother's neck.

ELECTRA:
  And I urged you on.
  I put my hand on the weapon with yours.   1225

CHORUS:
  You have caused the most terrible of sufferings.

ORESTES:
  Take hold, cover Mother's limbs with her robe
  and fit back her slit throat.
  You gave birth to us, your own murderers.

ELECTRA:
  Look, we are putting your robes around you,
  Mother, loved and unloved.   1230

1221: "I held my cloak over my eyes"—Like Perseus beheading the Gorgon, Orestes covers his eyes.

1225: Besides having the most vivid description (in the form of a reenactment) of the murder of Clytemnestra, this is the only version in which Electra is physically present and takes part.

Dei ex Machina

(The Dioscuri appear above the rooftop on the mēchanē.)

CHORUS:
> This is the end of great evils for the house.
> But, look! Here on top of the building
> there are appearing some divinities or some of
1235   the heavenly gods. This is not the way
> mortals approach. Why in the world are they coming
> into the clear sight of men?

DIOSCURI (CASTOR speaking):
> Son of Agamemnon, listen. Your mother's
> two brothers address you, the sons of Zeus:
1240   I am Castor, and this is my brother Polydeuces.
> Just now we have put down the violent disturbance
> of a ship at sea and arrived in Argos when we saw
> the murder of our sister here, your mother.
> She has met with justice but you did not do justice,
1245   and Phoebus—Phoebus is my king;
> I will hold my tongue—he is wise, but his oracle was not.
> Still we must go along with it. It is necessary now
> to do what Fate and Zeus have decreed about you.
> To Pylades give Electra to take home as his wife.
1250   And you—leave Argos. You are not permitted
> to walk in the city after killing your mother.
> The terrible fates, the dog-faced goddesses,
> will drive you wandering in madness.
> When you reach Athens, embrace the holy statue
1255   of Pallas Athena. As they swarm you with their hissing snakes,
> she will keep them off, so they cannot touch you,
> raising over your head the circle of the Gorgon's face.
> There is the Rock of Ares where the gods first sat
> to pass judgment in a case of murder

Mēchanē: The *mēchanē* (machine) was a crane that lifted actors above the scene building.

1252: "The dog-faced goddesses"—the Erinyes or Furies.

1259: "The Rock of Ares"—the Areopagus (Ares' hill or outcrop), the Athenians' homicide court, northwest of the Acropolis in Athens. Euripides attributes the founding of the court of the Areopagus to the gods' trial of Ares for killing Poseidon's son Halirrhothius, who had raped Ares'

when brutal Ares killed Halirrhothius 1260
son of the lord of the sea in anger
over his daughter's ungodly coupling, where a vote
most sacred in the eyes of the gods is secure from that time.
There you must risk trial for murder.
Equal votes cast will save you from 1265
the penalty of death. Loxias will take the blame
upon himself for commanding the murder of your mother.
And this law will be established for all time
that the defendant always wins when the votes are equal.
And the dreaded goddesses overcome by this distress 1270
will go down into a cleft of the earth right beside the hill,
which will be a solemn holy oracle for humankind.
You must go to live in a city of the Arcadians
by the streams of Alpheus near the sacred Lycian precinct;
the city will be named after you. 1275
This much I have to say to you. Aegisthus' body
will be given a proper burial by the citizens of Argos.
But as for your mother—Menelaus—he's just arrived
in Nauplia from the time he captured Troy—
he and Helen will bury her. Helen has come 1280

daughter. Aeschylus, *The Furies* (*Eumenides*) 481–84 represents Athena establishing the court for Orestes' trial.

1265–66: "Equal votes cast will save you"—See Aeschylus, *The Furies* (*Eumenides*) 735, 741, 752–53, on the vote of Athena, which favors the defendant in the event of a tie.

1271: "Cleft of the earth"—See Aeschylus, *The Furies* (*Eumenides*) 805; the cleft or chasm is at the northeast angle of the Areopagus.

1273–75: "You must go . . . the city will be named after you"—In other versions, Orestes is only temporarily exiled and returns to rule in Mycenae. The city dubiously named for him is Orestheion (mentioned in Thucydides, *The Peloponnesian War* 5.64.3 and Herodotus, *The Histories* 9.11), near the source of the Alpheus River. The Lycian sanctuary of Zeus is on Mount Lykaion, a mountain in Arcadia in the west central Peloponnesus, about twenty-two miles from Olympia (see map).

1276–80: In Homer's *Odyssey* (3.309–10), Orestes himself gives the funeral feast—of both Aegisthus and his mother—for the Argives.

1280–81: The story of Helen in Egypt appears in Herodotus' *Histories*, Stesichorus' Palinode (quoted in Plato, *Phaedrus* 243a–b), and the *Cypria*, as well as in Homer's *Odyssey*.

from the house of Proteus in Egypt and did not go to Troy.
To cause strife and death among mortals, Zeus
sent a phantom of Helen to Troy.
Let Pylades take his bride and go home

1285   to Achaean country, and let him take along
that man called your brother-in-law
into the land of the Phocians and give him a mass of wealth.
You now, set out over the neck of the isthmus
and go to the prosperous hill of Cecrops.

1290   For after completing your appointed sentence for murder
you will prosper, free of troubles.

ORESTES:
Sons of Zeus, may we approach
and speak with you?

CASTOR:
Yes, you are not polluted by these slaughters.

ELECTRA:
1295   May I be part of the dialogue, too, sons of Tyndareos?

CASTOR:
Yes, you, too. I attribute this act
of murder to Phoebus.

ORESTES:
How is it that though you are gods
and the brothers of the murdered woman
1300   you did not hold off the Furies from the house?

CASTOR:
Fate's grim necessity led to what had to be
and the commands of Phoebus, less than wise.

ELECTRA:
What Apollo, what oracles decreed
that I become Mother's murderer?

1283: "Phantom of Helen"—The reunion of the real Helen and Menelaus
in Egypt after the Trojan War is the subject of Euripides' *Helen*.

1289: Cecrops—a mythical king of Athens.

1292 ff.: The distribution of lines is uncertain.

CASTOR:
> Shared actions, shared fates;   1305
> one madness of your fathers
> tears through you both.

ORESTES:
> My sister, seeing you after so long,
> I am to lose the joy of your love so soon,
> and when I leave I will leave you behind.   1310

CASTOR:
> She has a husband and home. She has not
> suffered brutally, except that she is leaving
> the city of Argos.

ELECTRA:
> And what other grief is greater
> than to leave the borders of your homeland?   1315

ORESTES:
> And I will go away from my father's home
> and submit Mother's murder
> to the votes of aliens.

CASTOR:
>   Be brave. You will go
> to the holy city of Pallas. Have courage.   1320

ELECTRA:
> Press your breast to mine,
> dearest brother.
> The curses of Mother's murder
> sever us from our father's home.

ORESTES:
> Throw yourself into my arms. Embrace me. Raise the   1325
>   dirge
> as you would at my tomb if I were dead.

CASTOR:
> Alas, alas. Your cries of grief are terrible
> even for gods to hear.
> There is in me and the heavenly gods
> pity for mortals full of suffering.   1330

ORESTES:
I will not see you again.

ELECTRA:
And I will not come again into your sight.

ORESTES:
This is the last time you will speak to me.

ELECTRA:
Farewell, city.
1335   A long farewell to you, fellow women of the city.

ORESTES:
Most loyal—are you going now?

ELECTRA:
I am going. My face is wet with tears.

(Exit Electra and Pylades stage left.)

ORESTES:
1340   Pylades, good-bye.
Make my sister your bride.

(Exit Orestes, running, stage right.)

CASTOR:
Marriage will be their care. The dogs are here!
Run from them now, racing to Athens.
They will set upon you a frightening pace,
1345   snake-handed, black-coated,
bearing fruit of terrible pains.
We two must leave in haste, soaring
through stretches of the sky to the Sikel sea
to rescue the seafaring ships.
1350   We do not come to the aid of the polluted
but those who hold what's right, holy, and dear
in life; releasing them
from hard toils, we keep them safe.
Let no one choose to be unjust;

1348: Sikel—the sea between Sicily and Greece. Some scholars have taken this to be a reference to the Athenian failed invasion of Sicily in 415–413 B.C.E.

let no one side with perjurers.   1355
As a god, I have this to say to mortals.

(Exit the Dioscuri on the mēchanē.*)*

CHORUS:
Farewell! If anyone can fare well
and not be broken by bad luck,
he alone will prosper.

(The chorus files out in both directions.)

–END–

EURIPIDES

Phoenician Women

Translated, with Notes, by Cecelia Eaton Luschnig

Cast of Characters

JOCASTA	wife and mother of Oedipus
PAIDAGOGOS	servant, attendant to Antigone
ANTIGONE	daughter of Jocasta and Oedipus
CHORUS	of young Phoenician women
POLYNICES	exiled son of Jocasta and Oedipus
ETEOCLES	king of Thebes, son of Jocasta and Oedipus
CREON	brother of Jocasta
TIRESIAS	famous Theban seer
MENOECEUS	son of Creon
MESSENGER 1	Eteocles' lieutenant
MESSENGER 2	
OEDIPUS	former king of Thebes, son and husband of Jocasta

Nonspeaking Roles

TIRESIAS' DAUGHTER

Several extras are needed as attendants to Eteocles and Creon, and to convey the bodies in the exodos.

Phoenician Women was first performed at the Greater Dionysia around 410 B.C.E.

Phoenician Women

SCENE: *The setting is the palace of Cadmus at Thebes. The city is under siege. It is morning of the day of the battle of the Argives against the Thebans (known as the War of the Seven against Thebes). Stage right leads to the town and stage left to the battlefield.*

Prologue

Scene 1 (Jocasta's monologue)

> *(Enter Jocasta from the palace. She is dressed in black and her white hair is cut in mourning.)*

JOCASTA:
Morning sun, on swift steeds pulling out the daylight,   3
it was a tragic day for Thebes when you sent down

Title: The Greek name of *Phoenician Women* is *Phoenissae* (traditional Latin spelling) or *Phoinissai* (transliterated Greek); the play is named after the chorus of captive women from Tyre, who happened to be caught behind enemy lines inside Thebes when it came under siege by the Argives and their allies.

Prologue: The part of the play before the entrance of the chorus. Euripides usually begins his plays with a monologue by one of the characters (as in *Medea* and *Electra*) or by a god (as in *Alcestis* and *Hippolytus*). A character usually enters from the scene building and identifies it, here as the house of Cadmus. What slice of the epic banquet is being offered here? In most plays this monologue is followed by a dialogue (as here). This kind of monologue that gives the back story and situates us (the audience/reader) within the legend has been called "the Playbill prologue." Through selection, juxtaposition, choice of words, and parallel actions it also alerts us to the themes highlighted in the particular showing and telling of the story being staged. Although the tragedians used traditional material, each reworking of a myth or legend is a unique combination of innovation and convention.

3: The translation begins at line 3 because the first two lines in the manuscript are deleted by most editors as too pretentious:

> Cutting a roadway through the sky among the stars
> mounted aboard your gold embellished chariot . . .

5   your rays, the day that Cadmus reached this land
        crossing from Phoenicia's island in the sea.
        Cadmus married Harmonia, Cypris' daughter,
        and fathered Polydorus. From him they say
        Labdacus was born and from him came Laius;
10   this is where I come in. I am Menoeceus' daughter—
        and Creon is my brother, my own mother's son—
        they call me Jocasta, a name my father
        gave me. Laius became my husband. But when
        he was childless after years of marriage to me
15   he went to question Phoebus' oracle
        and ask for male children to carry on his line.
        The god intoned, "King of Thebes, keeper of fine horses,
        do not try to plant a crop of children against gods' will,

---

Her address to the rising sun indicates the time of day, confirmed in the next scene in which Antigone and her slave discuss what they see in the early dawn light.

5: Cadmus, descendant of Zeus and Io, brother of Europa, was the legendary founder and first king of Thebes, and patriarch of the line from Polydorus through the sons of Oedipus. The long history of Thebes is the *chronos* (time as a block) in which the *kairos* (critical time) takes place. For Jocasta it is compressed into a series of special days, days of passage for the members of the ruling family: Cadmus' literal passage to Thebes, marriages, births, comings of age, and deaths. These are the historical events that are enumerated to mark special days off from every span between sunrise and sunset.

6: Literally, "sea-girt Phoenicia." Cadmus came from Tyre, an island city of Phoenicia (joined to the mainland by Alexander; now Soúr in Lebanon). Through Jocasta, Euripides makes the Phoenician connection stronger than in other Theban tragedies.

7: Cypris—a name for Aphrodite, the Cyprian, so called because she came forth from the sea foam on Cyprus. Ares was the father of Harmonia.

8–9: The succession of kings of Thebes, after Cadmus.

10: It was a common practice to name a son after his grandfather. Creon's son, who has a part in this play, is named Menoeceus.

15: Phoebus—a name for Apollo; Laius went to the famous oracle in Delphi.

17: See the Introduction for a comparison of the oracles given to Laius in the Theban plays.

18: In Greek one speaks of "sowing" a woman's body.

for if you father a child, he that is born will kill you
and your whole house will wade in its own blood." 20
But he gave in to pleasure: under the influence of Bacchus
he planted in me a son and—when the baby was born—
the god's words came back to him and he knew his mistake.
He gave the infant to herdsmen to expose
in Hera's sacred meadow on craggy Kithairōn, 25
but first he pierced its ankles through with iron pins.
This is why Greece has named him Oedipus.
But instead, Polybus' horse herders took him,
brought him home, put him into their queen's arms.
The object of my birth pangs she put to her own breast 30
and convinced her husband the child was hers.
When he came to puberty, the hair reddening on his chin,
either my son intuited it or he heard somebody talking
and wanted to find out who his real parents were.
Off he went to Phoebus' temple; my husband Laius set out 35
for Delphi, too; he had to find out about the exposed child,
hoping that it was no longer alive. They fell into step
    together,
the two of them, where the road to Phocis splits off.
Laius' driver shouted out the command:
"Stranger, make way for the king's men." 40

21: He was either intoxicated or in a Dionysiac frenzy.

24: Exposure of unwanted children was a practice in the ancient world.

25: Kithairōn—a mountain near Thebes.

27: Oedipus—here interpreted as "Swollen Foot." On the theme of naming, see 12, 57–58.

28: Polybus was king of Corinth.

32: The Greeks perceived the first growth of beard (peach fuzz) as reddish.

33: An important theme introduced in Jocasta's speech is knowledge. Sophocles' *Oedipus Tyrannus* is universally recognized as a play about knowledge. Here Jocasta over and over shows that knowledge is reached by chance and leads to destructive actions.

38: In the various versions of this legend Laius and Oedipus meet at a crossroads; here both men are heading for Delphi and neither reaches it. Laius had disobeyed the earlier oracle; Oedipus never even gets to question the oracle. He has no reason to suppose that he has killed his father nor that he is destined to marry his mother, as he has been told in Sophocles' *Oedipus Tyrannus*.

But he, in pride, continued along, without a word.
The horses' hooves bloodied the tendons of his feet.
At that—why go through the details of our tragedy?—
son killed father and took the chariot home as a gift
45   for his stepfather. The Sphinx then came to torment us,
ravaging the city. And with my husband dead
my brother Creon offered my bed as prize:
if anyone could solve the monster's cunning riddle
he would win me as his wife. It happened somehow
50   that my son Oedipus figured out the Sphinx's song
[and for this he became king of Thebes]
and won the scepter of this kingdom as his prize.
In ignorance the poor wretch married his own mother;
in ignorance I, his mother, went to bed with my son.
55   To my son I bore two male children,
Eteocles and Polynices, known for his strength,
and two girls: Ismene, named by her father,
and the older of the two, Antigone—I chose her name.
When he learned he was bedding his mother
60   on top of all the sufferings he endured, Oedipus
inflicted bloody butchery on his own eyes

45: Sphinx—a winged female creature, part maiden, part dog; a symbol of death who posed a riddle to young men and devoured those who could not answer it. In brief, the best-known version of the riddle asks, "What goes on four feet at dawn, two at midday, and three in the evening?" Oedipus answered, "A human being."

51: Brackets around lines in the translation indicate sections of doubtful authenticity.

56: Literally, "the famous force of Polynices." Instead of naming him outright, Jocasta uses a periphrasis, putting a characteristic in place of his name. This is a common usage in Homer for strong men: "the might of Heracles" = "mighty Heracles." In a further twist, the characteristic is more suited etymologically to Eteocles, whose name means "true glory." Polynices means "full of strife."

57–58: Ismene plays a role in Aeschylus' *Seven against Thebes* and Sophocles' *Antigone* and *Oedipus at Colonus*. Euripides adds the information that Antigone is older.

61–62: See Sophocles, *Oedipus Tyrannus* 1268–80, for a full narrative of Oedipus' self-blinding. In Sophocles, Oedipus removes the brooches from the corpse of his dead mother.

and gored his eyeballs with my golden brooches.
And when our sons' cheeks began to darken
they hid their father under lock and key, hoping the story
of his unfathomable fate would pass out of memory.   65
Oedipus is alive still in the house. Sick from his tragic fate,
he brings down the most heinous curses on his sons,
willing them to split their estate with sharpened steel.
The two of them became terrified that the gods
would fulfill his curses if they lived together.   70
They agreed then that first the younger, Polynices,
would leave the country in voluntary exile,
and Eteocles would stay and hold the scepter.
At year's end they would change places. But once he sat
in the yoke of power, *he* refused to leave the throne   75
and sent Polynices away a refugee from his country.
And so *he* went to Argos and married into Adrastus' family.
He recruited a massive force of Argives, which now he leads
against the walls of our seven-gated city
to demand his father's scepter and a share in his country.   80
Trying to end their strife, I persuaded my son Polynices
to come under truce to my son Eteocles, before taking up arms.
He has sent a messenger to say he will come.

(Jocasta looks to the sky and assumes a posture of prayer.)

You who dwell in the shining recesses of the sky,
Zeus, preserve us and reconcile my sons.   85
You must not, if you are really wise, permit
the same unhappy man to always have bad luck.

(Exit Jocasta into the palace.)

67–68: See Aeschylus, *Seven against Thebes* 785–89, for Oedipus' curse on his sons to divide the estate by the sword.

77: Argos refers to both a city and an area (the Argolid) in the Peloponnese. In the play it is indistinguishable from Mycenae. The people are variously called Argives, Mycenaeans, Pelasgians, and Danaans (from King Danaus).

77: Adrastus—the Argive king, son of Talaus; best known for the expeditions against Thebes. He survived and went on to lead the expedition of the sons (*epigonoi*) of the Seven.

86–87: Scenes in Greek tragedy often end with a general reflection.

Scene 2 (Dialogue between Antigone and her minder, Paidagogos)

(From the rooftop, the voice of Paidagogos is heard. He appears on the roof first and then helps Antigone up onto the roof.)

PAIDAGOGOS:
Antigone, flower of your father's house,
your mother has heard your pleas and let you
90   leave your maiden's chamber to come up here
to the top story of the house to see the Argive army,
but wait there while I look up and down the street
to see if any of the townspeople are on the path
and a nasty slur fall on me, a slave, or on you,
95   a royal princess. I asked around and can tell
everything I saw and heard from the Argives
when I went to bring your brother the terms of the truce
from here to there and back here again from him.
Well, I don't see anyone coming this way from town.
100   Come, put your foot onto this old wooden ladder.
Look over the expanse of land and out by Ismenus'
waters
and Dirkē's stream; see how vast the enemy's army is.

ANTIGONE: *(Singing.)*
Hold out your old hand to my young one; hold it out
to help me lift myself up and steady my step
105   on the stair.

From the rooftop: This is a distinct scene, a set piece, but it is also innovative. It is reminiscent of the *teichoscopia* (view from the walls) in Homer, *Iliad* 3, in which Helen identifies the Greek warriors to the old men watching from the wall of Troy; its subject might also remind us of Andromache in *Iliad* 6 when she expresses her concern about defenses. Like Hector in the *Iliad*, the old man is certain that the besiegers have justice on their side. The rooftop is more commonly used for the appearance of gods (as in Euripides' *Electra, Heracles,* and *Hippolytus*), but Aeschylus' *Agamemnon* opens with a watchman on the roof.

90: Women had separate quarters in a Greek house, and unmarried girls were carefully guarded to preserve their virginity.

101–2: Ismenus (Hismenos) and Dirkē are the two rivers of Thebes.

PAIDAGOGOS:
Here, hold tight, my girl. We are just in time.
At this very moment the Pelasgian army is on the move,
dividing up into their separate companies.

ANTIGONE:
Goddess Hecate, daughter of Leto,
the whole plain   110
is flashing with bronze.

PAIDAGOGOS:
Yes, it's no puny force Polynices has led against our
    country,
but a thundering host of horsemen and ten thousand men in
    arms.

ANTIGONE:
Are the city gates shut tight with bars
and the bronze bolts, are they fitted into the stoneworks
of Amphion's wall?   115

PAIDAGOGOS:
No need to worry. We are safe inside the city.
Look there if you want to learn about the first company.

ANTIGONE:
Who is that with the white plume—
out in front, leading an army,   120
lifting a solid bronze shield lightly on his arm?

PAIDAGOGOS:
The leader of a company, my lady.

107: Pelasgian is another name for either Peloponnesian or Thessalian after a supposed founder, Pelasgus. (The word could be omitted in performance, or "Argive" or "enemy" substituted.)

109–10: Leto was also the mother of Artemis and Apollo. Hecate is closely connected with Artemis; she is goddess of the crossroads and is associated with magic and the moon.

115: Amphion, with his twin brother Zethus, ruled Thebes and built the walls around the city to the accompaniment of Amphion's lyre. Amphion married Niobe.

ANTIGONE:

But who? Where is he from?
Tell me, old man, what is his name?

PAIDAGOGOS:

125   He claims Mycenaean origin and lives
by the waters of Lerna. He is King Hippomedon.

ANTIGONE:

Ooh, how haughty he is and scary looking,
a giant sprung from the earth, just the way they look
130   in paintings, glowing bright as a star, like an alien creature.

PAIDAGOGOS:

See that man crossing Dirkē's water?

ANTIGONE:

He looks different. The style of his armor is strange.
Who is he?

PAIDAGOGOS:

He is Oeneus' son,
Tydeus. In his heart he carries the war-lust of Aetolia.

ANTIGONE:

135   Is he the one who married
the sister of Polynices' bride?
How alien he is in his armor, so outlandish.

PAIDAGOGOS:

All the Aetolians carry light shields, my child,
140   and are good shots with the javelin.

ANTIGONE:

Tell me, old man, how can you see everything so clearly?

PAIDAGOGOS:

I got to know the insignia on their shields
when I went to bring your brother the terms of truce,
and now I can recognize the men in their armor.

125–26: Hippomedon was an enormous man from Lerna.

134–40: Tydeus, an Aetolian, son of Oeneus, committed murder and had to go into exile. His son Diomedes is well known from the *Iliad* and the *Aeneid.*

ANTIGONE:
Who is this passing by the monument of Zethus—   145
he has curly hair and eyes like a Gorgon,
a young man by the look of him,
and is he leader of a company, since a crowd fully armed
follows at his heels?

PAIDAGOGOS:
That is Parthenopaeus, Atalanta's son.   150

ANTIGONE:
Well, I hope Artemis who roams the mountains
with his mother shoots him down with her arrows
and kills him—the man who came to destroy my city.

PAIDAGOGOS:
I hope so, too, my child. But they have justice on their
   side.
I'm afraid the gods may favor them and rightly so.   155

ANTIGONE:
Where is the man born of the same mother as I,
doomed to misery,
dear, dear old man, tell me, where is Polynices?

PAIDAGOGOS:
There he is, near the tomb of Niobe's seven daughters.
He is standing next to Adrastus.   160
Can you see him?

145: Zethus, twin brother of Amphion (115), was the strong, violent type; Amphion was the artistic and musical brother.

146: In Greek, *gorgos*, the adjective meaning "grim" or "fierce," from which *Gorgo*, the Gorgon, is derived. The best-known Gorgon was Medusa, whose severed head turned anyone who looked at her to stone. The head was ultimately fixed to Athena's shield or in the middle of her aegis.

150: Parthenopaeus ("maiden-faced")—son of Atalanta, the famous huntress who was raised by a bear.

159–60: Niobe was the daughter of Tantalus, wife of Amphion, mother of seven sons and seven daughters. She boasted about her children to Leto, who had only one of each. Leto, being a goddess, got her son and daughter, Apollo and Artemis, to kill all of Niobe's children. According to Pausanias (IX.5.9), they died in a plague.

ANTIGONE:
                    Yes, I see him, but not clearly.
I can just make out a faint outline, the shape of his body.
I wish I could race through the air
with feet like a cloud blown in the wind
165   to my own dear brother and at long last
throw my arms around his dear, dear neck,
poor refugee.
How splendid he is in his gold armor, old man,
glinting like the sun's rays at dawn.

PAIDAGOGOS:
170   He is coming home under truce to fill your heart
with joy.

ANTIGONE:
                    That one, old man, who is he,
the one mounted in the chariot guiding a team of white
    horses?

PAIDAGOGOS:
He is the seer Amphiaraus, mistress. The fresh sacrifices
he holds are streaming blood onto the thirsty ground.

ANTIGONE:
175   Selene, daughter of bright-banded Helios,
circle of golden moonlight,
how calmly and modestly he guides his course straight,
by applying the goad to the horses in turn.
But where is the man who insults our city so savagely,
180   Capaneus?

170–71: For a comparison of Polynices' mission with the embassy of
Menelaus and Odysseus to Troy to try to avert the Trojan War (*Iliad*
3.206), see Papadopoulou (2008, pp. 44–45) and scholia *ad* 170.

171–74: Amphiaraus—a seer who was tricked by his wife into joining the
expedition. In Aeschylus he is the one just and modest member of the Argive forces.

175: Selene is the Moon, daughter of the Sun (Helios), a lunar deity like
Artemis and Hecate.

180: Capaneus ("Smokey"), son of Hipponous. In Euripides' *Suppliants*,
his wife Evadne throws herself upon his burning funeral pyre.

PAIDAGOGOS:
        He is over there meticulously marking out
the approaches to the towers, gauging the walls up and
   down.

ANTIGONE:
  Oh no!
  Nemesis and loud-roaring thunder of Zeus
  and fiery bolt of lightning, beat down
  his overbearing arrogance.
  He is the one who claims he will enslave us,   185
  hand over the women of Thebes, captives of the spear,
  to Mycenae and Poseidon's streams
  and the waters of Lerna.
  Never, goddess Artemis,   190
  golden-haired daughter of Zeus,
  never let me suffer such bondage.

PAIDAGOGOS:
  My child, it's time to go back inside the house
  and stay in your maiden's chambers,
  now that you have seen what you longed to see.   195
  As havoc advances on the city, I see a mob of women
  making its way to the royal palace.
  Females are a breed of faultfinders:
  if they find the slightest grounds for criticism
  they pile it up out of all proportion. Women take a perverse   200
  pleasure in having nothing good to say about each other.

    (They exit down the ladder from the roof.)

    (Enter the chorus singing along the two side passages.)

182: Nemesis—daughter of Night (Nyx), personification of divine vengeance, whose duty was to curb excess. On the connection of the four goddesses Antigone invokes, see Craik's note on line 109.

187–88: Literally, "to Lerna's Trident and Poseidon's Amymonian waters."
The story is that Poseidon created the stream for Amymone by striking the
ground with his trident.

198–201: The old man ends with an unwarranted sneer about women—
a bow perhaps to the Eteocles of Aeschylus' *Seven against Thebes* who re-
proaches and harangues the chorus of Theban women throughout the first
half of the earlier play.

Parodos

CHORUS:

[Strophe 1]

Tyre's swollen seas left far behind, I came here
as living war-spoils for Loxias
from Phoenicia's island-city
205   to be a slave in Phoebus' house
where under the snowstruck ridges
of Parnassus he came to dwell.
Over the Ionian Sea with
circling oar I was sailing
210   on the sea's unplanted surface
past Sicily, with Zephyr's breezes
riding in the sky,
so lovely a sound.

[Antistrophe 1]

Hand-picked throughout the city,
215   most beautiful offerings to Loxias,
I have come to Cadmus' country,

Parodos: The entrance song of the chorus, made up of fifteen men, who
enter along the two *parodoi* or side entrances. In other Theban plays (Aeschylus' *Seven against Thebes*, Sophocles' *Antigone* and *Oedipus Tyrannus*)
the chorus is native to Thebes: in *Seven* they are women of citizen families;
in *Antigone* and *Oedipus*, Theban elders. The chorus here represents Phoenician captive women who are on their way to Delphi to serve in Apollo's
temple, but they have been caught in the hostilities and are now trapped in
Thebes. They would be dressed in exotic costumes as is suggested by Polynices' addressing them as foreigners (278–79).

202: Strophe ("turning") and antistrophe ("opposite turning") are metri-
cally matched stanzas, during which the chorus performs equal dance
movements and gestures but in opposite directions. Sometimes there is an
unmatched stanza in between two sets (as here, the mesode) or at the end
of an ode (epode).

203: Loxias—another of Apollo's cult titles.

207: Parnassus—a mountain near Delphi, sacred to Apollo.

211: Zephyr—the west wind.

to the land of Agenor's noble sons
sent here to Laius' towers,
the towers of our kin.
Like votive statues worked in gold   220
we are singled out as slaves of Phoebus.
But still the water of Kastalia
waits for us to wet
our hair's maiden glory
for Phoebus' service.   225

[Mesode]

Oh, rock gleaming with the fire's
twin-peaked flash above Dionysus'
frenzied crags
and you, vine, that every day
lets drop the ripened clusters   230
of the grape's flower;
holy dens of the serpent,
lofty lookouts of the gods,
sacred snowstruck mountain.
If only we could be whirling   235
in the chorus of the undying goddess,
fearless, by the glens of Phoebus
at Earth's navel, leaving Dirkē far behind.

217: Agenor—descendant of Io, ruler of Tyre, father of Europa, Cadmus, Phoenix, and Cilix. When Europa was carried off, the sons were sent to search for her and founded other settlements when they realized their quest was futile.

222: Kastalia—a spring near Delphi, used for ritual washing.

226–31: Dionysus is worshiped on Parnassus with torch dances. There was a legendary vine that produced fresh fruit every day. Both Dionysus and Ares are associated with Thebes.

232: This serpent or dragon is the Pytho, guardian of the oracle originally belonging to Themis, which Apollo killed when he took over the oracle at Delphi.

236: The undying goddess is probably Earth (Ge or Gaia).

238: Delphi was considered the center of the earth and Earth's birthplace. Sculptural representations of navels (outies) can be seen at the archaeological site, both inside the museum and outside.

[Strophe 2]

But now for us before the walls
240   the onset of impetuous Ares
fires up the blood of enemies
against this city—heaven help us.
For the troubles of kin are shared in common.
In common, too—if this seven-towered
245   land should suffer anything,
it is shared with the Phoenician people.
Common is the blood, common the children
of Io the horned.
In their troubles, we too have a share.

[Antistrophe 2]

250   And around the city a cloud
thick with shields outlines in fire
the choreography of bloody war,
which Ares soon will know,
when he brings the agony of the Furies
255   to the sons of Oedipus.
O Pelasgic Argos,
we fear your valor.
What comes from the gods we fear. For with justice truly
into this struggle rushes under arms the son
260   who comes to seek his birthright.

First Episode

(Enter Polynices stage left.)

POLYNICES:
    The gatekeepers have unlocked the bolts
    and let me pass freely inside the walls.

248: Io, descendant of Inachus, is the common ancestor of the Phoenicians
and the Thebans. She was loved by Zeus and turned into a cow by Hera,
who tormented her with a gadfly and sent her wandering. She gave birth to
Epaphus, ancestor of the Egyptian Danaus who founded Argos and of
Cadmus, the Phoenician founder of Thebes (see 676).

First Episode: An episode is the part spoken by actors, with songs sometimes mixed in (as in Jocasta's monody in this episode), that comes between

But now I'm afraid they will catch me in their traps
and not let me out again unbloodied.
That is why I turn my eyes in every direction   265
that way and this to look out for a trick.
The sword in my hand gives me confidence.
Whoa—who is that? Or am I startled by a sound?
To the brave everything is alarming   270
if they happen to set foot into enemy territory.
I trust my mother, who convinced me to come here
under truce; at the same time I do not trust her.
Well, help is at hand—the altar fires
are here and the palace is not deserted.   275
I'll slip my sword back inside its sheath
and ask these women who they are
and why they are standing in front of the palace.
Women, strangers to our land, tell me,
where have you come from, here to our Greek homes?

---

the odes. Episodes may use two or three actors. This is a three-actor scene:
Polynices, Jocasta, and Eteocles. This episode is unusually long and complex and can be divided into five parts:

1. 261–90: Enter Polynices carrying a sword, perhaps fully armed, alone.
2. 291–354: Enter Jocasta from the palace. There is a reunion of
   mother and son.
3. 355–442: Dialogue of Polynices and his mother.
4. 443–587: Enter Eteocles, perhaps along the opposite *parodos* (side
   entrance), probably with one or two attendants. This is the central
   agōn (debate scene).
5. 558–637: The dialogue deteriorates into a balanced match of insults.

261: We have a description of Polynices' golden armor (168–69), but we
do not know if (in the original performance) he entered fully armed or in
his tunic. He is carrying a sword and wearing a scabbard (268, 276).

266: Like the chorus of Aeschylus' *Seven against Thebes*, Polynices fears
every sound.

275: At this point Polynices would notice the women of the chorus as he
makes his way to the front of the palace.

278–79: Polynices is a native returning to his homeland after something
more than a year's absence, but he is made by the staging—the foreign
chorus being there to meet him—to be a stranger among strangers. He would
recognize the chorus as foreign by their attire.

CHORUS:

280   Phoenicia is the homeland that nurtured me;
      the sons of Agenor's sons sent us here
      as offerings to Phoebus, chosen from the spoils of war.
      Oedipus' illustrious son was prepared to send us
      to the sacred oracle and altars of Loxias
285   just when the Argives made war on the city.
      But tell me, who are you to have come
      into the seven-gated citadel of Thebes?

POLYNICES:

      My father is Oedipus, son of Laius;
      Jocasta, daughter of Menoeceus, gave me birth.
290   The people of Thebes call me Polynices.

CHORUS:

      Kinsman of Agenor's children,
      my rulers, who brought me here,

            (Singing.)

      I fall before you on bended knee, O king,
      as is the custom in my home.
295   You have come at last to your homeland.
      Oh, oh, mistress, come out, hurry.
      Throw open the gates.
      Do you hear, mother of Polynices?
      Why do you delay crossing through the high halls
300   and taking your son in your arms?

            *(Enter Jocasta from the palace, singing or chanting; later
            dancing around her son.)*

JOCASTA:

      Your Phoenician cry
      I heard, young women, and drag
      my elderly foot on quivering step. My son,
305   at last after days and endless days I see your face.
      Throw your arms around
      your mother's breast,

280: When the chorus speaks in an episode, the lines are spoken by one
person, the chorus leader.

hold out your cheek, and let your dark curls
hang down to cover my neck.
Ah, ah, appearing beyond hope,   310
at last in your mother's arms past expectation.
What can I say to you? How can I relive the pleasure
in every way with my hands and words
dancing happily
that way and this,   315
spinning around you as in the old days
full of joy? Ah, my child,
you left your father's home desolate,
a refugee driven off by your brother's wrong,
sorely missed by your family,   320
sorely missed by Thebes.
This is why I cut my gray hair in grief,
giving way to my tears in sorrow;
I took off my white dress, my son,
and wear instead   325
these dark and gloomy rags.
But inside the house your old father, eyeless,
forever in tears of longing
for his two sons,
unyoked now from the family,   330
rushed for the sword
and suicidal slaughter
or a noose hanging from the ceiling beams,
moaning curses on his sons,
with tears streaming all day long;   335
he is hidden in darkness.
And you, my son, I hear,
are yoked in the joy of matrimony
and have a foreign family;
you are busy with foreign kin,   340
anathema to your mother
and to Laius of days long gone—
doom of marriage far from home.
And I did not light the torch for you,

314: Jocasta dances around her son to protect him and to keep him close.
322: Cutting the hair is a sign of mourning.

345   a custom at our weddings
        for the happy mother.
        No wedding hymn to yoke Ismenus in marriage,
        no ceremonial bath for the bridegroom.
        All through Thebes there was silence for your bride's
            entrance.
350   My curse upon it: is it the sword
        or discord? Is your father to blame
        or has god made sport of
        the house of Oedipus?
        Deep in my heart has come the pain of these miseries.

CHORUS:
355   Giving birth holds a strange power over women,
        and all womankind is child-obsessed.

POLYNICES:
        Mother, I have both good and bad feelings about
        coming here into enemy territory. Still, all men are destined
        to love their homelands. If anyone says otherwise
360   he is playing with words, but home is where his heart is.
        So troubled was I and so fearful that some trick
        on my brother's part would kill me that with sword drawn
        I walked through the city casting my eyes every which way.
        One thing gives me the confidence to go on:
365   the truce and my trust in you, which led me
        inside the walls of my homeland. I have come here in tears,
        my eyes at long last gazing on the gods' shrines and altars,
        the gymnasia where I spent my youth, and Dirkē's stream,
        from which I was unfairly driven away to live
370   in a foreign city with tears gushing from my eyes.
        From one pain flows another as I see you again,
        your head shorn, your body draped in black.
        Ah me, I cry in anguish for my troubles.
        How terrible a thing is hatred inside the family, Mother,
375   and reconciliation is so hard to achieve.

344–49: At a Greek wedding the bride was escorted from her chamber in
a procession of the wedding party (family and friends), carrying torches
and singing the wedding song, and led to the door of her new husband's
home. A child who was a close relative of the bridegroom carried water for
his wedding bath.

How is my elderly father getting by in the house,
his eyes in darkness? How are my two sisters?
Do the poor girls cry over my exile?

JOCASTA:
A sadistic god is crushing the family of Oedipus,
starting when I first gave birth and broke the taboo;   380
then I married your father and gave birth to you.
Why speak of this? We must endure what gods give us.
How to ask what I want to know, for I'm afraid
I will hurt your feelings? Still, there are things I long to
    know.

POLYNICES:
Don't hold back. Please, ask anything you want to know.   385
Whatever you desire, Mother, is what I want most.

JOCASTA:
Then I'll ask first what I most want to know.
Losing your homeland—is it a terrible misery?

POLYNICES:
The very worst, even worse living it than telling it.

JOCASTA:
What is it like? What is so hard for refugees?   390

POLYNICES:
One thing is worst: not to be able to say what you think.

JOCASTA:
That is the role for a slave, not to speak freely.

POLYNICES:
A refugee must put up with any fool in power.

JOCASTA:
That is a problem: to be a fool among the fools.

POLYNICES:
It goes against the grain, but you act the slave to get by.   395

JOCASTA:
Exiles are nourished by hope, so the saying goes.

POLYNICES:
It leads us on with bright eyes, but it takes its time.

JOCASTA:
Didn't time show your hope to be empty?

POLYNICES:
It has an allure that sweetens my troubles.

JOCASTA:
400   How did you support yourself before your marriage?

POLYNICES:
One day I had enough; the next, nothing.

JOCASTA:
Your father has friends and allies—didn't they help?

POLYNICES:
Better be rich. Lose your fortune, lose your friends.

JOCASTA:
Didn't your high birth improve your status?

POLYNICES:
405   It's bad to be poor. High birth does not put food on the table.

JOCASTA:
Homeland, it seems, is a man's dearest possession.

POLYNICES:
No words can express how dear it is.

JOCASTA:
How is it you went to Argos? What goal did you have in
    mind?

POLYNICES:
Loxias had given a certain oracle to Adrastus.

JOCASTA:
410   What was it? What do you mean? I don't understand.

POLYNICES:
To join his daughters in marriage to a boar and a lion.

JOCASTA:
What do you have to do with these animal names, my son?

POLYNICES:
I don't know, but destiny called me to this opportunity.

JOCASTA:
  Yes, the god is wise. How did you attain this marriage?

POLYNICES:
  It was night when I arrived on Adrastus' doorstep.   415

JOCASTA:
  A homeless wanderer looking for a place to stay?

POLYNICES:
  That was it. And then another refugee arrived there, too.

JOCASTA:
  Who was he, this second unfortunate soul?

POLYNICES:
  Tydeus. They say he is the son of Oeneus.

JOCASTA:
  Why then did Adrastus compare you to wild animals?   420

POLYNICES:
  We came to blows over a place to sleep.

JOCASTA:
  Is that how Talaus' son figured out the oracle?

POLYNICES:
  Yes, and he gave his two daughters to the two of us.

JOCASTA:
  Are you happy in your marriage or not?

POLYNICES:
  To this day I find no fault in my marriage.   425

JOCASTA:
  How did you convince an army to follow you here?

POLYNICES:
  Adrastus made a vow to his two sons-in-law:
  [Tydeus and me—he's my brother-in-law]
  to restore us both to our homelands, starting with me.
  Many leaders of the Danaans and Mycenaeans   430
  are with us, providing a bitter service to me,
  but a needed one. For I lead this army upon
  my home city. I swear to the gods that not by my will

I take up arms against those I love. They choose it, not I.
435   Well, the resolution of these troubles depends on you,
        Mother: reconcile us, kin of one blood.
        Put an end to our troubles, mine, yours, the city's.
        The old chant goes—and I will repeat it—
        "Money is most precious to men
440   and holds great sway among them."
        I have come to get what is mine and am leading
        a vast army. A poor man has no respect.

CHORUS:
        Look, here comes Eteocles to take part in the truce.
        Jocasta, it's up to you, as their mother,
445   to say the right words to reconcile your sons.

        (Enter Eteocles stage right.)

ETEOCLES:
        Here I am, Mother. I have come as a favor to you.
        What has to be done? Let the debate begin.
        I have postponed posting the citizens around the walls
        and matching up my divisions, to hear from you
450   the mutual arbitration to which I gave my consent
        to admit *him* inside the walls under truce.

JOCASTA:
        Not so fast. Haste, you know, does not lead to justice,
        but slow deliberation sets the wisest course.
        Give up your glaring looks and angry snorting.
455   You are not looking at the Gorgon's severed head
        but at your brother who has come to meet you.
        And you, turn your face toward your brother,
        Polynices. If you look each other in the eyes
        you will speak more to the point and pay closer attention.
460   And I want to give you both some sound advice.
        When a friend is angry with a friend
        and they come together and meet face to face,

454–58: Jocasta gives an order, but do the brothers actually look at each
other? Jocasta's request cannot simply be ignored: whether Eteocles and
Polynices do as she asks or pointedly ignore her, it is a significant action
that affects the way we react to the scene (see Altena 2000, pp. 313–14).
455: See note on 146.

they should think only of the reasons why they have come
and keep no memory of past wrongs.
Yours is the first turn to speak, Polynices, my son,   465
since you have come at the head of an army of Danaans,
deprived of your right, as you allege. May one of the gods
be judge and conciliator of these troubles.

POLYNICES:
To speak the plain truth is a simple matter:
justice needs no elaborate disputation.   470
It has its own authority. But the unjust argument
because it is sick requires intricate medicine.
My only concern is with my father's estate,
both my share and *his*. In my desire to evade
the curses that Oedipus uttered against us,   475
I left the country on my own in voluntary exile.
I gave *him* the right to rule for one year's span
so that I would rule the next, taking my turn,
not coming out of hatred and envy of him
to cause the damage that is happening now.   480
And he agreed and swore an oath to the gods,
but now he breaks his promise and keeps for himself
both royal power and my share of the estate.
Even now I am ready to take what is mine,
dismiss the army to withdraw from this country,   485
and live in my own house enjoying my share;
then in turn yield an equal share for an equal time
to him and not lay waste my homeland
and *not* bring ladders to scale the battlements,
which I will do if justice is denied me.   490

465: As is common in a theatrical debate scene (*agōn*), reference is made
here to contemporary courtroom procedure in which the accuser speaks
first.

469–585: This is the central *agōn* (debate scene). Usually an *agōn* consists
of two matched speeches by the antagonists, neither of which prevails or
affects the outcome. Nearly every tragedy has a debate scene, which attests
to the popularity of such scenes with the Athenians, who were known for
their litigious spirit. Euripides here adds a third speech that should win
rhetorically and logically but is also without effect and is ignored by the
two contenders. On the debate as a conflict between "traditional beliefs
and sophistic relativism," see Meltzer 2006, pp. 1–27.

I call the gods to witness these words
that though all my deeds are just, without justice
I am most indecently deprived of my homeland.
These separate points I have spoken, not piling up
495   deceptive arguments but only what is right,
to wise men and, I think, to common folk, as well.

CHORUS:
I think so, too. Even though I am not native
to Greece, still you seem to speak to the point.

ETEOCLES:
If the same things seemed good and wise to everybody,
500   we would not have debates or strife,
but as it is nothing is the same or equal to people
except in name. And that is not the real thing.
I will speak, Mother, and hide nothing.
I would go to the risings of the stars in the sky
505   and down under the earth to attain this one thing:
to grasp in my hand the greatest god of all, Power.
This advantage, Mother, I am not willing to hand over
to anyone else, but I shall keep it for myself.
It would be cowardice to let go of the greater share
510   and accept the lesser. And besides this, I am ashamed
that *he* could come under arms to destroy our homeland
and achieve his desires. This would be a disgrace
to Thebes if in terror of the Mycenaean spear
I were to yield my scepter for him to wield.
515   He ought not to be making the truce with arms,
Mother; for words can achieve everything
that the arms of an enemy can conquer.
If he wishes to live in this country under other terms
he may do so. I will never step down of my own free
    will:
520   as long as I am able to rule, I will not be a slave to *him*.
Knowing this, come fire, come sword;
yoke the horses, fill the plain with chariots,

505: A typical polarity of which Greek is very fond.

506: Eteocles is an immoralist modeled on the likes of Euripides' well-known contemporaries, Alcibiades and Thrasymachus.

since I will not yield my power to him.
If one must do wrong, best do wrong
for Power; otherwise you might as well be good.   525

CHORUS:
It is not right to use fine words to support ugly deeds.
This is not good but galling to the eyes of justice.

JOCASTA:
Eteocles, my son, not everything
in old age turns out worse, but life's experience
has some things to say more soundly than youth.   530
Why do you go after Ambition, my son, of all gods
the most wicked? Don't do it. She is an unjust god.
She comes into homes and prosperous cities
and leaves those who welcome her in ruins.
And you are crazy for her. This is better, my son: 535
to honor Equality, who always binds kin to kin,
city to city, allies to allies. Equality is a constant
in human life. Less and more are always at war,
and this is the beginning of the day of hatred.   540
Measures and divisions of weights were established
for mankind by Equality, and she has defined the numbers.
Night's lightless eye and the fire of the sun
take equal steps through the year's orbit.
Neither of them by overreaching incurs the other's envy.   545
The sun and nighttime serve the needs of mortal men,
but you will not put up with an equal division of the estate
and share with him? What justice is in that?
Why do you pay homage to Power, so easy an injustice,
with such excess, and think it so important?   550
Is it honorable to have fame? If so, it's an empty honor.
Do you want to have a surplus in your house at such a cost?
What is the advantage in that? It is only a name.
To reasonable people having enough is sufficient.
We humans do not possess property to keep as our own;   555
we are but stewards of what belongs to the gods.

525: "Power"—in Greek *tyrannis*, also at 506.

536: Jocasta's talk about equality (*isotes*) adds a new, political cast to the
old theme of the equality of the brothers.

When it strikes their fancy, they take it back again.
Wealth is not forever; it lasts a day and is gone.
Listen, let me pose to you two questions:
560   Do you want to be king or to save the city?
Will you say, "To be king"? And if he beats you
and the Argive army defeats the Cadmeians,
you will see our city of Thebes overwhelmed;
you will see many young girls taken prisoner
565   and raped by the violence of enemy soldiers.
The wealth you seek will come at a cost to Thebes.
You are power-mad. That is all I have to say to you.
And now, Polynices, I have something to say to you.
Adrastus' favor to you was wrongheaded,
570   and you come like a fool to lay waste your city.
Listen, if—god forbid—you conquer this country,
for gods' sake how will you set up trophies to Zeus?
After seizing your homeland how will you make sacrifice
and put your name on the spoils beside Inachus?
575   "After burning Thebes to the ground, Polynices dedicated
these shields to the gods." I hope you will never
have this kind of fame among the Greeks.
And if you are beaten and his side triumphs, how will you
    return
to Argos leaving behind untold numbers of dead?
580   And someone will say, "Adrastus, you have crushed us
with your daughters' marriages. Because of one bride
we are ruined." My son, you are headed for disaster
both ways: to lose what you have there and to fail here.
Give up your excess; do give it up. When two men
585   confront each other in madness the result is tragedy.

CHORUS:
Oh gods, turn aside these catastrophes,
and somehow reconcile the sons of Oedipus.

565: When a city was captured, the men were killed and the women and
children were enslaved, becoming the property of their masters. Rape and
sexual slavery were common acts of war. Even the wise Nestor tells the
soldiers not to go home until each has bedded the wife of a Trojan in revenge for Helen's adultery (Homer, *Iliad* 2.354–56).
574: Inachus was a river/river god of Argos.

ETEOCLES:

   Mother, the contest of words is now over, but meanwhile
      time
   is being wasted for nothing. Your good intentions come to
      naught.
   For we cannot come together except on the terms I have   590
      stated:
   that I will wield the scepter as king of this country.
   Give up your long-winded admonishments and let me go.
   But you, get outside of the city walls or you will die.

POLYNICES:

   At whose hand? Who is so invulnerable that he could
   cast a murderous spear at me and not suffer the same doom?   595

ETEOCLES:

   He is right here and has not moved. Take a look at my hands.

POLYNICES:

   I see them. But wealth is a coward and runs for its life.

ETEOCLES:

   Yet you have come with a vast army to do battle with a
      nonentity?

POLYNICES:

   A careful general is better than an impetuous one.

ETEOCLES:

   You are a braggart, trusting in a truce that protects you from 600
      death.

POLYNICES:

   You are, too. Again I demand the scepter and my share of my
      country.

ETEOCLES:

   I take no orders from you. I will live in my own house.

588–637: The meter changes from iambic trimeter to iambic tetrameter,
which is used to indicate agitation, haste, and heightened emotions.

596–625: This is a long passage of *stichomythia,* a convention in tragedy
in which speakers each speak a single line of verse (or sometimes two;
sometimes the line is divided between the two speakers: this shows more
heated emotion and is called *antilabe*).

POLYNICES:
And have more than your share.

ETEOCLES:
                              I tell you, get out of the country.

POLYNICES:
Altars of my fathers' gods—

ETEOCLES:
                              which you have come to destroy—

POLYNICES:
Hear me.

ETEOCLES:
605   Who hears you, coming to wage war on your homeland?

POLYNICES:
Temples of the gods of white horses—

ETEOCLES:
                              who hate you—

POLYNICES:
I am driven from my homeland.

ETEOCLES:
                      Yes, because you have come to destroy it.

POLYNICES:
Unjustly, oh gods.

ETEOCLES:
                  Call on the gods in Mycenae, not here.

POLYNICES:
You are godless,

ETEOCLES:
                  but not like you, an enemy to my country.

POLYNICES:
You drive me out without my share—

606: Amphion and Zethus, the Theban version of the Dioscuri. See note on 115.

ETEOCLES:

                  yes, and besides that I will kill you.   610

POLYNICES:

    Father, do you hear what I suffer?

ETEOCLES:

                Yes, and he hears what you are doing.

POLYNICES:

    And you, Mother?

ETEOCLES:

          It is wrong for you even to speak of your mother.

POLYNICES:

    Oh city!

ETEOCLES:

        Go to Argos and call on the waters of Lerna.

POLYNICES:

    I will go, do not trouble yourself. Thank you, Mother.

ETEOCLES:

                     Get out of the country.

POLYNICES:

    I am going. Let me see my father.

ETEOCLES:

                   No, you cannot.   615

POLYNICES:

    My sisters, then.

ETEOCLES:

         You will never set eyes on them.

POLYNICES:

    Sisters . . .

ETEOCLES:

        Why do you call on them when you are their enemy?

POLYNICES:

    Mother, I'll say good-bye, then.

JOCASTA:
                         I suffer very much, my dear son.

POLYNICES:
   I am gone, no more your son.

JOCASTA:
                              I am very, very unhappy.

POLYNICES:
   Yes, he abuses us.

ETEOCLES:
620   And I am abused in return.

POLYNICES:
   Where will you be posted in front of the towers?

ETEOCLES:
                                   Why do you want to know?

POLYNICES:
   I will station myself opposite to kill you.

ETEOCLES:
                                 I desire exactly the same.

JOCASTA:
   Oh no! What are you doing, children?

POLYNICES:
                                  The deed itself will show.

JOCASTA:
   Will you not avoid your father's blood-curse?

ETEOCLES:
                                  The whole house can go to hell!

   (Exit Jocasta into the palace.)

POLYNICES:
625   Soon my sword will set to work and drip with blood.
      I call the gods to witness and the land that nurtured me
      that I am driven from my country in bitter anguish, without
          honor
      like a slave, not like the son of the same father Oedipus.
      And if you, my city, suffer harm, blame him, not me.

I'm here against my will, driven against my will from my home,   630
and you, lord Phoebus, protector of our doors and palace,
     farewell,
and my companions, images of the gods where sacrifice is made,
I do not know if I will ever address you again.
Hope is not yet asleep. I have confidence that with gods' help
I will kill this man and take control of the land of Thebes.   635

>   *(Exit Polynices stage left.)*

ETEOCLES:
Get out! Father gave you the name Polynices
with inspired foresight, a name full of strife.

>   *(Exit Eteocles into the palace.)*

First Stasimon

CHORUS:

[Strophe]

Cadmus came to this land
from Tyre; for him the four-footed
heifer, not forced to its knees,   640
lay down, fulfilling
the oracle that told him where to settle
on the wheat-bearing plains of his new home.
The divine voice proclaimed:
"where the beautiful stream of water   645
comes over the land
the green-bearing, deep-sown
fields of Dirkē."
And there by union with Zeus
his mother gave birth to Bromius.   650
While he was still an infant,

Exit Eteocles: The staging is not clear here. Eteocles may remain in front of the scene building through the choral ode.

642: While he was searching for his sister Europa, Cadmus received an oracle at Delphi that told him to follow a cow until it collapsed and to found a city on the site. Thebes is in Boeotia, from *bous,* "cow."

650: Bromius (Roarer), another name for Dionysus (Bacchus), son of Cadmus' daughter Semélē and Zeus.

coiling ivy, twining
its green shady tendrils,
cradled him in luxury,
655   adored in Bacchic dance by Theban maidens
and women in ecstasy.

[Antistrophe]

There it was, the bloodthirsty dragon
of Ares, cruel-minded guard,
watching over the running streams
660   and green runnels with its
eyes darting everywhere.
And this creature, when Cadmus the monster-killer
came for ritual water,
he killed it with a rock, crushing
665   its murderous head
with weapons hurled from his hands,
and by command of the motherless goddess,
Pallas, he cast the teeth fallen to the earth
into the deep-sown fields.
670   Then Earth sent up
an array in full armor above the
surface of the ground; iron-minded
murder joined them again with their own land,
and their blood soaked the earth that had revealed
675   them to the sun-drenched air of heaven.

[Epode]

And you, Epaphus,
offspring long ago of Io our foremother

657: A dragon, descendant of Ares, guarded the spring of Ares. Cadmus, needing water to sacrifice the heifer (640) to Athena, killed the dragon with Athena's help.

667: The motherless goddess is Pallas Athena, who sprang in full armor from the head of her father Zeus. Athena advised Cadmus to sow the teeth of the slain dragon in the earth. When he obeyed, grown men fully armed sprang from the earth. These are the Spartoi (Sown Men). They fought each other and all but five were killed.

676: Epaphus—see note on 248.

and child of Zeus,
I call, with foreign cry.
Io, with foreign prayers I call.   680
Come to this land, come.
Your descendants built it and occupied it.
Goddesses named together,
Persephone and dear
goddess Demeter,   685
queen of all, Earth, nurse of all.
Send torchbearing
goddesses; shield our land.
Everything is easy for gods.

Second Episode

(Enter Eteocles with a servant.)

ETEOCLES:

(To a servant.)

Go get Creon, son of Menoeceus,   690
brother of my mother Jocasta.
Tell him this—I want to communicate
my plans, both strategic and domestic, to him
before going into battle to face the line of spears.
But wait, here he comes just now to save you the   695
    trouble.
I can see him coming toward my house.

(Enter Creon stage right.)

683–88: Demeter and her daughter Persephone are torchbearers at the
Eleusinian mysteries.

690: Eteocles either enters from the palace or simply begins talking from
where he remained in front of the scene building, calling to a servant. By
695 Creon, entering stage right, becomes visible to Eteocles.

696: Allusions to earlier Theban tragedies bring out Eteocles' lack of control over affairs in *Phoenician Women.* In Sophocles' *Oedipus Tyrannus,*
Oedipus had sent Creon to the oracle. In *Seven against Thebes,* the Aes-
chylean Eteocles has sent a spy across enemy lines and announces his
arrival back into the city. Here Eteocles tries to send for Creon and is forestalled by Creon's coming along on his own.

CREON:
I have been all over trying to find you,
Eteocles, around the gates of the Cadmeians
and the guard posts searching for you.

ETEOCLES:
700   Good, I am eager to see you, too, Creon.
I found the truce utterly useless
when I entered into discussion with Polynices.

CREON:
I hear that he shows contempt toward Thebes,
secure in his ties with Adrastus' family and in the army.
705   These things we must leave in the hands of the gods;
I have come to report what is of most immediate concern.

ETEOCLES:
And what is it? I have not heard any news.

CREON:
A captive from the Argive army has fallen into our hands.

ETEOCLES:
What news does he have to tell us about them?

CREON:
710   That all around the towers the army of the Argives
is getting ready to encircle the city of the Cadmeians with arms.

ETEOCLES:
Then the city of Cadmus must march out in arms.

CREON:
Where? You are too young to see what you should see.

708: In Aeschylus' *Seven against Thebes,* this information comes from a spy Eteocles has sent out.

713: The fact that Creon is a better strategist than Eteocles takes away the one thing his namesake had in his favor in Aeschylus' *Seven against Thebes*—that he was an active and able commander, intelligent and swift in his decisions. In the earlier play there had been no older man to dampen his fire. But here, each of his suggestions is shown to be thoughtless, whereas in *Seven,* each of his choices was militarily and morally brilliant. Even his exit line "I will go" (748) is ruined by his appending a long speech (some of which editors have deemed suspicious) in which he ties up loose ends.

ETEOCLES:
Here outside the trenches, since soon we will fight.

CREON:
Our army is small, far outnumbered by theirs. 715

ETEOCLES:
I know they are bold in words.

CREON:
Argos has a reputation among the Greeks. .

ETEOCLES:
Take courage. I will soon fill the plain with their
   massacre.

CREON:
I hope so. But I see that this is a dangerous course.

ETEOCLES:
Well, I will not keep my army inside the walls. 720

CREON:
And yet, strategy is everything if you plan to win.

ETEOCLES:
Do you want me to turn to a different course?

CREON:
Yes, every possible course, before rushing into danger.

ETEOCLES:
What if we ambush them at night?

CREON:
Yes, if you fail you will be safe back here. 725 .

ETEOCLES:
Darkness levels the field and is an advantage to the bold.

CREON:
Night's darkness is frightening in case of disaster.

ETEOCLES:
Well, should I attack them at their dinner?

CREON:
It would be a surprise, but beating them is crucial.

ETEOCLES:
730   Yes, Dirkē's ford is deep if we have to retreat.

CREON:
Every course is inferior to keeping up one's defenses.

ETEOCLES:
But what if we charge the Argive army on horseback?

CREON:
Their army is encircled with chariots too.

ETEOCLES:
What should I do, then? Hand the city over to the enemy?

CREON:
735   Not at all. But make plans since you are a good strategist.

ETEOCLES:
What strategy do you think will work better, then?

CREON:
It is said they have seven men; that's what I heard.

ETEOCLES:
Posted for what? It is a small force.

CREON:
To be posted at the seven gates as leaders of companies.

ETEOCLES:
740   What do we do? I will not wait for an impasse.

CREON:
You also choose seven men to face them at the seven gates.

ETEOCLES:
To command companies or for single combat with the
    spear?

CREON:
Companies. Choose those who are the best warriors.

ETEOCLES:
I get it—to keep them from scaling the walls.

CREON:
745   Yes, and as fellow officers. One man cannot see everything.

ETEOCLES:
Should I choose them for bravery or tactical skill?

CREON:
Both. One is nothing without the other.

ETEOCLES:
I will do it. I will go around to the seven towers
and station officers at the gates as you suggest,
matching equals against equals on the other side.   750
It would take too long to give all the names
with the enemy encamped outside our walls.
I will go and not delay the action of my hand.
I pray that it turns out that I face my brother
and take him in battle with my spear and kill him,   755
the man who has come to destroy my homeland.
As for the marriage of my sister Antigone and your son
Haemon, if I should fall short of victory,
you must take care of it. Now at my departure
I reconfirm the betrothal already made.   760
You are my mother's brother. Why go on at length?
Take care of her, as is your duty for your sake and mine.
But as for Father, for blinding himself, he deserves
the charge of weak-mindedness. I have lost all respect
for him. He will kill us with his curses, if he gets the chance.   765
There is one thing left to do: if the soothsayer
Tiresias has any oracle to tell,
find it out from him. I have sent your son,
your father's namesake, Menoeceus,
to bring Tiresias here, Creon.   770
He will agree to speak with you,
but I have found fault with his prophetic skill
in the past and now he has cause to resent me.
This charge I lay upon you and the city, Creon:
if my side prevails, the body of Polynices—   775

752: Criticism of Aeschylus' *Seven against Thebes,* in which the central
scene is the naming of the attackers and defenders.

758: In Sophocles' *Antigone* the marriage of Haemon and Antigone is
forestalled by Antigone's death. Haemon, by then the last of Creon's sons,
commits suicide.

never inter it in Theban soil and put to death anyone
who tries to bury it, even a member of the family.
That is all I have to say to you. Now, attendants,
bring my armor, defense against enemy blows,
780   so that I may set out into the struggle that lies
before us with justice, bringer of victory.
I send my prayer to that most expedient of goddesses,
Caution; protect and preserve our city.

*(Exit Eteocles with attendants carrying the armor. Creon
remains to wait for Tiresias.)*

Second Stasimon

[Strophe]

Ares full of struggle, why, why are you possessed
785   of blood and death out of tune with the festivals of Bromius
and at the graceful dances of garland-crowned young women
do not let loose your hair and sing to the blowing of the
      flute
a song to which the graces set the dance,
but with men in arms inspiring the legions of Argives
790   with bloodshed for Thebes
you choreograph a revel with no sound of flutes?
Not under the thyrsus craze of fawnskins,
but with chariots and bits, you swirl the horses' hooves

777: Eteocles reduces Creon's responsibility (his defining trait in the Sophoclean *Antigone*) for refusing to bury Polynices by making it his own last request. It is the duty of family members to tend to their dead.

779: This line recalls Eteocles' last lines in Aeschylus' *Seven against Thebes* (675 ff.), in which he calls for his armor and perhaps arms himself on stage.

782: It is typical of the Euripidean Eteocles to pray to an abstraction rather than the traditional gods.

784–800: This strophe is an invocation to Ares referring to the present. Ares is invoked in language appropriate to Dionysus: the potential violence of the revel band is transferred to the war god. The image of the dance applied to the movements of war is compelling and terrible.

792: The thyrsus is a staff decorated with ivy carried by Dionysus and his worshipers in their ecstatic rites.

advancing upon Ismenus' stream;
on horseback you charge, inspiring against the Argives   795
the race of Sown Men,
a shield-bearing revel band
of enemies, against the stone walls,
decked out with bronze.
Strife is a direful goddess—
she has plotted troubles for the kings of the land,
for the children of Labdacus full of struggle.   800

[Antistrophe]

Sacred thickets, full of beasts,
snow-filled valley, eye of Artemis, Kithairōn,
you never should have nurtured the fruit of Jocasta's labor,
exposed for death, Oedipus, infant cast out of the house,
marred with gold-set pins.   805
The winged virgin, mountain-bred monster, never should have
     come—
sorrows for the land—
with its museless Sphinx songs
that once with bird claws on all its four feet
coming to the walls bore into the pathless light of the air
the children of Cadmus—Hades from below the ground   810
sent it against the Cadmeians. Godforsaken strife
thrives all the more among the children
of Oedipus in the halls and in the city.
What is not good never breeds the good,
illicit children,   815
their mother's birth pangs, pollution of their father,
and the man who went to bed with his mother.

801–17: The antistrophe refers to the recent past. It is full of life and breeding of a hostile, sinister, or monstrous kind, first the natural beasts (801) of
the mountain; then the brood of Jocasta (803), the nurturing (804) of Oedipus, a monster marred by prophecy and abuse; next comes the mountain-
bred portent (806), the Sphinx which carried off those born of Cadmus (808)
and was sent from Hades against the Cadmeians. Artemis' presence turns
the animals into beasts for the hunt and kill. Oedipus' exposure suggests
that the beasts should have preyed on him or the elements worked for his
death by exposure.

[Epode]

You bore, O Earth, once you bore,
820   as I learned—I learned the foreign tale at home—
from a beast-bred bloody-plumed dragon
the race grown from its teeth, for Thebes a most glorious shame.
And once to the wedding of Harmonia
gods came from heaven, and to the sound of Amphion's lyre
the walls of Thebes rose, and the towers rose to his lyre
825   at the crossing between the twin rivers
where Dirkē waters the green-growing plain
opposite Ismenus.
And Io the horned foremother of our race
bore kings for the Cadmeians,
830   an endless succession of good giving way to
more good; this city stands on the top
of Ares' circling crowns.

Third Episode

(Enter Tiresias with his daughter and Menoeceus stage right. Tiresias is wearing a crown of victory.)

818–32: In the epode there is yet more breeding (818–21, 826, 828–29). Here the result is mixed: even the savagery of the dragon and the teeth-bred generation is oxymoronically a glorious shame to Thebes. On the positive side, the gods came to the wedding of Harmonia; the walls of Thebes rose to Amphion's lyre; the plain between the rivers is fertile; and Io, the horned foremother, produced a royal line. The plain between Dirkē and Ismenus is now full of armed men hostile to Thebes. The very walls are under attack. One clear theme is change (831), the sine qua non of tragedy.

832: The crowns of the strophe (786) that decorated the heads of young girls in the choral dance have become at the very end of the epode (832) crowns or circlings of Ares, the exact meaning of which is unclear, with the outcome still unknown. Ares' dance is the image that carries through the ode from beginning to end, along with the breeding of strife and the ambiguity of good fortune, success, and victory. The god who is "full of struggle" (or suffering, 784) does not suffer himself but brings suffering to the human beings who are also called "full of struggle" (or suffering, 800). It is difficult to tell whether the ode is finally optimistic, despairing, or, as may be more likely, ambiguous. The crown reappears as a sign of victory on Tiresias' head.

Enter Tiresias with his daughter: Tiresias' daughter would have been a surprise. Usually he is accompanied by a boy, either his servant or his apprentice.

TIRESIAS:

    Lead me on, daughter, since you are the eyes
    to my blind feet, like a star to sailors.   835
    Guide my step here to level ground and walk
    in front so we don't trip. Your father is feeble.
    Hold tightly in your young hands the oracles
    that I took by reading the bird signs
    at my sacred place of prophecy.   840
    Menoeceus, my boy, son of Creon, tell me,
    how much longer is it to town and to your father?
    My knees are weary and it's difficult
    for me to make such a long journey.

CREON:

    Don't worry, Tiresias, you have almost reached   845
    your friends. Take him in hand, my boy.
    An old man's foot is like a wagon's wheel
    in need of support from another's hand.

TIRESIAS:

    Good. We are here. Why did you call me in haste, Creon?

CREON:

    I haven't forgotten. But gather your strength   850
    and catch your breath, to recover from the hard trek.

TIRESIAS:

    Yes, I am worn out. Just yesterday I was
    brought back here from the Erechthids;
    there was a war there, too, waged by Eumolpus.
    I gave glorious victory to the sons of Kekrops   855

838: The word here is *klērous*, or "lots"; perhaps the seer has drawn several from a collection of lots and has his daughter carry them as evidence. The daughter would be clutching tablets or scraps of papyrus (see Mastronarde 1994). The concept of a blind seer, unable to make out bird flight patterns or the entrails read at sacrifices, or even read the written lots that might record such things, boggles the mind.

853: Erechtheus was king of Athens. Erechthids are the children of Erechtheus, that is, Athenians. Erechtheus was fighting a war with the Eleusinians, who had as an ally the Thracian Eumolpus. Tiresias (or, in other versions, the Delphic oracle) told him that he should sacrifice one of his daughters to ensure victory. When he did so, his other daughters committed suicide.

and wear this golden crown, as you see,
which I was granted as the first fruits of the war-spoils.

CREON:
    I take your crown of victory as a good omen.
    We are at sea, as you know yourself:
860   Thebes is engaged in a great struggle with the Danaan army.
    Our king Eteocles has gone armed for battle
    to face the might of the Mycenaeans.
    He asked me to find out from you if there is
    anything in particular we can do to save the city.

TIRESIAS:
865   As far as Eteocles is concerned, my lips are sealed
    and I would keep the oracles to myself. But to you I will
      speak,
    since you desire to learn. This country has long been sick,
      Creon,
    ever since Laius fathered a son against the gods' will
    a husband he bred for his mother, unhappy Oedipus.
870   Then came the gory tearing out of his eyes,
    gods' devising, an exhibit to all of Greece,
    which the sons of Oedipus desired to conceal
    with the passage of time, trying to outrun the gods;
    but they made a terrible mistake. In giving their father
875   no respect, no way out, they turned the poor man
    savage. And he breathed on them deadly curses,
    being in torment and deprived of his rights.
    I tried everything in word and deed and reaped
    for my troubles the hatred of Oedipus' sons,
880   Creon. Suicidal death is upon them
    and many dead will fall on top of the dead,
    Argive and Cadmeian limbs commingled,
    will visit bitter lamentation on the land of Thebes.
    And you, unhappy city, will go down with them
885   unless someone heeds my words.
    This is best: that not any of Oedipus' descendants
    be a citizen or ruler of the country—
    they are god-maddened and will bring down the city.
    Since evil is more powerful than good,
890   there is one other means of preservation,
    but it is unsafe for me to speak of it

and bitter to those whom fortune has chosen
to provide a remedy to preserve the city.
I must go now. Good-bye. With all the others
I will suffer the future, if need be. What else can I do? 895

CREON:
Stay here, old man.

TIRESIAS:
Do not lay hands on me.

CREON:
Wait. Why are you rushing off?

TIRESIAS:
Not I, but your fortune is running from you.

CREON:
Say what it is that will save the city and its people.

TIRESIAS:
Now you want to know, but soon you will not.

CREON:
How could I not want to save my homeland? 900

TIRESIAS:
Then you want to hear? You insist upon it?

CREON:
What else could I feel more strongly about?

TIRESIAS:
Well, then, you can hear my oracles now.
First, I want you to give a clear answer to this:
where is Menoeceus, who brought me here? 905

CREON:
He hasn't gone anywhere. He is right next to you.

TIRESIAS:
Send him away, far from my prophecies.

CREON:
He is my own son and will keep secret what he must.

TIRESIAS:
Do you want me to speak in his presence?

CREON:
910   Yes, he will be glad to hear how to save the city.

TIRESIAS:
Hear, then, the course of my oracles:
what you must do to save the city of Cadmeians.
Since you insist on hearing—you must sacrifice
your son Menoeceus on behalf of your homeland.

CREON:
915   What are you saying? What story is this, old man?

TIRESIAS:
Just what has been revealed. You must do this.

CREON:
In a single breath your tongue has done much harm.

TIRESIAS:
To you, yes, but to our homeland great deliverance.

CREON:
No, no, I did not hear. Let the city go.

TIRESIAS:
920   He is not the same man now, but he changes his tune.

CREON:
Good-bye. I have no use for your oracles.

TIRESIAS:
Is the truth to be lost because your luck has changed?

CREON:
By your knees and gray hair, please . . .

TIRESIAS:
Why supplicate me? You ask what's impossible.

CREON:
925   Be silent. Do not tell these things to the city.

TIRESIAS:
You command me to do wrong. I cannot be silent.

CREON:
What will you do to me? Will you kill my son?

TIRESIAS:
Others will do that, but I will tell my story.

CREON:
Why has this curse fallen upon my son?

TIRESIAS:
You have every right to question my words now.   930
You must sacrifice him in the chamber
where the watcher of Dirkē's waters, earthborn dragon,
arose, and offer his blood as a libation to earth.
Because of Ares' ancient anger with Cadmus,
he demands death to atone for the serpent born of earth.   935
If you do this you will have Ares as your ally.
And if earth receives fruit for fruit and for blood
human blood, the land will favor your side,
which once sent up the golden-helmeted crop
of Sown Men. Out of that race one must die   940
who is a child born from the dragon's jaw.
You are the last of us left here of the Sown Men,
unmixed both on your mother's and your father's side,
you and your children. The coming marriage of
    Haemon
precludes his sacrifice, for his status is not unwed.   945
He has not yet touched her, but still he has a bride.
This young colt, roaming free, may die for the city
and preserve the land of his fathers.
A bitter homecoming he will cause for Adrastus
and the Argives, casting dusky death over their eyes,   950
and he will make Thebes glorious. Of two destinies
you must choose one: save your son or save your city.
You have heard all that I had to say. Daughter,
take me home. Anyone who practices the art of prophecy
is a fool. If he reveals offensive things   955
he will reap resentment from all who hear his omens;
but if, out of pity for those who come to him, he lies,
he wrongs the gods. Only Phoebus should
tell the gods' will to men, for he has no one to fear.

(Tiresias and his daughter begin their slow departure,
leaving by the same side passage where they entered.)

CHORUS:

960   Why are you speechless, Creon, gaping in silence?
     I too am just as dumbfounded as you.

CREON:

     What could anyone say? It is obvious what my words
     must be. I will never reach such a point of misery
     that I would offer my son as a sacrifice for the city.
965   For all mankind love of children is a way of life,
     and no one would offer his child for slaughter.
     Let no one try to flatter me into killing my son,
     but I am more than willing to die—I have reached
     a ripe age—to keep my homeland safe.
970   Come, my boy, before the whole city learns of it;
     reject the crazy ramblings of that oracle monger
     and go into exile—leave the country as quick as you can.
     He will tell this to the leading citizens and officers,
     going around to the seven gates and company commanders.
975   If we act quickly you can be saved,
     but if you are slow we are lost and you will die.

MENOECEUS:

     Where should I go, then? What city? What foreign
       friends?

CREON:

     Wherever you will be farthest from this country.

MENOECEUS:

     It is yours to command and mine to obey.

CREON:

     After you go past Delphi . . .

MENOECEUS:

                    Where must I go next, Father?
980

CREON:

     To the Aetolian country.

MENOECEUS:

                    And from there, where next?

CREON:

     To Thesprotian territory.

MENOECEUS:
                    The sacred site of Dodona?

CREON:
  Yes, you understand.

MENOECEUS:
                    What protection will I get there?

CREON:
  The god will be your guide.

MENOECEUS:
                    What will I do for money?

CREON:
  I will provide you with money.

MENOECEUS:
                    Thank you, Father.   985
  But you go now. I will go see your sister,
  Jocasta, at whose breast I was first nursed
  when I lost my mother and was an orphan.
  I will go speak to her and then look to my safety.   990
  But go now. Don't hinder me on your side.

      (Exit Creon stage right.)

  Women, do you see how well I calmed my father's fear,
  cheating him with words to achieve my aim?
  He is trying to send me away, deprive the city of its destiny,
  and make a coward of me. It is forgivable   995
  in an old man. But for my part there is no excuse
  if I become a traitor to my homeland, which gave me life.
  Just so you know—I will go and save the city
  and give my life to die for this country.
  It is shameful—when some men, who are free of oracles
  and do not come under divinely imposed obligation,   1000

982: Dodona in Epirus (northwest Greece) was the most important oracle
of Zeus, site of his speaking oak. Zeus was a protector of suppliants.

987–89: Another relationship for Jocasta, foster mother of Menoeceus. In
Sophocles' Antigone, Creon's wife is alive and kills herself when she hears
of the death of Haemon, the last of her sons.

stand by their shields and are not reluctant to die
fighting before the towers for their homeland—
but will I betray my father and my brother,
betray my city, too, and like a coward flee the country?
1005 Wouldn't I be seen as a deserter wherever I live?
I will not, by Zeus in the heavens and bloody Ares
who once established the Sown Men, who rose up
from the earth, to be kings of this country.
I will go now to stand upon the highest tower
1010 and immolate myself into the deep, dark den
of the dragon where the prophet directed,
and I will preserve the homeland. My word is final.
I go now to offer my death to the city, no paltry gift,
and I shall deliver the land from its sickness.
1015 If everyone would take advantage of whatever
opportunity offers to benefit the common welfare
of his country, future cities would experience
less dissension and people's lives would be better.

(Exit Menoeceus stage left.)

Third Stasimon

CHORUS:

[Strophe]

You came, you came,
O winged brood of earth,
1020 brood of the underground monster Echidna,
snatcher of Cadmeians,
full of death, full of sorrow,
half girl,
deadly freak
1025 with whipping wings,

1018–66: The third stasimon is a lamentation for the men who were victims of the Sphinx, the dragon, and the family bloodlust. It describes the lament and repeats it and at the same time becomes a dirge for the latest victim.

1020: An echidna is a viper and symbol of treachery; as a supernatural monster, she is half nymph and half snake, an eater of raw flesh. See Hesiod, *Theogony* 295–305.

flesh-eating claws,
who snatched the young
from Dirkē's lands
to music without the lyre,
avenging Fury,
sorrows and more sorrows you kept bringing to our land   1030
with your murders. A killer sent by the gods
did this.
Keenings of mothers,
keenings of girls
they sobbed in the houses.   1035
A cry of woe,
a strain of woe,
another and then another cried out
in succession; up and down the city
the moaning roared like thunder,
and there was the same sound of sorrow   1040
when the swooping monster Sphinx
caused one more of the men to vanish from the city.

[Antistrophe]

In time he came,
sent by Delphi,
Oedipus, unhappy man,
here to the land of Thebes.   1045
They welcomed him then for heartache later,
for he joined his mother
in marriage; no marriage there,
the wretch, after his glorious victory
in riddles,
and he poisoned the city.   1050
Through blood he wades;
into unclean struggle—
he has sent his children there by his curses,
unhappy man. Amazed, we are amazed

1029: Erinys, a fury or spirit of vengeance/family justice, an avenger.
1036–37: The wailing sounds of the mothers and maidens (*ieieion boan,*
ieieion melos, an untranslatable sad sound) are made in the present by the
maidens of the chorus, mourning for the orphan boy.

1055   at the one who is gone to death
        for his native land,
        leaving behind the same songs of sorrow for Creon,
        but he has gone to make the seven-towered gates of the land
        glorious in victory.
        I pray, adored
1060   Pallas, we will be mothers like that
        and be blessed in our children—
        you caused the blood of the dragon
        to flow down—struck with a stone—
        you stirred Cadmus' mind to his work
1065   and there fell on this land, by godsent rapture,
        a doom.

Fourth Episode

(Enter Messenger stage left.)

MESSENGER:
    Halloo! Is there anyone at the palace gates?
    Open up. Send Jocasta out of the house.
    Halloo, I call again. Though it is a long way, still
1070   come out and hear me, noble wife of Oedipus.
    Cease from your laments and tears of grief.

JOCASTA:
    My dear, it is you who stands beside Eteocles in battle,
    and shields him from hostile missiles—
    you have not come to announce his death,
1075   have you? What news do you have to report?
    Is my son dead or alive? Please, tell me.

MESSENGER:
    He is alive. Of that terror I can relieve you.

JOCASTA:
    What is it, then? Are our seven circling towers still standing?

MESSENGER:
    They stand unscaled. The city is not taken.

1072: Compare with Electra, who does not recognize the Messenger even though he is one of her brother's slaves and had just left her house (Euripides, *Electra* 761–69).

JOCASTA:
Have they faced the peril of battle with the Argives?   1080

MESSENGER:
Yes, peril in the extreme, but Theban Ares
prevailed over the Mycenaean spear.

JOCASTA:
In the name of the gods, tell me one thing, if you know—
about Polynices. I care about him—is he alive?

MESSENGER:
Both your sons are alive up to this moment.   1085

JOCASTA:
Bless you. But how did you, from your post on the towers,
drive away the Argive army from our gates?
Tell me so that I may go and bring pleasure
to the old blind man inside with the news that the city is safe.

MESSENGER:
Creon's son stood on the highest tower to die   1090
for his country, staining his sword dark with blood
as he thrust it through his throat, our land's salvation!
Your son, then, divided the companies into seven
and assigned commanders to the seven gates, guards
against the enemy, and he stationed horsemen   1095
in reserve for horsemen, infantry for fellow shield-bearers
so that there would be a quick defense
for trouble spots along the walls. High on the battlements
we spot the white shields of the Argive army
pouring down from Teumessus, and near the trench   1100
they are charging the city of the Cadmeians at a run.
From their side and from our walls, at the same time
exactly, bugles trumpet a paean call to war.
First to the Neitan gate a company bristling
with close-packed shields marched forth   1105

1090–92: Menoeceus dies before the fighting begins, but his death has no
obvious effect on the war, which has its own natural back-and-forth
rhythm. At this point there is no way of knowing whether the city is saved.
1100: Teumessus—a hill about five miles from Thebes, where the Argives
had probably camped overnight.

under command of the huntress' son, Parthenopaeus.
On his shield he carried his family crest:
Atalanta taking down the Aetolian boar with arrows
shot from far away. Then to the Proetid gate advanced
1110   the prophet Amphiaraus with fresh-slaughtered victims
on his chariot, displaying no violent insignia
on his shield but calmly carrying arms without sign.
To the Ogygian gate strode King Hippomedon.
In the middle of his shield the insignia showed
1115   all-seeing Panoptes spotted all over with eyes.
Some of the eyes opened with the risings of stars,
others were shuttered with their settings—
we were able to see this later, after he had died.
Up to the Homoloid gate Tydeus led his company.
1120   On his shield he carried a lion skin with bristling mane.
And on the right the figure of Prometheus the Titan
was carrying a torch to set ablaze the city of Thebes.
At the Krenaian gate your son Polynices led his force.
On his shield he bore the sign of Potnian horses
1125   running wild. They were rearing in alarm.
Inside the rim, right under the handle, there were pivots
cleverly circling to make the horses appear mad.
And his heart no less set on war and battle,
Capaneus led a company to the Electran gate.
1130   On the iron-backed circle of his shield there was fixed
an earthborn giant bearing on his shoulders an entire city,
which he had pried up from its foundations with levers—
he wanted to show us what our city was going to suffer.
Adrastus was poised to breach the seventh gate.
1135   His shield was covered with a hundred snakes
in silhouette, and he wore hydras on his left arm—
an Argive boast. The serpents held in their jaws
Theban children they were seizing from the walls.
I was able to look at their shields when I brought

1115: Panoptes is Argus, who guarded Io. He had eyes all over his body so
that while some slept others were open.

1125: The Potnian horses were from the town of Potniae near Thebes,
where there was a well whose water drove animals mad if they drank from
it. The most famous were Glaucus' maddened horses, who killed and devoured their master.

a message to the shepherds of the contingents. 1140
We fought first with bows and arrows and javelins
and far-shooting slings and pounded them
with stones. We were beating them in battle
when a sudden cry went up from Tydeus and your son:
"Sons of Danaans, before you are crushed with missiles, 1145
why do you hold back from rushing the gates, all together,
infantry, cavalry, and drivers of chariots?"
When they heard the shout, no one was a laggard.
Many fell, blood gushing from their heads.
On our side you could see men tumbling from the walls 1150
thick and fast like divers, the breath knocked out of them
watering the parched earth with streams of their blood.
And then the son of Atalanta, an Arcadian, no Argive,
like a hurricane falling upon the gates is shouting
for fire and pickaxes to dig down the city. 1155
But Periclymenus, son of the sea god, stopped him
as he raged in his fury, hitting him on the head with a rock
the size of a wagon, a cornice from the battlements.
It shattered his blond head, smashed the sutures
of his bones, and bloodied his just-reddening cheek. 1160
He will not come back alive to his mother,
the beautiful huntress, daughter of Mainalos.
When he saw that we were successful at this gate,
your son went on to the next and I followed him.
I saw Tydeus and a thick phalanx of men armed 1165
with Aetolian spears flinging at the topmost lip
of the towers so that men in flight were leaving
the steep sides of the battlements. Again, like a hunter
with his hounds, your son rounded them up
and posted them back on the towers. On to the other gates 1170
we hurried after we had settled this disorder.
Capaneus—how can I put into words how wild he was?
Holding a long-reaching ladder to scale the wall,
as he approached he was making the boast

1140: In Homer the commanders are called "shepherds of the people."
1156: Besides Eteocles, Periclymenus is the only Theban defender named.
1160: Reddening cheek refers to the first growth of his beard, indicating
how young he was (see note on 32).

1175   that not even Zeus' sacred fire could prevent him
       from leveling the city from its highest turrets.
       As he was saying this, though pelted by rocks
       he kept crawling up, crouched under his shield,
       setting his feet on the ladder's rungs one by one.
1180   Now he was passing the copestone of the walls
       when Zeus struck him with lightning. The earth bellowed.
       All our hearts were struck with terror. And from the ladder
       he swung around in a circle; his limbs went separate ways;
       his hair flew up to the sky; his blood spurted to the ground;
1185   his hands and legs were spinning like Ixion's wheel.
       He fell to the earth, his body a ball of fire.
       When Adrastus saw that Zeus was his army's enemy,
       he restrained his Argives on the other side of the trench,
       but our side, seeing the happy omen from Zeus,
1190   kept up our assault—drivers of chariots, cavalry,
       infantry—and into the midst of Argive arms
       we closed on them with spears. It was total chaos.
       They were dying, falling over the sides of their chariots;
       wheels popped off; axles piled up on axles
1195   and dead bodies heaped on top of bodies.
       And so we have kept safe the towers of our homeland
       up to the present day. Whether our country will stay lucky
       in the days and years to come depends on the gods.
       But for now one of the gods has kept us safe.

       CHORUS:
1200   Oh glorious victory. If the gods have in mind
       something better, I pray our good fortune will last.

       JOCASTA:
       What concerns the gods and fortune is going well.
       My sons are alive and our country has survived.
       Poor Creon has reaped the bitter harvest
1205   of my marriage and Oedipus' tragedy,
       losing his son for the common good, but grief
       to him. But, please, take up your story again.
       What are my sons planning to do next?

1185: "Ixion's wheel"—In punishment for an attempt to rape Hera, Ixion
was bound for eternity to a burning (or flying) wheel.

MESSENGER:
Let the rest be. Up to now things are still going well.

JOCASTA:
What you just said makes me suspicious. I can't let it go.   1210

MESSENGER:
Your sons are safe. What more do you need to know?

JOCASTA:
To hear if the future still brings good news.

MESSENGER:
Let me go. Your son will be missing his aide.

JOCASTA:
You are hiding some trouble, trying to keep me in the dark.

MESSENGER:
I would prefer not to spoil the good news by telling the bad.   1215

JOCASTA:
You will tell it unless you can fly up to the sky.

MESSENGER:
Very well, then. Why couldn't you just let me go
after the good news and not make me tell the bad?
Your two sons are getting ready—it's a deplorable
act of daring—to fight apart in single combat.   1220
Speaking to the Argives and Cadmeians
in public, a speech that should never have been made,
Eteocles went first. Standing on a steep tower
he ordered silence to be heralded to the army
and spoke: "Commanders of the Greek land,   1225
chief men of the Danaans who came here,
and people of Cadmus, do not for Polynices' sake
nor for mine, squander your lives.
To free you from this peril, I will myself
alone stand to face my brother in battle.   1230
And if I kill him I will live alone in my house,
but if I am defeated I will hand it over to him alone.
You, Argives, give up the struggle and return
to your country; do not leave your lives here;
the people of the Sown Men lying dead are enough."   1235
That is what he said, and then your son Polynices

jumped up from the ranks and applauded his speech,
and all the Argives shouted their approval and so did
the people of Cadmus, since they thought it was right.
1240 At this the generals made a truce and in no-man's-land
between the armies they swore oaths to abide by it.
Then they covered their bodies in their bronze armor,
gray-headed Oedipus' two sons in their youthful prime.
They were outfitted by their friends, our commander,
1245 by the Sown Men, the other by the chiefs of the Danaans.
They stood there gleaming in arms and did not blanch
with fear, furiously eager to hurl the spear at each other.
One after another their friends came up to them
with words of encouragement, saying this sort of thing:
1250 "Polynices, it is in your power to raise an image of Zeus
as a trophy and to bestow a glorious reputation on Argos."
But to Eteocles in turn: "Now you are fighting for the city.
If you win glorious victory, the scepter is yours to wield."
With words like these they exhorted them to battle.
1255 The prophets made sacrifice of sheep and observed
the burning tips and fissures; in the moisture of the flesh
opposite the top of the flame they found two meanings:
one a sign of victory, the other of defeated men.
If you have any means to stop them, words of wisdom
1260 or magical charms, go, restrain your sons
from this terrible battle. The danger is great
and the prize will be tragic tears for you
if you are to lose both your sons on this day.

JOCASTA:
Antigone, daughter, come out of the house,
1265 but not to dance at the maidens' festivals;
now god-ordained fate propels you,
and you must come along with your mother
to stop two good men, your brothers, veering
toward death from dying at each other's hands.

1255–58: For interpretations of this difficult passage, see Mastronarde 1994.

1265: The various coming-of-age celebratory rituals in which girls participated.

(Enter Antigone from the scene building.)

ANTIGONE:
What, Mother? What new alarm for our family   1270
are you calling out in front of the house?

JOCASTA:
My daughter, your brothers' lives are over.

ANTIGONE:
What is it?

JOCASTA:
              They are set on fighting a duel.

ANTIGONE:
Oh no, what are you saying, Mother?

JOCASTA:
              Not words of comfort. You must come with me.

ANTIGONE:
Leave my maidens' chamber? Where are we going?

JOCASTA:
                                        Through the army.   1275

ANTIGONE:
I feel awkward in front of a crowd of men.

JOCASTA:
                          Shyness does not suit your situation.

ANTIGONE:
What will I do?

JOCASTA:
                You must settle your brothers' quarrel.

ANTIGONE:
How, Mother?

JOCASTA:
                Fall down on your knees at my side.
Lead us to where they plan to fight. There must be no
    delay.
Hurry, daughter, hurry, because if I get there before   1280

my sons' spear-fight my life will go on,
1283   but if they die I will lie down with them in death.

   (*Exit Messenger stage left, followed by Jocasta and Antigone.*)

Fourth Stasimon

CHORUS:

[Strophe]

Aiai, aiai!
1285   Trembling, trembling with dread I hold my heart.
Through my flesh
pity flows, pity for the unhappy mother.
Two children—who will shed whose blood?
1290   Ah me, for the troubles, oh Zeus, oh earth,
brother's neck, brother's life
with weapons, in bloodshed
sorrow, more sorrow,
1295   which dead man murdered will I keen?

[Antistrophe]

Feu da, feu da!
Paired beasts, murderous souls,
brandishing spears,
they fall, savage falls; both will soon shed blood.
Unhappy ones, why in the world did they come
1300   to the thought of single combat?
With alien call the keening cry
of tears for the dead we shall shrill.
The fate of death is almost here.
1305   This day's light will decide the future.
Hapless death, hapless death from the Furies.

1282: [if you are slow we are lost and you will die] is omitted here because it is repeated from 976 where it is more appropriate to the situation.
1284: Aiai is an untranslatable tragic noise, as is *feu da* at 1296.

Exodos

(Enter Creon stage right, carrying Menoeceus' body.)

CHORUS:
I see Creon in a cloud of sorrow coming here
to the house, and so will end my present lamentations.

CREON:
Ah. What to do? Shed tears in pity   1310
for myself or for the city, which is under a cloud
of gloom like the journey across Acheron?
My son is gone; by dying for his country
he won a glorious reputation but bitterest gall to me.
Mournfully I lifted him from the dragon's den;   1315
I carried him in my arms, victim of suicide.
My whole house is wailing. But here I am,
an old man, looking for my aged sister Jocasta
to wash and lay out my dead son.
Those not yet dead must give honors   1320
to the dead and pay respect to the gods of death.

CHORUS:
Your sister is gone, Creon. She left the house
and her daughter Antigone has gone with her.

Exodos: Everything that comes after the last choral ode. This one falls into
three parts:

1. 1308–1479: Another long messenger's speech, delivered to Creon.
2. 1480–1581: The Messenger leaves and three corpses are brought
   back by Antigone and attendants; Oedipus comes out into the light.
3. 1582–1766: The family of Oedipus comes to an end.

The exodos is a four-character scene—Creon, Messenger, Antigone, and
Oedipus—but the actor playing the Messenger would leave after his speech
and return as Oedipus.

Enter Creon: Creon's entrance with Menoeceus' body is reminiscent of the
scene at the end of Sophocles' *Antigone* when he comes in carrying the
body of Haemon, the last of his sons.

1312: Acheron—the river of sorrow in Hades.

1319: Women were associated with transitional events in human life, such
as birth and death, and with the physical body.

CREON:
Where? On what errand? Tell me.

CHORUS:
1325 She heard that her sons were going to face each other
in single combat of spears for the royal house.

CREON:
What are you saying? I was tending to the body
of my son and heard nothing about this.

CHORUS:
Your sister left some time ago, Creon.
1330 I expect the life-and-death struggle
has already been fought by the sons of Oedipus.

CREON:
Ah me. I see evidence of this,
the tragic face and bearing of a messenger
coming here; he will report the awful news.

(Enter Messenger stage left.)

MESSENGER:
1335 Oh horrors! What story or what words shall I speak?

CREON:
We are ruined. Your words promise disaster.

MESSENGER:
Horrors! No other word will do. I bring great sorrows.

CREON:
On top of the troubles we have already suffered.
What more do you have to tell?

MESSENGER:
Your sister's sons are dead, Creon.

CREON:
1340 Oh no. You tell of a great tragedy for me, for the city.
House of Oedipus, did you hear this,
the sons dead, meeting the same doom?

CHORUS:
So awful, the house itself would weep if it were able.

CREON:
> Ah me, this is the heaviest, most tragic fate.   1345
> [Ah me, unhappy in my sufferings, wretched as I am.]

MESSENGER:
> If you knew the bad news on top of this . . .

CREON:
> How could there be more misery than this?

MESSENGER:
> Your sister is dead with her two sons.

CHORUS:
> Raise a wail, raise a wail of women   1350
> beating their hands over the head.

CREON:
> Poor Jocasta. What an end to your life and marriage
> you have suffered, all because of the Sphinx's riddle.
> How did it happen, the death of her two sons,
> a struggle caused by Oedipus' curse? Tell me.   1355

MESSENGER:
> The success of our homeland before the towers
> you already know. The surrounding walls are not so far
> that you could fail to know all that happened there.
> When aged Oedipus' two young sons
> had arrayed themselves in their armor of bronze,   1360
> they stepped into no-man's-land and took their stands—
> two commanders, two leaders of their men—
> for single combat and a test of valor with the spear.
> Looking toward Argos, Polynices sent out his curse:
> "Goddess Hera, I belong to you since I joined   1365
> in marriage the daughter of Adrastus and dwell in his land.
> Grant to me that I kill my brother and in victory
> soak my right hand with his hated blood,"

1350–51: Literally, "white-armed beating of hands over the head." Lightness was a sign of beauty and delicateness, and it was traditional to depict women's flesh as white, whether because they spent most of their time indoors or because they used white lead as a cosmetic.

1365: Hera was the chief god at Argos.

and he prayed for this most sordid crown, to kill his own kin.
1370   Tears of pity for their doom welled up in many eyes.
They looked into each other's eyes, exchanging glances.
And then Eteocles, looking toward the temple of Pallas
Athena of the golden shield, prayed, "Daughter of Zeus,
grant to my hand to hurl a victorious spear
1375   from my arm, striking my brother's heart
and to kill the man who came to lay waste my homeland."
And when the torch was let go like the blast
of an Etruscan trumpet, signal of murderous battle,
they rushed at terrifying speed upon each other.
1380   Like boars whetting their savage jaws
they came together, chins dripping with foam;
they raced on with spears. They crouched behind their shields
so the steel would glance off without success.
If one spotted the other's eye rising above the rim
1385   he directed the spear at his face, hoping for the first kill,
but cleverly they turned the eye to the shields'
eyelets so that the spear had no effect.
In shock for their friends, more sweat was dripping
from the onlookers than from those actually engaged.
1390   Then Eteocles' foot brushed aside a rock
that was rolling under his step and he let his leg slip
outside the shield. Polynices rushed to meet him with the spear,
catching sight of the opportunity for his weapon to strike;
he pierced through the leg with his Argive spear
1395   and the entire Danaan army raised a cry of triumph.
During this struggle, seeing the shoulder exposed,
Eteocles, though first wounded, threw his spear powerfully
through Polynices' chest and drew a cheer
from the citizens of Cadmus. But he broke the tip of his spear.
1400   Faced with the loss of his spear, Eteocles backs up a step.
He lifts up a slab of marble, and heaves it,
breaking Polynices' javelin in two. The battle was tied,
the hands of both were deprived of their shafts.
Then, grasping the hilts of their swords,
1405   the two came together setting shield to shield;
standing firm on each side they made a great din of battle.
Somehow Eteocles, from his familiarity with the country,

1378: The battlefield trumpet was considered an Etruscan invention.

thought of the Thessalian stratagem and brought it into play.
Backing away from the present standoff,
he sets his left foot behind him   1410
and, protecting his abdomen, advances
on his right foot, and straight through the navel
he thrusts his sword and fixes it into his brother's backbone.
Poor Polynices, cramping up his sides and stomach,
stumbles in the pools of his own blood.   1415
And his brother, thinking he had won the contest,
throwing his sword onto the ground, began stripping the body,
keeping his mind not on himself but on his object—
and that is what tripped him up. Still breathing a little,
and holding onto his weapon even after his mortal fall,   1420
with one last effort Polynices, who had fallen first,
stuck his sword into his brother's liver.
Their mouths full of dust, the two lie fallen side by side.
They have left behind the royal power undivided.

CHORUS:
It is a tragedy. Oedipus, I grieve for your sorrows.   1425
A god, it seems, has fulfilled your curses.

MESSENGER:
Listen now to this—there was worse to follow.
While her two fallen sons are giving up their lives,
their unhappy mother throws herself onto the scene
on scurrying feet with her young daughter in tow.   1430
Seeing them wounded with mortal blows,
she cried out, "My sons, I am here too late
to help." Throwing herself on each in turn
she sobbed, she howled in grief for her lost labor
of nursing them, and their sister stood alongside her,   1435
"Keepers of Mother's old age, you betray my marriage,
my dear, dear brothers." And then, a dying gasp
whistling from his chest, King Eteocles
heard his mother, and placing on her a clammy hand,
he let out no further sound, but from his eyes   1440
he spoke with his tears to show her a sign of love.
But the other, Polynices, was still breathing and, looking

1408: The Thessalian stratagem may have been a wrestling technique; see
Mastronarde's (1994) note on 1409–13.

toward his sister and his gray-haired mother, spoke to them:
"We are done for, Mother. I feel sorry for you
1445   and my sister and my dead brother.
He was loved, he lost my love, but still I loved him.
Bury me, Mother, you too, my sister, here
in my homeland, and though the city is angry,
persuade them with soothing words so that I may have
1450   that much of my country, though I have lost my father's house.
Shut my eyelids with your own hand,
Mother," and he placed it on his eyes himself,
"and farewell. Already darkness closes in on me."
Both sons together breathed out their pitiful lives.
1455   And when their mother had witnessed this tragedy,
overwrought with grief, she snatched the sword
from between the bodies and performed a horrific act.
She thrust the iron straight through her neck. She lies there dead
between her beloved sons, her arms embracing both.
1460   Then the army rose up in strife of words.
We argued that my master was victor,
and they that theirs was. The leaders were quarreling,
one side that Polynices had struck the first blow,
another that both were dead so there was no victory.
1465   In the midst of this, Antigone slipped off unseen.
But they—the men—rushed to arms. By lucky forethought,
the people of Cadmus were sitting under arms
so that we got the jump on them, still unarmed,
when, without warning, we fell upon the Argive army.
1470   No one could withstand. The plains were filled with men
in flight, and blood was streaming from untold numbers
fallen to the spear. And as we were victorious in battle
some were setting up a victory statue to Zeus,

1456: This would be the sword Eteocles threw down at 1417. The sword
is the usual masculine suicide weapon. Women are more likely to choose
hanging, but here Jocasta uses what opportunity has presented. Stabbing
herself in the neck, however, is feminine; men aim for the heart or liver (see
Loraux 1987).

1466–75: Thebes is saved—not necessarily by the heroism of Menoeceus,
nor by the seven defenders, nor even by the single combat of the enemy
brothers, but because the Theban fighting men had the good sense to keep
their arms at the ready. The citizen army prevails.

others stripping shields from the Argive dead
and bringing the spoils inside the walls.   1475
Others with Antigone are carrying the bodies
of the dead here for their loved ones to mourn.

*(Enter Antigone and a procession of extras carrying the
bodies from the battlefield, stage left.)*

Of the city's struggles some have turned out
most happily, others most tragically.

(Exit Messenger stage right.)

CHORUS:
No longer is the tragedy of this house   1480
just a report, for all can see now
the fallen bodies of these three
here before the palace—in a shared death,
they have drawn fate's dark lot.

ANTIGONE:
Not veiling the soft skin of my cheek,   1485
covered with ringlets or like a bashful girl
hiding the red blush of my face under my eyes,
I carry myself along, a Bacchant of the dead
throwing the cloth from my head,   1490
casting off my soft saffron robe,
leading a procession of mourning for the dead.
Alas, ah Polynices, you were well named. Ah Thebes,
your strife, not strife, but death on death   1495
overthrew the house of Oedipus
with blood of horror, blood of gloom.
What musical lament,
what song in tune
with my tears, my tears—house, my house   1500
I call upon you
bearing three bodies, kindred blood,
mother and sons, the Fury's delight
that destroyed all the house of Oedipus

1489: Bacchant—Intense emotion is common to both Bacchic ritual and
funeral lamentation, both practiced by women in groups (see Segal 1997,
p. 363).

1505 when he read the riddle clear to him
of the savage singing Sphinx,
hard to fathom, and he killed her.
Ah me, ah me,
what Greek, what foreign speaker
1510 or who else of well-born men
from ages past endured so many evils
of human blood,
such sufferings brought to light
in misery? How can I mourn?
1515 What bird, then, in the high-leaved branches
of oak or pine
in laments of a solitary mother
sings along with my pains?
Woe with woeful sounds
1520 I weep, soon to pass
a lonely lifetime
in tears always,
tears streaming from my eyes.
On which of them should I cast
1525 the first offering of locks torn from my hair?
Here by my mother's two
breasts once full of milk,
or on the fatal wounds
of my brothers' bodies?
1530 *Otototoi!* Leave your
home, coming with blind eyes,
aged father; show yourself,
Oedipus, reveal your wretched life,
you who in the house have cast over your eyes
1535 dark gloom and drag out a slow-footed life.
Do you hear? Wandering
in the halls, unhappy man,
resting your aged feet on the bed?

(Enter Oedipus from the palace.)

OEDIPUS:
Why, daughter, do you bring me
1540 with a staff for my blind feet out into the light

1530: *"Otototoi"*—an untranslatable wail of grief.

from my bed of pain, from my dark chamber
with most piteous tears,
a gray unseen image of air,
a ghost from below,
a dream in flight?   1545

ANTIGONE:
   You will bear the unhappy telling of news,
   Father. Your sons no longer look upon
   the light, nor your wife who always helped you
   with kind support for your blind step.
   Father, it's so sad.   1550

OEDIPUS:
   Ah me for my sufferings. I am left to grieve
   and cry out. Three lives—by what doom,
   how did they die? Tell me, child.

ANTIGONE:
   Not in reproach or mocking   1555
   but with sorrow I speak. Your spirit of vengeance
   weighted down with swords
   and fire and brutal battles has come over your sons.
   Ah Father, ah me.

OEDIPUS:
   Woe . . .

ANTIGONE:
              Why do you mourn?   1560

OEDIPUS:
   My children.

ANTIGONE:
                 You have waded into misery.
   But what if you could still see the sun's passage through
        the sky
   and look on these bodies of the dead
   with the sight of your own eyes?

1562: See 3, where Jocasta invokes the Sun starting his course through the
sky as the day and the play begin.

OEDIPUS:

1565   The evil fate of my children is clear,
        but my poor wife, daughter, how did she die?

ANTIGONE:

        Letting fall tears of grief
        clear to all,
        she offered her breast, yes, offered to her children
        a suppliant, holding it out in entreaty.
1570   She had found her sons at the Electra gate
        beside the meadow where lotus grows,
        amid spears in fraternal slaughter;
        their mother found them like lions in their den,
        battling, already wounded,
1575   the cold deadly spilling of blood,
        Hades' portion, gift of Ares.
        From between the corpses she seized a bronze sword
        and dyed it red inside her flesh; in grief for her sons she fell
            between them.
        On this day, Father, upon our house
        the god who brings these things to pass
1580   has brought together all the heartbreak.

CHORUS:

        This day has been the beginning of many evils
        for the house of Oedipus. I pray for a happier life.

CREON:

        Desist now from your wailing since it is time
1585   to be mindful of the funerals. Oedipus, listen
        to my commands. Your son Eteocles handed over to me
        the leadership of the country, entrusting to me the dowry
        for Haemon and the marriage of your daughter Antigone.
        You, I will not allow you to live any longer in this country.
1590   Tiresias in fact told me clearly that Thebes will never
        be prosperous while you are living inside its walls.
        Go then. I say this not in a spirit of insult or hostility
        toward you; because of your vengeful spirit
        I am afraid that the land will suffer more disaster.

OEDIPUS:

1595   My destiny! From the start you brought me forth
        to sorrow and suffering, if any man ever was.

Even before I came into the light from my mother's womb,
Apollo had declared to Laius that still unborn
I would become my father's murderer. Oh the misery—
and when I was born, the father who gave me life   1600
tried at once to kill me, believing I was his enemy
because he was destined to die at my hand. He disposed of me,
still crying for my mother's milk, to be devoured by wild beasts.
I was saved from that fate, and how I wish Kithairōn
had gone to the bottomless pit of Tartarus   1605
because it did not destroy me, but my destiny gave me
to Polybus as my master to be his slave.
Then I killed my father and to my misery
I entered the bed of my doomed mother and fathered sons,
my own brothers, and now I have destroyed them.   1610
I inherited Laius' curses and passed them on to my children
for I was not naturally so devoid of intellect
that I devised these horrors against my own eyes
and the lives of my children without the hand of the gods.
And now in my misery what am I to do?   1615
Who will guide my blind step? The dead woman here?
If she were still alive I know she would.
Or my pair of noble sons? They too are lost to me.
Am I still young enough to find a livelihood?
How can I? Why do you cause my death, Creon?   1620
Yes, you will kill me if you drive me out of my country.
I will not wrap my arms around your knees
to beg and appear a coward. I will not betray
my own nobility, not even in my broken condition.

CREON:
Thank you for not pleading at my knees;   1625
I still would not allow you to remain in this country.
Of these dead—this one is to be laid out in the house,
but this one who came here to lay waste his homeland
with a foreign army, Polynices' corpse,
cast it out unburied beyond the borders of the territory.   1630
This proclamation will go out to all the Cadmeians:

1605: Tartarus—the lowest region of the world, beneath Hades, where the
gods imprisoned their enemies.
1622: That is, in an act of supplication.

If anyone is caught tending this body
or covering it with earth, he will be put to death.
[But leave him unwept, unburied, for birds to scavenge.]
1635   And you, Antigone, leave now the lamentation
for these three dead and go inside the house.
Conduct yourself as befits a young woman preparing
for tomorrow and the marriage to Haemon that awaits you.

ANTIGONE:
Father, how we are sunk in troubles and misery.
1640   I pity you more than the dead.
For to you one thing is not heavy and another less so,
but you were born unlucky in everything, Father.
But tell me, newly named king, why do you abuse
my father by driving him from his homeland?
1645   Why do you make decrees over a pitiful corpse?

CREON:
It is Eteocles' decision, not mine.

ANTIGONE:
It is senseless and you are a fool to go along with it.

CREON:
How so? Am I wrong to carry out his last wish?

ANTIGONE:
Yes, if it is a wicked and wrong decision.

CREON:
1650   What is this? Is it wrong to throw him to the dogs?

ANTIGONE:
The penalty you exact is not lawful.

CREON:
It is. He was not born an enemy to the city, but he became one.

ANTIGONE:
Then he gave up his life to his doom.

1637–38: Antigone combines associations of the wedding with the funeral procession she is enacting (see Seaford 1994, pp. 350–52).

1651: Basic Panhellenic values forbade withholding burial from a fallen enemy (see Euripides, *Suppliants* 526).

CREON:
And now let him pay the penalty to the grave.

ANTIGONE:
What wrong did he do, if he came for his share of his   1655
homeland?

CREON:
Just so you know, this man will not be buried.

ANTIGONE:
I will bury him even if the city forbids it.

CREON:
Then you will bury yourself along with his corpse.

ANTIGONE:
Well, it is glorious for two kin to lie side by side.

CREON:
Take hold of her and drag her inside the house.   1660

ANTIGONE:
No, you don't, since I will not let go of his dead body.

CREON:
Fate has decided this, young woman, not what you choose.

ANTIGONE:
This too is decided—not to abuse the dead.

CREON:
No one will put dust on this body nor pour ablutions on him.

ANTIGONE:
I will. In the name of my mother Jocasta, I beg you, Creon.   1665

CREON:
You are wasting your efforts. You will not have your way.

ANTIGONE:
Let me pour water over the body.

CREON:
That would be one of the things forbidden by the city.

ANTIGONE:
But let me put bandages around his raw wounds.

CREON:
1670   There is no way you will honor this corpse.

ANTIGONE:
Oh my dear, dear one. At least I will kiss your mouth.

CREON:
Do not ruin your marriage with your grieving.

ANTIGONE:
I will never—as long as I live—marry your son.

CREON:
But you must. How will you escape the marriage?

ANTIGONE:
1675   That night I will be one of Danaus' daughters and kill him.

CREON:
Look at the audacity with which she taunts me.

ANTIGONE:
Let this weapon know it, the sword of my oath.

CREON:
Why are you so eager to avoid your marriage?

ANTIGONE:
I will go into exile with my unhappy father.

CREON:
1680   You show nobility of spirit, along with your lunacy.

ANTIGONE:
And I will die with him, too, so you know the rest.

CREON:
Go, then. You will not murder my son. Leave the
country.

(Exit Creon into the palace.)

1675: Literally, "That night will turn me into one of Danaus' daughters,"
that is, a killer of her husband. All but one of the fifty daughters of Danaus
(the Danaids) killed their husbands, the fifty sons of Aegyptus, on their
wedding night.

1677: She touches the sword with which Jocasta killed herself.

OEDIPUS:
My daughter, I admire your spirit, but . . .

ANTIGONE:
If I marry, you will have to go into exile alone.

OEDIPUS:
Stay and be happy. I will endure my troubles. 1685

ANTIGONE:
You are blind. Who will take care of you?

OEDIPUS:
I will fall wherever fate takes me and lie on the ground.

ANTIGONE:
Where is Oedipus of the famous riddle?

OEDIPUS:
He is gone. One day blessed me. One day ruined me.

ANTIGONE:
May I not have my share of your miseries, then? 1690

OEDIPUS:
Exile is disgraceful for a daughter with her blind father.

ANTIGONE:
Not for a sensible one, Father, but noble.

OEDIPUS:
Help me so I can touch your mother.

ANTIGONE:
Here, reach out your hand and touch the dear, dear old
woman.

OEDIPUS:
Mother, most unhappy partner. 1695

ANTIGONE:
She lies there pathetically, all her troubles around her.

OEDIPUS:
And the bodies of Eteocles and Polynices, where are they?

1689: See Sophocles, *Oedipus Tyrannus* 438, "This day will give you birth
and destroy you."

ANTIGONE:
The two lie stretched out next to each other.

OEDIPUS:
Lay my sightless hand on their unhappy faces.

ANTIGONE:
1700   Here. Put your hand on your dead sons.

OEDIPUS:
Dear, unhappy dead of an unhappy father.

ANTIGONE:
Dear name, dear to me, Polynices.

OEDIPUS:
Now, daughter, Loxias' oracle is coming to pass.

ANTIGONE:
What oracle? Are you telling more troubles on top of these?

OEDIPUS:
1705   That I will die a refugee in Athens.

ANTIGONE:
Where? What rampart of Attica will welcome you?

OEDIPUS:
Sacred Colonus, home of the horse god.
But come, tend to your blind father,
since you are set upon sharing my exile.

ANTIGONE:
1710   Go into gloomy exile. Stretch out your dear hand,
aged father, with me
as guide, like a breeze escorting a ship.

OEDIPUS:
Here, here, I set out,
1715   my poor child, you be a guide to my feet.

ANTIGONE:
I am, yes, I am full of woe,
saddest of all the Theban girls.

1707: Colonus was the region of Athens, sacred to Poseidon, where Oedipus died. See Sophocles, *Oedipus at Colonus.*

OEDIPUS:
Where do I put my aged step?
Where set my cane, child?

ANTIGONE:
This way, this way, come to me.   1720
This way, this way, put down your foot
like a potent dream.

OEDIPUS:
Ah, ah! To drive me, an old man,
from my homeland into most gloomy exile.
Ah me, ah me! I have suffered terrible, terrible things.   1725

ANTIGONE:
Why "suffered"? Why say "suffered"? Justice does not see the
    wicked
and does not punish men's perverse deeds.

OEDIPUS:
I am he who reached the song
of glorious victory towering to the sky,
solving the impenetrable riddle   1730
of the half-human girl.

ANTIGONE:
You bring up the Sphinx's disgrace;
do not speak of past good fortune.
This sad tragedy has awaited you
to become a refugee from your homeland,   1735
Father, to die somewhere else.
And I am going far away from my home,
leaving tears of longing to the friends of my youth,
a refugee, a girl no more.
Alas. The goodness of my feelings   1740
toward my father's sufferings
will bring me glory.
Unhappy for your misery and my brother's
who is gone from our home, an unburied corpse,
to be pitied. Even if I must die, Father,   1745
I will bury him in the darkness.

OEDIPUS:
Go to your companions.

ANTIGONE:
  Enough of my sufferings.

OEDIPUS:
  You—pray at the altars.

ANTIGONE:
1750 Enough of my troubles.

OEDIPUS:
  Go to the enclosure of Bromius,
  sacred untrodden space in the mountain of the Maenads.

ANTIGONE:
  For whom once I put on
1755 the Theban fawnskin when I danced
  on the sacred ground of Semélē in the mountains,
  offering the gods a favor with no return?

OEDIPUS:
  Citizens of a glorious land, this is Oedipus
  who understood the famous riddles and was a great man,
1760 who alone restrained the power of the murdering Sphinx,
  now myself without honor, pitiful, I am driven out of the land.
  But why do I sing these sad songs and mourn in vain?
  As mortals we must bear the gods' compulsions.

  (Exit Antigone and Oedipus stage right.)

CHORUS:
  Victory much revered, sustain
1765 my life
  and never cease to crown it.

  (Exit chorus by the two side passages.)

–END–

1700–1763: The lament breaks down in non sequiturs. Creon disposes of the remaining members of the house of Oedipus. Oedipus laments his fate, once more reciting the crucial events of his life. What about Antigone? Her future is in doubt.

1764–66: The chorus files out with the usual meaningless tagline.

EURIPIDES

Bacchae

Translated, with Notes, by Paul Woodruff

Cast of Characters: *Bacchae*

DIONYSUS   god of intoxication, son of the god Zeus and the mortal Semélē, also known as Bacchus, Iacchus, Evius, and Bromius

CHORUS   of Bacchae (also known as Maenads), the women celebrants of Dionysus

TIRESIAS   a blind seer

CADMUS   founder and former king of Thebes, grandfather of Dionysus and Pentheus

PENTHEUS   king of Thebes, cousin of Dionysus

AGAVĒ   daughter of Cadmus, mother of Pentheus

A SOLDIER IN PENTHEUS' ARMY

FIRST MESSENGER

SECOND MESSENGER

Bacchae was first produced posthumously with *Iphigenia at Aulis* not long after 406 B.C.E. Euripides' plays won first prize in that year's Greater Dionysia.

The Daughters of Cadmus

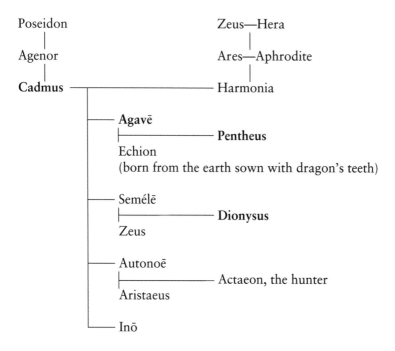

Poseidon
|
Agenor
|
Cadmus ——————————— Harmonia

Zeus—Hera
|
Ares—Aphrodite
|

—— **Agavē**
|————————— **Pentheus**
Echion
(born from the earth sown with dragon's teeth)

—— Semélē
|————————— **Dionysus**
Zeus

—— Autonoē
|————————— Actaeon, the hunter
Aristaeus

—— Inō

Bacchae

Prologue

DIONYSUS:

(dressed as a celebrant in his own religion)

I have arrived. I am Dionysus, son of Zeus,
come to Thebes, where my mother gave me birth
in a firestorm, struck by lightning. Her name
was Semélē; her father, Cadmus, had founded
this city. I have changed from divine to human form,   5
and here I am.

(pointing to various features of the landscape)

      There's the Ismenus River, the other one is called Dirkē.
Over here, by the house, is the marker for my mother's grave,
where she was struck by thunder. The ruins of her home
are still smoking from the living flame of Zeus. That
is how angry Hera was at my mother—violent, deathless rage.
      Cadmus, now, he's done well,   10
to keep this ground off limits, sacred to his daughter.
The vines that cover it, however, these are mine;
I set them around, made them copious and green.
My journey? I began from Lydia, where the sand is rich
in gold, then passed through Phrygia, then the sun-struck   15
plains of Persia, saw Bactria's walled towns, faced
the rigors of Media, and so came to rich Arabia. Then across
Asia, where fine-towered cities lie along the salt sea,
teeming with Greeks and other peoples mixed.
      I came here—my first Greek city—   20

1: Dionysus appears in the role of a human being, a foreign male leader of
a troop of Bacchic women. Such troops were not led by men in actual cult
practice; instead they felt the presence of the god as their leader.

only after I had started initiations there
and set those places dancing, so that mortals
would see me clearly as divine. Now Thebes
is my choice to be the first place I have filled
25 with cries of ecstasy, clothed with fawnskin, put thyrsus
in hand—this ivy-covered spear—because my mother's
sisters—of all people, *they* should have known better—
said Dionysus was no son of Zeus. They said
Semélē was seduced by some man or other and
30 put the blame on Zeus (as Cadmus cunningly advised her)
for her mistake in bed, and Zeus killed her—they yawped
everywhere—because she pretended to be his wife.

That is why I have stung these women into madness, goaded
them outdoors, made them live in the mountain, struck
35 out of their wits, forced to wear my cult's panoply.
All the females, all the women of Thebes—I sent them
crazy from their homes. Even the king's daughters are running
wild with them under fir trees, or seated on rocks in the open.
This city must fully learn its lesson, like it
40 or not, since it is not initiated in my religion.
Besides, I must defend my mother, Semélē,
and make people see I am a god, born by her to Zeus.

Well, now, Cadmus has given his rights as king
to Pentheus, the son of his daughter Agavē,
45 and Pentheus wages war on the gods through me,
shoves me away from libations, pays no attention
to me in his prayers. For that, I'll show him
I am truly god, and I'll show the Thebans too.
Then, once I've put this place in order, I'll
50 turn to another country, reveal myself there.
But if Thebes reacts in anger, sends military
force to drive my Bacchae from the mountain,
I'll lead my Maenads like an army into battle.

21: Initiations—The core of Dionysus-worship as represented in this play
is an experience of initiation that leads, among other things, to a clarity of
vision in matters relating to the god.
53: "I'll lead my Maenads like an army"—In an early version of the story
Pentheus goes to battle against the Maenads. Maenads were women who

It's to do this that I have taken human form
and changed myself into a man.
Now come, my sacred band of women,   55
that came with me from the bulwark of Lydia,
Mt. Tmolus, companions in my journey from abroad.
Take up the drums, the native drums of Phrygia,
the ones I discovered, I and Mother Rhea.
Surround this royal home of Pentheus, and strike.   60
Make the city of Cadmus take notice. Meanwhile,
I'll join the Bacchae on the slopes of Mt. Kithairōn,
and take my part in their dances.

Choral Entry-song

(The chorus enters, responding to his call.)

CHORUS:
Out of Asia
from the sacred mountain, I hasten   65
my sweet labor for the Thunderer.
I strain my voice—but it's no strain—
shouting praise of Bacchus.
You, on the road! You, on the road!
You, in the houses!
Come out! Let everyone
keep holy silence now.   70
For I shall sing the age-old hymn
to Dionysus.

---

celebrated Dionysus by dancing themselves into a frenzy on a mountainside,
out of the sight of men.

57: Mt. Tmolus—famous for its gold dust–bearing rivers. Lydia and Phrygia
are both in western Asia Minor (modern Turkey).

59: Rhea—a name for the mother goddess, whose worship was distinct
from that of Dionysus.

62: Mt. Kithairōn—a mountain near Thebes. Maenads feel that the god is
present in their rituals, although no human men are present. Dionysus proposes to join them, but probably not in human form.

66: Thunderer—Bromius, "the Roarer," a name for Dionysus.

68: Bacchus—another name for Dionysus.

[Strophe 1]

O
blessed are they
who know in their happiness
gods' initiations,
live life in holiness,
75   minds tuned to festival,
dancing on mountaintops,
sacred cleansing
in honor of Bacchus.

They celebrate the rites also
of the mother, great Cybélē
80   and they shake aloft their thyrsus
over heads enwreathed in ivy,
serving Dionysus.

Run, Bacchae! Run, Bacchae!
Bring the god, the son of a god,
85   Thunderer Dionysus,
down from the mountains of Phrygia,
down to Greece, to broad avenues,
Bromius.

[Antistrophe 1]

Born
suddenly in labor
pangs brought on by force:
90   Zeus' thunderbolt took wing,
struck him out the womb.
His mother lost her life
in the flash of lightning.

For a womb, Zeus took him
95   straight into the cavern of his thigh

73: A strophe is a large metrical unit, which is matched by its antistrophe.
83: Bacchae—the women celebrants of Dionysus, also known as Bacchants
and, by outsiders, as Maenads.

and sewed him up secretly
with golden fasteners
to hide him from Hera.

He was born when, as the Fates
said, his time came: a god   100
with his bull's horns, and crowned
with his snake crown. That is why,
in their wild hair, the Maenads weave
predator serpents.

[Strophe 2]

Oh, Thebes, Semélē's motherland,
may you be crowned in ivy,   106
and may you run green with creeping
vines, run fruitful and green.
Join the Bacchae, celebrate
with boughs of oak and fir.   110
Wear dappled fawnskins,
garland with locks of white
lamb's wool. And round your rebel stalks
weave holiness. Make haste: let all the land dance,
for now the Thunderer leads our revels.   115

To mountain! To mountain!
There waits a throng of women-born
now stung to leave their work
at loom and shuttle, stung by Dionysus.

[Antistrophe 2]

Oh, caverns of the band of youths,
sacred chambers that gave birth to Zeus   120

98: As the wife of Zeus, Hera was hostile to the children he fathered with
other women.

113–14: "And round your rebel stalks weave holiness"—The chorus
strangely puts *hubristas* ("insulting," modifying "stalks") next to the im-
perative "make holy," suggesting that the stalks (large woody stems of
fennel) threaten some danger that is cancelled by the holy purpose to which
they are put.

125
on Crete, where Corybants,
thrice-crested in the caves, invented
this taut cowhide drum,
gave it the beat of a swift Bacchic dance
below flutes, sweet-wailing.
This was their gift to the Mother, to Rhea—
the drumbeat of Bacchic praise.

130
Then satyrs in ecstasy
brought it from the goddess mother
and set it to the dances
we celebrate in each third year,
a joy to Dionysus.

[Epode]

135
He gives delight on mountains
when from the festive throng he runs
clothed in sacred fawnskin, falls earthward,
hunts goat-kill blood, raw flesh-eating joy,
140
yearning for mountains in Phrygia, Lydia—
with Bromius in the lead.
    VoHé
    VoHé

It flows milk, the ground flows wine, it flows
the nectar of bees.

As smoke streams from incense
145
of Syria, Bacchus waves

121: Corybants—the young men who protected the infant Zeus by banging drums and dancing. Dancing priests of Cybélē, called Corybantes, were a novelty in Athens at the time of this play.

135: "He gives delight on mountains"—It is unclear whether this is the god delighting the dancers or the dancer delighting the god. According to Segal, "Probably the god is meant" (1997, p. 23). If so, then who is it who falls? Segal takes it to be the victim in the hunt, but the syntax requires that it be the god. Perhaps the god is incarnate in the animal. But the passage is probably corrupt (Seaford 1996).

142: "*VoHé*"—the Bacchic joy-cry. Most translations print *euoi* or *evehe*, which look more like the Greek, but are not readily pronounceable in English.

his flaming torch aloft;
he darts, he runs,
he dances, he puts
them on fire if they stray.
Shouting, he rouses them,   150
his long hair softly tossing to the sky,
and adds to their sweet cries his thundering call:
"Run, Bacchae! Run, Bacchae!
Rich from the gold-flow of Tmolus,
sing praise to Dionysus   155
over thundering drums
and cry *VoHé*
to the glory of the god
with shouts and Phrygian war-cries."   160

When the ebony flute, melodious
and sacred, plays the holy song
and thunderously incites the rush of women
    to mountain, to mountain,
then, in delight, like a colt with its mother   165
at pasture, she frolics, a lightfooted Bacchant.

Scene One

TIRESIAS:
Where's the gatekeeper? Call Cadmus to come out,   170
Agenor's son, who left his home in Sidon
and ringed this city of Thebes with towers.
Hurry up! Someone tell him Tiresias
wants him. He'll know why I'm here.
We made an agreement, he and I, to tie a thyrsus,   175
and—though I'm old and he's older—
to wear fawnskins and wreathe our heads in fresh ivy.

CADMUS:
Here you are, dear friend. I recognized your voice
from inside the house—such a wise voice, a wise man's voice.
And I'm ready. Look, I have my costume for the god.   180
As well I might. Considering he's my daughter's son
whom they've now discovered is a god, Dionysus,
we should build him up as best we can.
        Where should we go to dance? Where plant

185   our feet and toss our heads, gray as they are?
        Be my guide in religion, Tiresias, the old leading
        the old, since you're so wise. I hope I'm never tired
        of rattling my thyrsus on the ground, night and day.
        Isn't it delightful to forget how old we are?

TIRESIAS:
        I feel just the same as you:
190   I'm growing young, my feet want to dance.

CADMUS:
        So how shall we get to the mountain? By chariot?

TIRESIAS:
        No. That's no way to give honor to the god.

CADMUS:
        Then let me guide you as we walk, old as I am.

TIRESIAS:
        Don't worry. The god will lead us there—both of us.

CADMUS:
195   Are we the only men in Thebes who'll dance for Bacchus?

TIRESIAS:
        The only ones in our right minds. The rest are mad.

CADMUS:
        We're wasting time. Come, take my hand.

TIRESIAS:
        Of course. And you take mine: we'll be a team.

CADMUS:
        I'm not the one to look down on gods. I'm human.

TIRESIAS:
200   We don't try to be clever with the gods;
        our traditions—which are old as time itself—
        came from our forefathers. No sophistic arguments
        will throw them down, no, not from the best brains of all.

203: Some sophists taught people to use argument strategies like wrestling holds to throw their enemies; some also used arguments to undermine belief in the gods.

CADMUS:

Won't folks say I ought to be ashamed, taking up dancing
now that I'm so old, and putting ivy on my head?   205

TIRESIAS:

The god won't care who's young, who's old:
we all must dance, because he wants
honor from all of us, together. He'll not exclude
anyone who gives to him the glory he desires.

CADMUS:

Tiresias, I know you cannot see this shining light,   210
so let me be your prophet and put it into words for you:
Here's Pentheus coming home in a hurry—
Echion's son, I made him king. My goodness,
he *is* in a flutter. Strange! What do you suppose he'll say?

PENTHEUS:

       (addressing the audience)

I happened to hear, when I was out of town,   215
there's trouble in the city—a revolution:
These women of ours have left their homes
and run away to the dark mountains, pretending
to be Bacchants. It's this brand-new god,
Dionysus, whoever that is; they're dancing for *him*!   220
They gather in throngs around full bowls
of wine; then one by one they sneak away
to lonely places where they sleep with men.
Priestesses they call themselves! Maenads!
It's Aphrodite they put first, not Bacchus.   225
Those I've captured are chained by the hand,

204–5: Recent editors assign these lines to Cadmus, though older editions
treated them as part of Tiresias' speech, with the meaning, "*Let* them say I
ought to be ashamed, old man that I am, to take up dancing now, with ivy
on my head!"

208–9: "He'll not exclude anyone"—Some Dionysiac rituals excluded men,
but generally the religion broke down all barriers, and even slaves could
take part in some rituals. Signs of distinction, such as Cadmus' royal chariot, would be inappropriate in this more than democratic cult (192).

225: Aphrodite—goddess of love.

and they are under guard in public jail.
As for the ones who got away, I'll hunt them
down out of the mountains—even my aunt
230   and my mother Agavē, and Actaeon's mother as well.
I'll catch them all in iron cages! I'll put a stop,
right now, to this dirty business, this Bacchism.
Also, I hear there's a foreigner come to town,
a wizard with magic spells from Lydia, who has
235   long blond curls—perfumed!—upon his head,
and the bloom of wine, the grace of Aphrodite,
on his cheeks. Day and night he plays around
with young girls, showing off his "VoHé"
mysteries. Just let me get him in this house!
240   I'll stop him rattling his thyrsus and shaking his hair,
once I have his head cut from his shoulders.
And *he's* the one who says Dionysus is a god,
that *he* was sewn up in the thigh of Zeus—
when actually he was burnt to ashes by lightning,
245   along with his mother, because she lied when she named
Zeus as her lover. That's a hanging offense, isn't it?
One insult after another. I don't care who he is . . .

(catches sight of Tiresias and Cadmus)

What's this? Another marvel? Our expert reader
of omens in fancy fawnskins—is that you, Tiresias?
250   And my very own grandfather—what a laugh!—
playing Bacchant with a thyrsus. Shame on you, old man.
You both should have some sense at your age.
Why don't you shake that ivy off? And let
the thyrsus go, out of your hand, grandfather.
255   Tiresias, you talked him into this. You just want
to make a profit bringing in this new divinity so you
can check out more bird-omens and run more sacrifices.
If your gray hair hadn't stopped me, you'd be
sitting in chains surrounded by Bacchic women
260   for importing bad religion: because when women

_____

230: Actaeon—son of Autonoē, grandson of Cadmus, and cousin of Pentheus and Dionysus, whose fate is frequently mentioned as parallel to that of Pentheus. He was torn apart by his own hunting dogs for an offense to the goddess Artemis. See 337 ff.

get their sparkle at a feast from wine,
I say the entire ritual is corrupt.

CHORUS LEADER:
Sacrilege! Friend, have you no respect for gods?
For Cadmus? Who planted the crop of earthborn men?
You are Echion's son: You'll disgrace your own family!   265

TIRESIAS:
When a prudent speaker takes up a noble cause,
he'll have no great trouble to speak well.
You, on the other hand, have a tongue that runs on smoothly
and sounds intelligent. But what it says is brainless.
True, boldness can help a man speak powerfully,   270
but he'll turn out bad for the city because he'll have no sense.
This "new divinity," the object of your ridicule,
has more greatness in his future here in Greece
than I can say. Young man, there are two
first principles in human life: the goddess Demeter—   275
or earth—you may use what name you like—
who nourishes us by means of the dry element;
and the second one balances her exactly, that's
Semélē's child, who discovered, in the wet element,
a drink from grapes, a drink he delivered to us.   280
This brings relief from pain for long-suffering mortals
when they are filled with the vineyard's bounty;
it grants sleep, lets them forget the evils of the day,
and there is no other cure for trouble.
We pour him out as libation to the gods, god that he is,
so that what good we have we have by way of him.   285
Now, do you think it's silly he was sewn in the thigh
of Zeus? I'll explain to you how fine this really was.
When Zeus had plucked him from the lightning fire
and raised the newborn to Olympus as a god,
Hera wanted to throw him down from heaven.   290
But Zeus contrived a defense worthy of a god:
he broke off a piece from the sky that circles the earth
and made a surrogate to give Hera as a hostage.

293: Hera evidently thought she had the real Dionysus, whom she kept as
a hostage for her husband's good behavior. But Zeus sent the real Dionysus
to be raised by nymphs in a place of safety.

So that was how he saved the real Dionysus
from Hera's violent rage. After a while,
295   people began to say he'd been "sewn in thigh."
They put "sewn in thigh" for "showing sky" because
they heard that Zeus fooled Hera by "showing sky" to her.
Let me add, this god gives prophecy or foresight:
whatever is Bacchic—or maddened by his *force*—
300   has foresight aplenty, and when the god enters people
in force, he maddens them and makes them tell the future.
Also, he has his share of the war god's power, too:
Sometimes an army is in full gear, standing in order,
and they're struck by a panic before a weapon is touched.
305   That madness comes from Dionysus too.
Besides, you will come to see him on the crags of Delphi
with his torches, leaping on the twin-peaked mountain
shoulder, waving and shaking his Bacchic wand—
you'll see he's great everywhere in Greece.
        Now, Pentheus, take my advice.
310   Do not brag about your power in controlling men;
and whatever your judgment should be, if it is ailing
do not judge that it is sound. Accept this god into your land;
pour him libations, join his Bacchic dance, put wreath on head.
It is not Dionysus who will force virtue on women
315   in matters of sex. You must look for this in their natures.
Even in a Bacchic revel, a woman who is really virtuous
will not be corrupted. Look. You are delighted
when the people crowd your palace gates
320   and the city resounds with the name of Pentheus.
In my opinion, it's the same with Dionysus—
he too is pleased by being honored. I, therefore,
along with Cadmus—sneer at him if you will—
are wreathing our heads in ivy for the dance.

297: The pun in Greek is between *mēros* (thigh) and *homēros* (hostage).
Explanations based on word play or imagined derivations were common in
sophistic rhetoric of the period.

300: I have not been able to translate the Greek pun here; it is between
mania (frenzy) and *mantikē* (future-telling).

306: Prophecy is mainly the business of Apollo at Delphi; Tiresias is suggesting that Dionysus has a share of Apollo's power, as well as that of the
war god Ares.

We are gray-haired, the pair of us, but still we must dance.
I'll make no war on gods; I do not accept your argument.   325
I am sorry to say it, but you are mad. Totally mad.
And no drug could help you, even though you're as sick
as if you had been drugged.

CHORUS LEADER:
  Old man, Apollo's not insulted by your claims;
  you are being sensible when you honor Dionysus,
  great god that he is.

CADMUS:
  Tiresias' advice is excellent, my boy. Stay home   330
  with us, don't cross the threshold of the law.
  You are flitting about, you know, so thoughtless,
  the way you think.
         Suppose you're right, the fellow's not a god—
  well, let him have the title anyway, as far as you care.
  Tell a lie. It's a good cause: you'll make Semélē famous,   335
  mother of a god. And our whole family reaps the glory.
  Look what happened to Actaeon, your cousin—
  he died horribly. His own dogs (he'd reared them himself
  to eat raw meat) tore him in pieces, and all because
  he bragged he was a better hunter in the mountains   340
  than Artemis. Don't let that happen to you. Here,
  put on this ivy. Join us. Let's give honor to the god.

PENTHEUS:
  Keep your hands off me! Go ahead and be a Bacchant,
  but don't you wipe that foolishness off on me.

         (pointing to Tiresias)

  This "teacher" here infected you with silliness.   345
  I will punish him.

         (turning to his guards)

                 Send someone right away
  to where he has his Seat of Divination.

331: Law—*nomos*, which can also mean "custom." Why does Cadmus
appeal to this in defense of a brand new religion? The chorus will do the
same (387, 891–96, and 995).

Pry it up, turn it upside down, use levers,
and make a mess of the whole place. Take his sacred
350   head-wrappings and toss them out, leave them to
the wind and rain. I can't hurt him any worse than that.
You others, sweep the city. Track down that foreigner,
the one who looks like a girl. He carried this new disease
to our women, put this filth in our bedrooms.
355   If you catch him, bring him here in chains
so he can pay the penalty—death by stoning—and learn
what a serious crime it is to play Bacchus in Thebes.

TIRESIAS:
Abomination! You haven't the faintest idea what you are
     saying!
You've become a complete lunatic; this is no temporary
     madness.
360   Let's be on our way, Cadmus. We must win over the god
with prayers—for this man's sake, violent as he is,
and for the city's too. Otherwise the god may take
a terrible revenge. Come with me, on your ivy-covered staff.
Try to keep me upright, and I'll do the same for you.
365   It would be a shameful sight for two old men to fall. Still,
we have to go, bow down to Bacchus as the son of Zeus.
Pentheus' name means "grief"; I hope he brings no grief
upon your family. This is not fortune-telling—
I'm looking at facts: he who speaks foolishness is a fool.

FIRST CHORUS:

[Strophe 1]

370   O Reverence, queen of gods,
Reverence, who over earth
spread golden wing,
Have you heard Pentheus?
Have you heard the outrage,
375   insult to Thunderer
son of Semélē—he who is first
of all the blessed powers
for joy at festivals
where heads are wreathed?
     His domain

is sacred dances
laughter by flutesong   380
relaxation of care,
whenever grapes shine
on feasting of gods,
or when, at ivy-wreathed festivals,
sleep steals round men from the wine bowl.   385

[Antistrophe 1]

Mouths that run unchecked,
lawless and senseless,
end in disaster.
But a life lived in peace   390
with good sense holds
family together,
stays unshaken.
Far away, the sky dwellers,
heavenly powers, may be;
but they are watching us.
Wisdom? It's not wise   395
to lift our thoughts too high;
we are human, and our time is short.
A man who aims at greatness
will not live to own what he has now.
That, I believe, is the life of men   400
whose judgment is foul.
          They are insane.

[Strophe 2]

Oh, let me be in Cyprus,
Aphrodite's land,
where cupids dwell   405
and cast their spells upon our minds,
and where the river of a hundred mouths

395: "It's not wise to lift our thoughts too high"—This famous couplet, *to
sophon d'ou sophia / to te mē sophon phronein,* uses a play on the two main
senses of *sophos*—wise, clever—and contrasts two uses of intelligence. "It's
not wise to be a wiseass, or to think oneself beyond the level of a mortal."

makes rainless Paphos fruitful,
with water from afar.
410   Or there, on the sacred slope of Mt. Olympus,
lovely Pieria, home of the Muses—
Take me there, Thunderer, Thunderer,
leading spirit of the joyful cry,
to the land of the Graces,
415   the land of Yearning, the land
where Bacchic revels are the law.

[Antistrophe 2]

Divine, son of Zeus,
he rejoices in feasting,
he loves Peace the blissgiver,
420   cherisher of young men, goddess.
To rich and poor alike
he grants delight of wine
without pain.
And he hates the man who does not try—
425   each day, each longed-for night—
to live a flawless life
and wisely steers away,
in heart and mind,
from men who stand out above others.
430   What is ordinary,
what the crowd thinks right,
is good enough for me.

Scene Two

SOLDIER:
Pentheus, we are here. Mission accomplished.
We have hunted down this wild thing
435   you sent for, but we found the beast was gentle,
made no attempt to escape, willingly held out
its hands, did not turn pale or lose its blush of wine.
Instead, he laughed and had us take him prisoner.
440   He waited and made my task an easy one.

409: The river is the Nile, which was thought to issue in springs at Paphos,
on the island of Cyprus.

I was ashamed. I said, "This isn't my idea, Stranger.
Pentheus sent me under orders to capture you."
Now, about these Bacchic women you'd arrested,
chained, and locked up in the public jail—
they're free, they escaped to the mountains,   445
they're dancing around up there, calling on the god.
The chains simply fell off their feet, all by themselves,
and the doors—no human hand touched them,
but they were unlocked. So many miracles this man
has brought to Thebes! Well, the rest is your concern.   450

PENTHEUS:
You may release his hands. He's in my net; he won't
escape me now, no matter how quick he is.

   (looking him over)

Well, well. Not bad. You're actually quite good-looking.
I mean, to women. Of course, that's why you came to Thebes.
This long hair of yours—you're no wrestler, are you—   455
these curls along your cheek—oh, they'll swoon for you—
and this fine complexion—you had to work on that,
staying out of the sun, in the shadows, hunting,
with your pretty face, for sex, Aphrodite's business.

So tell me this first. Where are you from?   460

DIONYSUS:
Right away, sir. It's a simple story.
No doubt you've heard of Mt. Tmolus, where flowers grow?

PENTHEUS:
I have. Runs round the city of Sardis, circles it.

DIONYSUS:
That's where I'm from. Lydia is my country.

PENTHEUS:
What was your reason for bringing this cult religion to   465
   Greece?

DIONYSUS:
Dionysus made me an initiate himself, and he's a son of Zeus.

463: Sardis is the capital of Lydia in western Asia Minor.

PENTHEUS:
What do you have there—some Zeus who spawns new gods?

DIONYSUS:
No. It was here he joined Semélē in marriage.

PENTHEUS:
Did he take you by force in a dream, or did you see him?

DIONYSUS:
470 Face to face. And he personally taught me the rituals.

PENTHEUS:
Tell me about these rituals. What do they look like?

DIONYSUS:
They may not be revealed to those who are not Bacchants.

PENTHEUS:
What's the good of these rituals to people who celebrate them?

DIONYSUS:
Hearing that is forbidden you, but knowing it would be of
value.

PENTHEUS:
475 What a neat quibble. Now I really want to hear.

DIONYSUS:
Keep up that irreverence and the dance will turn hostile.

PENTHEUS:
Now, you say you saw the god clearly. What did he look like?

DIONYSUS:
Whatever way he wanted. I had no control of that.

PENTHEUS:
Another clever diversion! You didn't say a thing.

DIONYSUS:
480 Speak wisdom to a fool and he'll think you have no sense at all.

PENTHEUS:
Are we the first to whom you've brought this divinity of yours?

DIONYSUS:
Outside Greece, everyone is already dancing for him.

PENTHEUS:
That's because foreigners have so little sense compared to us.

DIONYSUS:
In this case more, much more. They just have different
customs.

PENTHEUS:
You practice this cult by night or by day?   485

DIONYSUS:
Mostly at night. Darkness lends solemnity.

PENTHEUS:
Darkness is just a filthy trap for women.

DIONYSUS:
Some people can dig up dirt in daytime too.

PENTHEUS:
You'll have to be punished for this—this wicked cleverness.

DIONYSUS:
And you for stupidity, for irreverence to the god.   490

PENTHEUS:
Tough talk for a Bacchant! You get lots of exercise . . . with
words.

DIONYSUS:
What penalty do you propose? What horrible thing will you do
to me?

PENTHEUS:
Let's start by shearing off your pretty goldilocks.

DIONYSUS:
That's sacred! I grow my hair in honor of the god.

PENTHEUS:
Next, hand over your thyrsus.

DIONYSUS:
Take it away yourself. The one I carry belongs to Dionysus.   495

493: Growing long hair as a dedication to a god and later cutting it as a
religious offering had been common practice among men in ancient Greece.

PENTHEUS:
And we'll lock you up and keep you under guard.

DIONYSUS:
The god himself will set me free, whenever I want.

PENTHEUS:
Sure he will, whenever you stand among your Bacchae and
summon him.

DIONYSUS:
500   Even now he's very near, and he sees what I am suffering.

PENTHEUS:
Then where is he? He hasn't revealed himself to me.

DIONYSUS:
He is where I am. You do not see him because you lack
reverence.

PENTHEUS:
Grab him! He has insulted me—and Thebes.

DIONYSUS:
I proclaim: do not tie me. Believe me, I am sane and you are
crazy.

PENTHEUS:
505   But I say, tie him up. Believe me, I have you in my power.

DIONYSUS:
How do you live? What are you doing? Who are you? You
don't know!

PENTHEUS:
I am Pentheus, son of Agavē. My father was Echion.

DIONYSUS:
Misfortune becomes you, with a name like that.

PENTHEUS:
Get out! Lock him up over there in the horse-stalls.
510   Let him stare at gloom and darkness.
There's a place for you to dance.

508: Pentheus' name and misfortune—the Greek word for grief is *penthos*.
See 1244.

(Chorus starts to beat the drum.)

These women you brought—
they're as guilty as you. We'll sell them as slaves,
or I'll keep them myself, make them work at the looms.
Either way, I will stop that damn noise.

DIONYSUS:

I am prepared to go. Mind you, what cannot happen   515
cannot injure me. But you! Dionysus will punish
you for these insults, and you say he does not exist!
When you abuse us, you are trying to put *him* in chains.

SECOND CHORUS:

[Strophe 1]

Fair-maidened River Dirkē, queen
of waters, daughter of Achélous,   520
you who bathed
the infant child of god—
when Zeus the father pulled him,
from undying fire, into his thigh,
did you not hear the cry of Zeus?   525

"Go, twice-born Dithyrambus,
into my male womb.
I now reveal you,
with your Bacchic name, to Thebes."

But now, blessed Dirkē,   530
you cast me out when I bring
wreaths and feasting to your shore.
Why do you reject me? Why do you run from me?
A time will come—I swear by all the joy
that you may squeeze from Dionysus'   535
grapes—a time when you *will*
pay attention to the Thunderer.

520: The Achélous, the largest river in Greece, has no geographical link to
the smaller Dirkē River of Thebes, but stands here for all flowing waters.
526: Dithyrambus—a name for Bacchus.

[Antistrophe 1]

What anger, oh what anger
shows now from the earthborn
spawn of a serpent,
540   Pentheus, begot
by Echion, the earthborn—
a wild-eyed monster
without a human face who
like a deadly giant wrestles with the gods!
545   Soon he will have me in his snares,
although I belong to the Thunderer.
Already he has my comrade in the sacred dance
imprisoned at home,
hidden in darkness.

550   Do you see this, son of Zeus,
Dionysus? Those who speak for you
are bound by force.
Come down from Olympus
waving your gold-faced wand
555   and put down the insults of this deadly man.

[Epode]

Where are you now, Dionysus, waving your thyrsus?
Where on Nysa are you leading the dance,
on the mountain that feeds wild things?
Where? On the Corycian Peaks?
560   Perhaps at rest on Mt. Olympus,
in the wooded glades where Orpheus,
once upon a time, struck movement
into trees, and wild beasts, too,
followed the music of his cithara.

539: According to the myth of Thebes' origin, Cadmus peopled his city by sowing the teeth of a serpent he had slain, and from them sprouted men to be his army (see *Phoenician Women* 667–75, with note).

544: The Olympian gods had, according to the myth, secured their power by defeating a race of earthborn giants with the help of Heracles.

559: Nysa is probably a mythical mountain; Mt. Parnassus, with its Corycian Peaks, is near Delphi.

You are the blessed place, Pieria.   565
You are honored by the god of joyful cries.
He comes to set you dancing in his worship.
He will cross swift-flowing
rivers with his Maenads
whirling in their dance—the River Axion   570
and Lydias, father of waters,
who gives happiness and wealth to men
from the most beautiful flow of water
(so I have heard), for it fattens
the land with fine horses.   575

Scene Three

DIONYSUS:

> *(calling from offstage in his own voice, as a god)*

> *Iō!*
> Hear me, hear my call!
> *Iō* Bacchae, *Iō* Bacchae!

HALF-CHORUS 1:
> What's this? Oh, what? Where does it come from,
> this roar of the joy-god, summoning me?

DIONYSUS:
> *Iō, Iō,* I call again,   580
> son of Semélē, son of Zeus.

HALF-CHORUS 2:
> *Iō, Iō,* master, master!
> Come to our sacred dance,
> Thunderer, Thunderer!

DIONYSUS:
> Queen of commotion, shake the earth's foundations!   585

HALF-CHORUS 1:
> Ah! Ah!
> Now the house of Pentheus will rattle down in ruins.

565: Pieria, on the slope of Mt. Olympus.
566: "The god of joyful cries"—Evius, from the cult-cry represented as *VoHé.*
571: The Axion and Lydias rivers are in Macedon.

HALF-CHORUS 2:
Dionysus rises in the house!
Worship him!

HALF-CHORUS 1:
590   We worship. Oh, yes!

HALF-CHORUS 2:
Do you see? The stone crosspieces—
they're sliding off the columns!
The Thunderer!
He's raising Bacchic cries within the roofs.

DIONYSUS:
Strike, lightning bolt, brightly!
595   Burn the house of Pentheus,
burn it to ashes!

HALF-CHORUS 1:
Ah! Ah!
Look at the fire! Do you see how dazzling it is,
by the tomb of Semélē?
Where she, in former days,
left the flame of Zeus, thunderstruck?

HALF-CHORUS 2:
600   Fall to the ground, you trembling
Maenads, fall. For the lord
comes, he will cast this house
down to the dust. He is son of Zeus!

DIONYSUS:

(coming on stage in human form)

What frightened foreigners you women are—
605   down on the ground as if you had been struck!
Don't you see—it was Bacchus who shook the house
        apart?
Rise up, take courage, leave off trembling.

CHORUS LEADER:
It's you! Our great light in dancing to Bacchus!
How glad I am to see you! I was desolate, alone . . .

DIONYSUS:

> Did you lose hope when I was sent inside?   610
> Did you think I was trapped in Pentheus' dark jail?

CHORUS LEADER:

> What else could I think? Who would protect me if you were
>   lost?
> But how did you get free from that unholy man?

DIONYSUS:

> I saved myself. It was easy. No trouble.

CHORUS LEADER:

> But I thought he tied your hands with knots of rope?   615

DIONYSUS:

> There I made a fool of him. He thought he'd tied me up,
> but he never laid a hand on me—he only fed himself on hope.
> In the stable, where he planned to jail me, he came upon a bull,
> and it was this he bound up, hoof and leg. He was panting
>   fiercely   620
> as he tied the knots, biting his lips, sweat streaming down his
>   body.
> I was very near; I sat peacefully and watched. That was when
> Bacchus came, shook down the house, and raised the flames
> over his mother's tomb. When the king caught sight of that,
> he thought his house was on fire, ran up and down,   625
> told all his slaves to bring water from the river. What a waste
> of time! Then he let that job go because he thought I had
>   escaped,
> so he grabbed his black sword and ran indoors. Now,
> the Thunderer—this is only how he appeared to me—I think
> he formed an image of me in the courtyard for Pentheus   630
> to attack; he rushed up slicing clean air, trying to cut me down.
> Still Bacchus added outrage to outrage against him:
> shook the house down to the ground, totally ruined,
> so Pentheus could see what a painful mistake he had made,
> putting me in jail. He's exhausted now, leans back   635
> and drops his sword—this man who dared do battle
> with a god! I left the house peacefully, and joined you here.
> Pentheus is nothing to me. But now—I hear his footsteps—
> he'll be here any minute. What will he say this time?

640   Well, never mind; even if he blows up a storm he will not
       bother me. A wise man trains his temper to be good and calm.

PENTHEUS:
   I've been tricked! It's horrible. That foreigner got away.
   The one I overpowered a few minutes ago and put in chains.
   Aha! There's the man!

   (to Dionysus)

645   What's this? What are you doing
   in the forecourt of my house? How did you get out?

DIONYSUS:
   Relax. Let peace lie firm beneath your anger.

PENTHEUS:
   How did you break prison and get outside?

DIONYSUS:
   Didn't you hear me? I told you Someone would set me free.

PENTHEUS:
650   Who? You keep saying strange new things.

DIONYSUS:
   He who grows the clustering grapes for humankind—
   that good deed, for which you held Dionysus to blame.

PENTHEUS:

   (shouting to his soldiers)

   Lock the gates! That's an order. Close off the city all around.

DIONYSUS:
   What's the point? A god can leap over walls.

PENTHEUS:
655   What a wiseass you are—cunning, except where it counts.

DIONYSUS:
   Where it counts the most, I was born cunning.

   *(He spies the messenger running down from the
   mountain.)*

                                             Wait.
   You'd better listen to this man first. Pay attention.

He's bringing you news from the mountain.
We will wait, trust us, we will not run away.

FIRST MESSENGER:
Pentheus! Ruler of Thebes! I'm here from Mt. Kithairōn,   660
where white snow glistens, never failing.

PENTHEUS:
What's so important about the news you bring?

FIRST MESSENGER:
I saw the Bacchae in their sacred power, white
thighs shooting like arrows from the land.   665
I'm here because I have to tell you—and the city, sir—
what awe-inspiring things they do, beyond fantasy.
But first I'd like to know whether you'll give me complete
freedom to report what I saw there—or must I watch
my tongue? I am afraid of your quick temper, sir—   670
so hot, so like a king, but too much.

PENTHEUS:
Say anything. You'll be safe as far as I'm concerned.
It's wrong to lash out at a law-abiding citizen.
But for every horror you tell me about the Bacchae
I'll add to the sentence of punishment we'll give   675
this person, for laying his clever schemes on women.

FIRST MESSENGER:
Our herds of cattle climbed into the mountain
meadow, just as the sun began to warm the earth.
And there I see them—three troops of women dancers,   680
one led by Autonoē, the second by your mother Agavē,
the third by Inō. They were all asleep, totally relaxed,
some leaning back on pine boughs, others laid
their heads on oak leaves on the ground.   685
They had let themselves go, in a sensible way,
not as you said, sir, intoxicated by wine and flute,
not running off by themselves in the woods for sex.

Your mother leapt to her feet, wide awake
with a shout of ecstasy—Bacchae all around her—   690
she'd heard the longhorns mooing.
The others shook cozy sleep out of their eyes

and sprang upright in close drill—an amazing sight—
young and old, unmarried girls too.
695   First they let their hair down to their shoulders,
and those who had loosened their fawnskin garments
hitched them up and belted the spotted skins
with snakes that licked their cheeks.
Some of them cradled young gazelles or wolf cubs,
700   and gave white milk for them to suck.
These were ones who had just given birth,
and their breasts were swollen, their babies left behind.
All crowned themselves with ivy, oak, and flowering
vines. One took her thyrsus, struck a rock,
705   and water leapt out, pure as dew.
Another set her staff in solid ground
and the god sent her a fountain of wine.
If anyone was thirsty for a drink of milk
she scrabbled her sharp fingers in the earth
710   and it came, spurting white. Sweet streams of honey
too came dripping from the ivy-covered wands.
And all in all, if you'd been there and seen these things
you'd come praying to the god whom you condemned.
Then we got together, cowherds and shepherds,
715   shared our stories, words clashing,
told each other the awe-inspiring things they did.
One man spoke up, a drifter who'd practiced
the art of words in town, "Hey, all of you who live up here
on the sacred mountain, wouldn't you like to hunt down
720   Agavē, yank Pentheus' mother out of her Bacchic dances,
and earn some favors from the king?" We thought
he'd spoken well, and so we laid an ambush,
hiding in the bushes. And they, at the appointed time,
spun into a Bacchic dance, shaking the thyrsus
725   and crying, "Iacchus," to the thunderborn child
of Zeus, all with one mouth, and the entire mountain
danced for Bacchus, wild beasts too, all racing into motion.

By chance, Agavē's leaping brought her next to me
and I sprang out—I meant to capture her—
730   and I gave up the ambush where we were hiding.

695: Women in ancient Greece tied up their hair before sleeping.

She raised a shout, "Oh you running dogs of mine,
these men are hunting *us!* Now follow me,
follow! A thyrsus is a weapon in your hands."
So we were the ones who ran away, to escape
being torn apart by Bacchae. And they attacked   735
our livestock as they were grazing on new grass.
No sharp weapons, but you'd have seen one woman
tear apart a young cow with her bare hands—
it was bellowing, its udder was swollen with milk. Others
ripped grown cows to pieces. You'd see ribs and feet   740
hurled every which way, hooves flying, pieces hanging
in the pine trees, smeared with blood and dripping.
Bulls in all their pride stumbled headlong:
They once had rage tossing on their long horns;
now more hands than you can count pull   745
them down—young girls' hands. And strip off the flesh
that covered them, faster than a king could wink one eye.
Then they took off like a flock of birds and raced
to the fields below, along the River Asōpus,
where Thebes grows bumper crops of grain.   750
Two villages, Hysiae and Erythrae, are settled there
beneath the heights of Mt. Kithairōn. And the Bacchae
fell on them like enemies on a rampage, tore
the towns to shreds, stole children from the houses,
put booty on their shoulders. (And even though   755
they did not tie it down, nothing fell to the dark earth,
not bronze, not iron. And the fire they carried in their hair
never singed a curl.)

        The village men were in a rage
at being plundered by the Bacchae; they grabbed weapons,
and then—sir, it was a terrible thing to see—   760
the men could not draw blood with their javelins,
but the women hurled the thyrsus and injured them
so badly they turned tail and ran—women over men!
Only a god could make that happen.
Then they returned to where they had begun their dance,   765
to the springs the god had opened for them,
and washed off the blood, while the snakes licked
every drop clean from the skin of their cheeks.
This god, your majesty, whoever he is—

770   you'd better accept him for our city. He has great power
in other ways, but above all, I've heard it said
that he's the one who gives us wine to ease our pain.
If you take wine away, love will die, and
every other source of human joy will follow.

CHORUS LEADER:
775   I'm nervous about speaking freely to a king,
but even so, I have to say it:
No god is greater than Dionysus.

PENTHEUS:
This outrageous behavior of the Bacchae
is catching on like wildfire already. We'll be
the laughingstock of Greece. No time for delay:
780   You, go to the south gate.
Call up our heavy infantry in their armor,
our cavalry, fleetfooted, and our light troops,
bearing small shields, the men
of singing bowstrings. Tell them all:
785   We will make war upon the Bacchae. This
is worse than anything—that the source
of so much trouble to us is women.

DIONYSUS:
You hear what I say, Pentheus, but you do not
take it to heart. Even though you've treated me badly,
I tell you, it's wrong to take up arms against a god.
790   Keep the peace. Dionysus will not stand for it if you drive
the Bacchae from mountains filled with cries of joy.

PENTHEUS:
Don't you lecture me! You just got out of your chains—
You don't like being free? Should I restore your penalty?

---

*788–846: Persuasion of Pentheus—Does the god use rhetoric or magic?
Probably rhetoric, because 849 ff. implies that Pentheus is still sane at the
end of the scene. Like any expert in persuasion, Dionysus plays on Pentheus'
desires, both conscious and unconscious. Because he is speaking to an ambitious young soldier, he cleverly casts the operation in a military light,
playing on the ambiguity of* stolē *("outfit" in the sense of a woman's dress,
but also in the sense of equipment for an expedition).*

DIONYSUS:

Sooner than I'd suffer a pang of anger, if I were mortal
and he a god—I'd offer a sacrifice when he goads me.   795

PENTHEUS:

I'll make an offering—from the blood of women. They
deserve to die for raucous disturbances on Mt. Kithairōn.

DIONYSUS:

You will run away, all of you. You have tough bronze shields,
but you will be routed by the Bacchic thyrsus. What a
disgrace!

PENTHEUS:

It's impossible to wrestle this foreigner to the ground!   800
Jail him or let him go, he keeps on talking.

DIONYSUS:

Sir, there's still a way to make this come out well.

PENTHEUS:

Really? You want me to give in to my own women, my
slaves?

DIONYSUS:

I'll bring the women here—no weapons.

PENTHEUS:

The hell you will. It's another trick you've invented, against me.   805

DIONYSUS:

Not at all. My only wish is to use my skill to save you.

PENTHEUS:

It's a plot! You've promised the Bacchae to keep up the dance
forever.

DIONYSUS:

Yes, I have promised, as you say . . . but to the god.

PENTHEUS:

Bring me my weapons! And you, shut your mouth.

795: Dionysus puns on the words for sacrifice and anger, which are close
in sound.

DIONYSUS:

810   *Wait.*

    Would you like to see the women gathered on the mountain?

PENTHEUS:

    Of course. I'd give a pot of money for that.

DIONYSUS:

    Really? Isn't this great passion of yours rather sudden?

PENTHEUS:

    Well, it would hurt me to see them if they're drunk, but . . .

DIONYSUS:

815   Still, while you hated it, you'd enjoy the spectacle.

PENTHEUS:

    Yes, of course, and I'd be quiet and sit under a pine tree.

DIONYSUS:

    They'll track you down, no matter how sneaky you are.

PENTHEUS:

    OK. I'll stay in the open. You give good advice!

DIONYSUS:

    Will I be leading you, then? And will you undertake this
       journey?

PENTHEUS:

820   Yes, don't waste a minute. Lead on!

DIONYSUS:

    First, let's fit you out, cover your hide with a linen dress.

PENTHEUS:

    What? Change rank from man to woman?

DIONYSUS:

    They'll kill you if they see you as a man.

PENTHEUS:

    Good point, as before. You've been pretty cunning all
       along.

810: "*Wait*"—This translates Greek "*A*," an exclamation that does not fit
into the metrical scheme, and probably here expresses protest.

DIONYSUS:
  We owe it to Dionysus. He's our inspiration.   825

PENTHEUS:
  Good strategy. Now, how do we implement it?

DIONYSUS:
  Just step inside your house and I'll fit you out.

PENTHEUS:
  How? As a woman? That's disgusting!

DIONYSUS:
  Changed your mind? Don't want a view of the Maenads?

PENTHEUS:
  As for my outfit, what did you propose to cover me with?   830

DIONYSUS:
  Start with your head. I'll give you a wig with long hair.

PENTHEUS:
  And what next? Another decoration?

DIONYSUS:
  A dress. Full-length. And a headband around your hair.

PENTHEUS:
  Anything else you'd like to add?

DIONYSUS:
  A thyrsus for your hand, and a spotted fawnskin.   835

PENTHEUS:
  No. I couldn't put on a woman's outfit.

DIONYSUS:
  But you'll cause bloodshed, if you attack the Bacchae directly.

PENTHEUS:
  Right. Then I should go first to observe the situation.

DIONYSUS:
  That's cunning. Otherwise, you'd use trouble as bait for
    trouble.

PENTHEUS:
  But how can I sneak through the city without being seen?   840

DIONYSUS:
We'll use empty streets. I'll be in front.

PENTHEUS:
Most important: I don't want the Bacchae laughing at me.
Let's go inside—I'll make a decision.

DIONYSUS:
As you wish. My plan works either way.

PENTHEUS:
845   I will set out—either marching under arms
or in the manner you advised.

(Exit.)

DIONYSUS:
That man! Women, he's on the edge of the net:
His death will give justice, and he's coming to the Bacchae.
Dionysus, the work is yours to do. I know you're very near.
850   Pay him back. First, drive him out of his wits.
Fill him with a skittish frenzy. He'll never want
to take on a woman's dress in his right mind.
But if he marches right outside his senses, he will get
dressed.
And I have a longing to see him jeered in Thebes,
855   as he's led through the city looking like a woman—
in return for those threats he made, trying
to be formidable. Now I'm off to get the fine clothes
I will fit to Pentheus for his trip to Hades when
his mother kills him. Then he will know the son of Zeus,
860   Dionysus, and realize that he was born a god, bringing
terrors for initiation, and to the people, gentle grace.

THIRD CHORUS:

[Strophe]

To dance the long night!
Shall I ever set my white foot
so, to worship Bacchus?
865   Toss my neck to the dewy skies

842: "Laughing at me"—that is, in triumph.

as a young fawn frisks
in green delight of pasture?

She has run away now from a fearful
hunt, away from watchful eyes,
above tight-woven nets—   870
while the dogleader cheers
the running of his hounds.

She strains, she races, whirls and prances
on meadows by rivers, delighting
in absence of men   875
and under shadow-tresses
the tender shoots of the wildwood.

[Refrain]

What is wise? What is the finest gift
that gods can give to mortals?
A hand on the heads
of their enemies, pushing down?   880
[No.] What is fine is loved always.

[Antistrophe]

Never hurried, never
failing, a god's

877–81 and 897–901: Refrain—The meaning of this is disputed. Some
early versions take the answer to be the traditional Greek secular principle:
the finest gift from the gods is putting down your enemies. But most recent
scholars believe that the chorus is putting vengeance into question on religious grounds. On this view, the last line implies a negative answer, which
I have supplied in brackets, for the sake of clarity (Seaford 1996, Esposito
1998, Leinieks 1996). Probably the audience knows what worship of Dionysus promises: the only source of joy that cannot be taken away by time
and change is initiation, the Dionysiac equivalent of "treasures in heaven"
(cf. 73 ff.). (If this is the message, Dionysus himself seems to have missed it;
but in other traditions, too, gentle deities have been thought to be ruthless
with unbelievers.) Nussbaum takes the refrain to be ambiguous on the point
(1990, p. xiii).

881: [No]—This is how the chorus thinks the question should be answered,
but it is not explicit.

fist comes down on men
885   who love to be hard-hearted,
who hold back what is due to gods
in the madness of bad judgment.
Ingenious, how the gods
keep time's long foot a secret
890   while hunting down irreverent men.
No one should ever be above the law,
neither in thought nor action.

The cost of these beliefs is light:
power lies
with whatever thing should be divine,
895   with whatever law stands firm in time
by nature ever-natural.

[Refrain]

What is wise? What is the finest gift
that gods can give to mortals?
A hand on the heads
900   of their enemies, pushing down?
[No.] What is fine is loved always.

[Epode]

Happy the man who has come away
safe on the beach from a storm at sea,
happy the man who has risen above
905   trouble and toil. Many are the ways
one man may surpass another
in wealth or power,
and beyond each hope there beckons another
hope without number.
Hope may lead a man to wealth,
hope may pass away;
910   but I admire a man when he
is happy in an ordinary life.

Scene Four

(Enter Dionysus.)

DIONYSUS:
  You who long to see what is forbidden,
  you who seek what must not be sought,
  you, Pentheus, come out and let me see you here
  before your house in a woman's gear, a Maenad's,   915
  you who spy against your mother and her troops.

  (Enter Pentheus.)

  Why, you look just like one of Cadmus' daughters!

PENTHEUS:
  Hey, I think I am seeing two suns, I'm seeing double—
  Thebes, the seven-mouthed fortress, all double.
  And you're a bull, ahead of me in procession;   920
  I see new horns sprouted on your head.
  Were you ever a wild animal? You're being a bull now.

DIONYSUS:
  The god is with us; he's not angry anymore.
  He has made peace with us, and now you see things as you
    should.

PENTHEUS:
  How do I look now? Is this the way Inō stands?   925
  Or my mother Agavē?

DIONYSUS:
  When I see you I think it's one of them.
  But this little curl of yours is out of position;
  it's not where I set it under your headband.

PENTHEUS:
  I think I shook it up and down indoors, dancing   930
  like the Bacchae. That made it leave its post.

DIONYSUS:
  I'll put it back in order; that's my duty,
  to serve you. Hold your head straight.

PENTHEUS:
  Sure. You arrange it. I'm in your hands.

918: "Seeing double"—Seaford 1996 suggests the effect is due to the mirror used at a stage of initiation.

DIONYSUS:
935   Your sash is loose, your pleats are uneven,
        and your dress has slipped below your ankles.

PENTHEUS:
        I guess it has. But only on *this* side.
        Over here my dress hangs right.

DIONYSUS:
        You will surely think I am your closest friend when you
            see
940   how modestly the Bacchae dress—more so than you'd
            expect.

PENTHEUS:
        Should I hold my thyrsus this way, or in my right hand?
        I want to look like one of them.

DIONYSUS:
        Right hand. And lift it in time with your right foot.
        I'm delighted at your change of mind!

PENTHEUS:
945   Will I be strong enough to lift Mt. Kithairōn
        to my shoulders, Bacchae and all?

DIONYSUS:
        Yes, if you wish. Your mental state
        used to be unhealthy. Now it is as it should be.

PENTHEUS:
        Should we bring crowbars? Or do I barehanded
950   thrust my arm or shoulder underneath the summit?

DIONYSUS:
        Mind you, you must not smash the Nymphs' temples
        or the places where Pan loves to play his pipes.

PENTHEUS:
        That's right. A strong fist is not what conquers
        women. I'll hide myself in the fir trees.

DIONYSUS:
955   You'll find the hiding place a man should have
        if he goes to trick the Maenads as a spy.

PENTHEUS:
  Yes, I can imagine them like birds in a thicket,
  held in a sweet tangle of sex!

DIONYSUS:
  And that is why you're assigned guard duty.
  Perhaps you'll catch them . . . unless you're caught first.   960

PENTHEUS:
  Take me through the middle of Thebes.
  I am the only man in the city who dares to do this.

DIONYSUS:
  Only you. You bear the city's pain alone,
  and the contest you will face is meant for you.
  Follow me. I am your guide and your protection.   965
  Someone else will bring you back.

PENTHEUS:

        (interrupting)

                                      My mother!

DIONYSUS:
  Everyone will be impressed . . .

PENTHEUS:

        (interrupting)

                                  That's why I'm going!

DIONYSUS:
  You will be carried . . .

PENTHEUS:

        (interrupting)

                          You'll spoil me!

DIONYSUS:
  In your mother's arms.

PENTHEUS:
                          You'll pamper me to pieces.
  You'll make me tender, by force.

DIONYSUS:
  I will indeed.

PENTHEUS:
970   I will have what I deserve.

DIONYSUS:
  You are wonderful and terrible; wonders and terrors await
      you
  where you go. You will win glory towering high as heaven.

  (Exit Pentheus.)

  Now, Agavē, stretch out your arms,
  and you too, her sisters, Cadmus' daughters.
975 I am bringing the boy for a great contest,
  which I will win—I and Dionysus.

  (Exit Dionysus.)

FOURTH CHORUS:

[Strophe]

  Run, swift hounds of madness, run to mountain!
  Find where Cadmus' daughters hold their celebration,
  Sting them to fury at the man
980 who parties in a woman's outfit
  and spies in madness on Maenads.

  His mother will be first. She'll see him
  on smooth rocks, or in a tree lurking.
  She'll call the Maenads to her.

985 "Who is this
  who longs for us, for the mountain-runners of Cadmus?
  To mountain, to mountain, he came, he came!
  Oh, Bacchae, who
  could his mother have been? No women's blood in him;
990 he's a lion's whelp, or the cub of Gorgons from Libya."

[Refrain]

  Now, Vengeance, out in the open!
  Now, Swordbearer, slice through his throat!

He is godless, lawless, and unjust;   995
he is Echion's son, the earthborn.

[Antistrophe]

His judgment wrong, his feelings tuned against the law,
he can't abide your worship, Bacchus, or your mother's.
Intelligence gone mad,
spirit struck to arrogance, he has appointed   1000
himself to suppress the unconquerable by violence.

Death makes judgment sound, hears no
excuses. When you face the gods, remember
your mortality, if you'd live a painless life.

Wisdom you may have;   1005
I'd rather hunt for other virtues,
great ones and more plain: for a good life,
live reverently,
through night and day,
and if customs reach beyond justice,
cast them out, and honor the gods.   1010

[Refrain]

Now, Vengeance, out in the open!
Now, Swordbearer, slice through his throat!
He is godless, lawless, and unjust;   1015
he is Echion's son, the earthborn.

[Epode]

Be seen as a bull, be seen many-headed,
be seen as a serpent, or lion blazing fire.
Bacchus, come with laughing face,   1020

1005: "Wisdom you may have"—The chorus has no wish to be wise in the
sense of clever; there is a quieter wisdom, however, which they cherish. See
395 and 1150.

1017–18: "Be seen as a bull, be seen many-headed, be seen as a serpent, or
lion blazing fire"—These are visible forms Dionysus takes, and this may be
a standard prayer calling for an epiphany of the god—an event in which
the god shows himself to mortals in all his power.

after the beast-catching man who hunts Bacchae;
tangle him in your fatal net, as he falls
beneath a pack of Maenads.

Scene Five

SECOND MESSENGER:
Oh, this house, this family! All Greece thought it lucky,
1025 once. That old man who came from Sidon, sowed
the earthborn crop from a serpent in the ground!
How I grieve for you! And I'm only a slave.

CHORUS LEADER:
What is it? What news from the Bacchae?

SECOND MESSENGER:
1030 Pentheus is dead, the child of Echion.

CHORUS LEADER:
Lord Bacchus! Great god revealed.

SECOND MESSENGER:
What are you saying? What did you mean? Woman,
you can't be happy over this calamity to my master?

CHORUS LEADER:
I'm a foreigner. I sing a hymn of praise that's strange
1035 to you. Because I am free at last from the fear of prison.

SECOND MESSENGER:
Do you think we are so unmanly here in Thebes
that we will not punish you for this?

CHORUS LEADER:
Dionysus! Dionysus holds me
in his power. Not Thebes.

SECOND MESSENGER:
1040 I sympathize, but you women should not rejoice
when evil has been done. It is not proper.

CHORUS LEADER:
Tell me, I want to know exactly how he died.
He was unjust, he was a fountain of injustice.

1037: A line with this meaning has evidently dropped out of the mss.

SECOND MESSENGER:
  We left the outskirts of Thebes and crossed
  the Asōpus River, then headed for the heights
  of Mt. Kithairōn. Pentheus and I   1045
  (I was following my master) and the foreign stranger
  who was our guide on that observation patrol.

  First we occupied a grassy hollow,
  maintaining silence—walking carefully, no talking—
  so that we could see without being seen.   1050
  Between two cliffs, we spotted a ravine
  laced with trickling streams, shaded by pines.
  And there were the Maenads, sitting happily at work.
  Some were rewinding ivy tendrils
  around a thyrsus that had come undone;   1055
  others, like colts set free from a decorated yoke,
  tossed back and forth the singing of a Bacchic hymn.
  Pentheus, poor man, could not see the whole crowd
  of women. "Stranger," he said, "from where we stand
  my eyes can't reach as far as those phony Maenads.   1060
  But if I climb some tower of a fir tree on the high ground there,
  I could accurately observe the Maenads' shocking behavior."

  Then I saw the stranger do something amazing.
  He grabbed a fir tree by its topmost shoot in the sky
  and pulled it down, down, down, to the black earth,   1065
  bent like a bow or like a round wheel
  when the compass scribes its running arc.
  That's how he pulled down the mountain tree,
  and bent it to the earth. No mere human could have done it.
  He seated Pentheus in the fir branches   1070
  and let the trunk go straight, gently easing up
  with his hands, careful not to shake him off.
  The tree towered straight up in the air
  with my master seated on its back.
  But they saw him, better than he saw the Maenads.   1075
  Just before he came into view, sitting on high,
  the stranger disappeared altogether, and out of the sky
  came a voice—it must have been Dionysus,

1056: "Decorated yoke"—a symbol of marriage.

shouting to rouse the young women:
"I have brought him to you, girls—the one
1080 who ridiculed me and my worship.
Now you must pay him back."
And with this pronouncement came
sacred fire, linking heaven and earth.
Then, silence in the sky, and silently the wooded glen
1085 restrained its leaves, wild creatures gave no cries.
The women did not know what sound they'd heard;
they stood stock still and cast their eyes about.
Again, he gave command. Then Cadmus' daughters
knew surely this was a command from Bacchus,
1090 and they ran with the speed of a dove;
the Bacchae followed, darting down the ravine
past jagged rocks and snow-melt torrents, while the god
1095 breathed madness in them. When they saw my master
sitting in the fir-tree they started to throw slingstones
up at him with great force; some climbed a facing
pinnacle of rock and hurled fir-boughs like javelins.
Others made missiles of the thyrsus and let
1100 fly at Pentheus—a cruel volley, but it fell short.
He was higher than their zeal could reach, up
there on his miserable seat, caught with no defenses.
In the end they struck at his tree roots with thunder-
bolts of oak branches, trying to pry them up. But those
1105 were no iron crowbars, and their efforts led nowhere.
So Agavē said, "Come on, stand in a circle, Maenads,
and grab the trunk. Let's catch this tree-mounting
beast; and keep him from telling the world
the secret of our dances to the god." Thousands of hands
1110 took the fir-tree and plucked it right out of the earth.
And he fell, ground-plummeting, from on high,
his high perch, wailing all the way down.
That was when Pentheus learned he was near to disaster.
His mother was the first at the killing. She was priestess,
1115 and she rushed to attack him. He tore off his headband
in hopes she would recognize him, not kill him.
He reached out to her cheek, miserable Agavē's,
and said, "I am yours, Mother, your child Pentheus.
You gave me birth in the house of Echion.
1120 Pity me, Mother. I have made mistakes.

But do not kill your own son because of them."
She was foaming at the mouth, face twisted, eyes
rolling, not thinking as she ought to think. She
was possessed by Bacchus and did not believe him.
Grabbing his left wrist with her hands, she braced   1125
her foot against his ribs—what a horrible fate for him—
and tore off his shoulder—but not by brute strength.
The god made it come off easily in her hands.
On the other side Inō was taking him apart,
breaking off bits of meat. Autonoē and the mob of Bacchae   1130
all went after him then. Then there was screaming everywhere.
He kept crying in pain as long as he had breath; they
were howling in triumph. Off went one with a forearm,
another took his foot—with its hunting boot. And his ribs
were stripped, flesh torn away. They all had blood on their 1135
hands. They tossed Pentheus' meat like balls in a game of catch.
The body is spread around: one piece by a rugged
cliff, another deep in the woods under heavy foliage,
impossible to find. His head—this is horrible—
it turned out that his mother took it in her hands.   1140
She's got it planted on the tip of her thyrsus,
and she's carrying it straight down Kithairōn (thinks
it's a mountain lion's), leaves her sisters to dance
for Bacchus. She's gleeful about her hunting (her luck
was cruel). She's inside the walls now, shouting   1145
and praising Bacchus: "My hunting partner," she calls him,
"who helped me run the dogs and catch my prey!
Glorious victory!" (But all she's won is tears.)
        I'm going now, before Agavē reaches home.
I won't be underfoot when there's a disaster.
But this is the highest glory: have a sound mind and reverence 1150
     for
whatever belongs to gods. This too is the most wise
of all pursuits a human being can follow.

FIFTH CHORUS:
     Strike up the dance for Bacchus,
     raise a cheer for the downfall
     of serpent-spawn Pentheus,   1155
     who fitted himself out as a woman,
     took for a thyrsus the staff

that promises Hades,
and paraded after a bull—to his downfall.

1160   Bacchae of Cadmus,
your glory-song turns to a dirge, your fame to tears—
a fine contest, to end with blood streaming
from a hand thrust
against a child.

CHORUS LEADER:
1165   Now I see her, she rushes home eagerly—
Pentheus' mother, Agavē. Her eyes are rolling
wildly. Welcome her, as a band of Bacchic revelers.

Exodos (Final Scene)

*(Enter Agavē, with the head of Pentheus on a stick, his
hair curled round it like ivy on a thyrsus. She enters
immediately into the rhythms of the chorus and soon
becomes part of their dance.)*

AGAVĒ:
Bacchae from Asia!

CHORUS LEADER:
                    What are you shouting about?

AGAVĒ:
1170   We're bringing it home from the mountains,
a fresh-cut curling
shoot of the vine. Our hunting was blessed.

CHORUS:
I see. Come, you are one of us.

AGAVĒ:
I caught him, with no ropes or snares.
A lion's cub—
1175   he's young, can you see?

CHORUS:
From a wild place! Where?

AGAVĒ:
Kithairōn.

CHORUS:
> Kithairōn?

AGAVĒ:
Slaughtered him!

CHORUS:
> And the first blow? Whose was it?

AGAVĒ:
Mine. It was my privilege.
The sacred dancers call me "Blessed Agavē."   1180

CHORUS:
Who else?

AGAVĒ:
> Cadmus . . .

CHORUS:
Cadmus?

AGAVĒ:
> His daughters.
They got to the beast after I did, after me.
Oh, we had such luck in our hunting.

> *(Here the lyric rhythm of the piece begins to repeat the
> pattern set at Agavē's entrance.)*

AGAVĒ:
So join me in the feast.

CHORUS:
> What feast? Join you? In misery?

AGAVĒ:
He's young. The young bull just begins   1185
to grow curls down his cheeks
and the hair on his head is soft.

CHORUS:
His hair, at least, would suit a beast from the countryside.

AGAVĒ:
Bacchus, dogdriving hunter, was cunning.
Cunningly he roused Maenads   1190
against this beast.

CHORUS:
   The lord is a hunter!

AGAVĒ:
   You praise?

CHORUS:
                  I praise

AGAVĒ:
   Soon Cadmus' people . . .

CHORUS:
                        and your son Pentheus . . .

AGAVĒ:
   He'll praise his mother
1195   for catching this big game, this lion's cub.

CHORUS:
   Outstanding catch!

AGAVĒ:
                        Outstanding hunt!

CHORUS:
   Do you rejoice?

AGAVĒ:
                  I exult!
   It was magnificent, magnificent,
   what the hunt achieved, for all to see.

CHORUS:
1200   Then show it to the city people now, wretched woman.
   Show them your victory—the game you brought from the
      hunt.

AGAVĒ:
   Come, all you who dwell in the fine-walled city
   of Thebes! Come and look at the big game
   we daughters of Cadmus chased and caught.
1205   We didn't need any throw-strap javelins
   or even nets. We used our own white arms,
   just the fingers on our hands. We have made
   spearthrowing obsolete, put weaponmakers out

of business. With hands alone we caught
this beast and tore it limb from limb.   1210

Where's my father, the old man? I want him
here. And Pentheus, my son—where is he? I want him
to take a great strong ladder and lean it on the house
so he can nail this to the beam-ends, now that I've
come with the head of a lion I hunted down.   1215

> *(Enter Cadmus, followed by servants carrying the
> remains of Pentheus covered on a stretcher.)*

CADMUS:
This way. That horrible thing you carry
is Pentheus. This way, in front of the house.
It took me endless trouble to find the body
in the ravines of Kithairōn and bring it here,
all torn apart, no two pieces in the same place.   1220
It was very hard to find them in the woods.
I didn't hear from anyone what my daughters had done—
the reckless maniacs!—till I was back in the city
after coming down from the Bacchic dance
with old Tiresias. So I hurried back to the mountain   1225
and here I am, bringing the boy who was killed
by Maenads. I saw Autonoē up there—that was
Actaeon's mother—and Inō too, still afflicted,
raving in oak-thickets, bitten with frenzy. But Agavē—
someone said she'd danced her way down here   1230
in Bacchic style, and it's quite true what I heard.
I am looking at her now, and what a miserable sight she is!

AGAVĒ:
Father, no one can brag about his daughters more
than you; we are the best daughters a man could have,
by far. All of us, but me especially.   1235
I gave up weaving, left my shuttles beside the loom,
turned to more important work—big-game hunting,
barehanded. And I brought you this with my own arms—
Do you see? It's the hero-trophy I captured,

1215: Heads of sacrificial victims and possibly of game were hung high on
buildings.

1240 so you could hang it on your house. Take it,
 Father. Put out your hands. Show off my success
 at hunting to your friends, announce a banquet.
 You are blessed, blessed! We have achieved such things!

CADMUS:
 [Grief beyond measure—I can't take it in.
1245 Achieved? Wretched hands! It's murder.]
 A fine victim for a sacrifice! You strike him down for the
  gods
 and then invite all Thebes and me to the feast!
 Oh, I grieve more for your disaster than for mine.
 The god had a right to destroy us, this lord of thunder.
1250 But he went too far, considering he was born in our
  family.

AGAVĒ:
 Well, you're hard to please! That's old age for you,
 always puts a scowl in a man's eye. I wish my son
 would follow my example, and be a lucky hunter
 whenever he goes after game with the boys
1255 from Thebes. But all he can do is wage war
 on gods. He needs you to give him a piece
 of your mind, Father. Who will call him
 into my sight, so he can see me in my good fortune?

CADMUS:

   (crying in horror)

 When you know what you've done,
1260 you'll feel the most terrible agony of pain. But if you stay
 in the state you're in forever, you'll be
 unlucky to the end, and never have the faintest idea.

AGAVĒ:
 What do you mean? It's not beautiful? It's painful?

CADMUS:
 First let your eyes look at the sky. Up here.

AGAVĒ:
1265 I'm looking. Why did you suggest I look at this?

1244–45: Most editors delete these lines.

CADMUS:
　Is it the same? Or do you think it changes?

AGAVĒ:
　It's brighter than before, a new glow comes through it.

CADMUS:
　And that fluttering sensation, still have that in your soul?

AGAVĒ:
　I don't know what you mean. But I am somehow coming
　back into my mind, I'm moving away from the old thoughts.　　1270

CADMUS:
　Can you listen now and answer clearly?

AGAVĒ:
　I've forgotten what we were saying, Father.

CADMUS:
　When you married, what house did you go to?

AGAVĒ:
　You gave me to Echion—a Sown Man. So they say.

CADMUS:
　And who was the son born at home to your husband?　　1275

AGAVĒ:
　Pentheus, from my marriage to his father.

CADMUS:
　Tell me, now. Whose face do you have in your arms?

AGAVĒ:
　A lion's. At least that's what they said, the hunters.

CADMUS:
　Look straight this time. It won't take long to see it.

AGAVĒ:
　Oh! What am I looking at? What am I carrying in my arms?　　1280

CADMUS:
　Look carefully, and you will learn the answer clearly.

_____

1274: Sown Man—grown from a serpent's tooth planted in the ground (see
note on 539).

AGAVĒ:
> I see horrible pain. I am so miserable.

CADMUS:
> You don't think it looks like a lion anymore?

AGAVĒ:
> No. It's Pentheus. I have his head.

CADMUS:
1285   We mourned for him before you even knew who he was.

AGAVĒ:
> Who killed him? How did he come into my hands?

CADMUS:
> Truth is horrible; it always comes at the wrong time.

AGAVĒ:
> Tell me. What will it be? My heart is pounding.

CADMUS:
> You killed him, you and your sisters.

AGAVĒ:
1290   Where did he die? At home? What kind of place?

CADMUS:
> The place where—before this—dogs tore Actaeon apart.

AGAVĒ:
> But why did he come to Kithairōn? Were the gods against
> him?

CADMUS:
> He went to jeer at the god, and at your Bacchic dances too.

AGAVĒ:
> What about us—how did we come to land up there?

CADMUS:
1295   You were mad. The whole city had gone into Bacchic
> frenzy.

AGAVĒ:
> Dionysus destroyed us. Now I understand.

1291: Actaeon—the son of Autonoë. See 337ff.

CADMUS:

  He was insulted outrageously when you did not believe he was
  a god.

AGAVĒ:

  And my son's body, that I loved so much. Where is it, Father?

CADMUS:

  I brought it here, after a long search. It was hard to find.

AGAVĒ:

  Has he been fitted together decently?   1300

> *(Here there is a gap in the only surviving manuscript for
> this part of the play. We must imagine the scene: Cadmus
> or the chorus answers, "No," and Agavē restores the head
> to the body, mourning for her son as she hugs each limb.
> See the section on the play's lost speeches.)*

AGAVĒ:

  And Pentheus—did he have any part in my mindless folly?

CADMUS:

  He *did* turn out like you—with no reverence for the god.
  And so he tied everyone together in one injury [to the god]—
  you women, and himself. As a result, he ruined my house
  and me. You know I have no male children, and now   1305
  I see this offshoot of your womb, poor woman,
  dying the worst death possible, the most shameful.

  (To the corpse)

  In you, Child, our home found its eyes.
  You held my family together, as the son of my daughter,
  and you were a terror to the city. No one wished   1310
  to insult the old man, once he saw your face,
  because you made them pay a fair penalty.
  Now I'll lose my rights, I'll be cast out of my home—
  Cadmus the Great, who sowed the race of Thebans
  and brought a splendid crop to harvest.   1315
  Oh dearest of men—even though you are
  no more, I count you, Child, among the friends I love—
  never again will you caress my beard,
  embrace me, call me "Mother's father,"
  ask, "Has anyone done you wrong, old man?   1320

Dishonored or disturbed your heart? Caused you pain?
Tell me, and I'll punish the man who wrongs you, Father."
Now I am miserable and you are wretched,
your mother's pitiful, and her sisters are wretched too.

1325 If there is anyone who despises the divine,
he should look at this man's death and believe in gods.

CHORUS:
I feel for you, Cadmus. But that grandson of yours
deserved his punishment, painful as it is for you.

AGAVĒ:
My life's turned upside down, Father, as you see . . .

*(Here again a passage has dropped out of the manuscript.
We must imagine that Agavē offers to help her father as
they go into exile together. She is interrupted by Dionysus,
who makes his appearance as a god for the first time in
the play, high above the royal house. His speech ends with
prophecies for each of the principal characters. Cadmus is
the last to hear his fate.)*

DIONYSUS:
1330 You, Cadmus, will be transformed into a serpent, while your
        wife
will turn into a wild animal, changed to the form of a
        snake—
Harmonia, daughter of Ares, whom you took as wife, though
        you
were mortal. The oracle of Zeus says that you will drive
an oxcart, you and your wife, at the head of a troop of
        foreigners.

1335 You will take and sack many cities with an enormous army,
but when they plunder the shrine and oracle of Apollo,
they will cause themselves to have a miserable return
journey. You and Harmonia, however, will be rescued by
        Ares,
and he will settle you to live in the Land of the Blessed.

1340 I pronounce this fate as Dionysus, born of no mortal father,
for I am the son of Zeus.
If you had known how to keep your minds
sound—which you did not wish to do—you would have had
good fortune, and the son of Zeus would have been your ally.

CADMUS:
Dionysus, hear our prayer. We have done wrong.

DIONYSUS:
You learned too late. When you should have known us you   1345
did not.

CADMUS:
We know that now. But you are too severe in prosecuting us.

DIONYSUS:
I am a god, and you committed an outrage against me.

CADMUS:
Anger does not become a god. You should not be like a human
being.

DIONYSUS:
Zeus, my father, agreed to all this long ago.

AGAVĒ:

> *(with a cry of despair)*

It is a decree, then. Old man, we are banished. How miserable!   1350

DIONYSUS:
Why put it off? It will be, by necessity.

> *(Dionysus probably exits on this line.)*

CADMUS:
My child, what terrible misery we all face—you, your sisters,
and me. I will arrive as a stranger in a foreign land—
me an old man. Worse than that, the god has   1355
fated me to lead a ragtag army of foreigners against Greece.
I and my wife Harmonia, daughter of Ares,
will come in the form of wild serpents
at the head of a troop of spearmen
against the tombs and altars of Greece.   1360
And I will have no relief from evil and misery,
no voyage down the Acheron to be at peace below.

1362: The Acheron was one of the rivers of the underworld. Cadmus does
not mention here his destination in the Land of the Blessed, probably because endless life seems no consolation to him (Dodds 1960).

AGAVĒ:

(embracing him)

Oh, Father, I'll be bereft of you in my exile.

CADMUS:

Why are you wrapping your arms around me
1365   like a swan with its white-haired useless parent?

AGAVĒ:

But where can I turn, when I'm an outcast from my
    country?

CADMUS:

I don't know, Child. I'm not much help.

AGAVĒ:

Farewell my house, farewell my native land.
I am leaving you now. So unlucky,
1370   my marriage undone. An exile.

CADMUS:

My child, you should go where Aristaeus . . .

AGAVĒ:

I weep for you, Father.

CADMUS:

And I for you, my child, and for your sisters.

AGAVĒ:

It's terrible how
1375   lord Dionysus brought
this calamity on your house.

CADMUS:

Because it was terrible what you did to him;
he had no honor to his name in Thebes.

1371: "Where Aristaeus . . . "—probably Mt. Kithairōn, where Actaeon,
the son of Aristaeus and Agavē's sister Autonoē, was torn apart by his own
dogs. The idea would be that she may meet with her sisters there and share
the journey into exile. The text breaks off here, but this is probably Cadmus' meaning. Alternatively, Cadmus may be advising his daughters to seek
the protection of Aristaeus.

AGAVĒ:
Farewell, Father.

CADMUS:

Fare *well,* sad Daughter,
though that will be hard where you are going.   1380

AGAVĒ:
Friends, take me where I can find my sisters
so that we may be exiles together.

I'd like to go far away from the curse of Kithairōn,
where I can't see Kithairōn,   1385
where there's no display of a thyrsus to remind me.
Leave that to other worshipers of Bacchus.

CHORUS:
Many are the shapes the gods will take,
many the surprises they perform.
What was thought likely did not transpire,   1390
and what was unlikely the god made easy.
That is how this matter ended.

–END–

Bacchae: The Lost Speeches

Of the two surviving manuscripts for *Bacchae,* one breaks off after line 755, and the other—our only manuscript source for the second half—is missing at least one large section, and probably two, with the result that we do not have Agavē's lament or the beginning of Dionysus' prophecy.

Editors lack consensus as to whether the lament of Agavē came in the gap after line 1300 or the gap after line 1329. Wilamowitz, Murray, and Dodds support the later position and are followed in English reconstructions by Arrowsmith, Williams, and Bagg. Kirk, Seaford, and Leinieks place the lament after 1300, using arguments laid out by Robert, making what in my view is a better case. The arguments turn mainly on what makes the best sense in context.

We have three kinds of information for the lost speeches: ancient summaries, fragments, and ancient or medieval texts that imitated *Bacchae.* Reconstructions of the lost speeches are to be found, for example, in Roux, Leinieks, and Esposito.[1]

1. Ancient Summaries

a. The Hypothesis

The ancient summary known as the Hypothesis does not mention the lament, but does report on the prophecy: "Dionysus appeared and made an announcement to all. He then made clear what would happen to each one in actual fact, so that no outsider would despise him as human on the basis of mere words."

b. Apsines

Writing in the third century about how to arouse pity, the rhetorician Apsines mentions the missing lament twice:

---

1. Willink's 1966 article on the text of the *Bacchae* is helpful on both the papyrus and the Byzantine imitation.

Agavē, after recovering from her madness and recognizing that her own child has been torn to pieces, accuses herself, and so arouses pity. (9.587)

By this device, Euripides consciously arouses pity for Pentheus: Holding each of his limbs in her hands, his mother laments in accordance with each of them [the limbs]. (9.590)

2. Fragments

a. From an ancient footnote to Aristophanes

For if I had not taken this personal defilement into my hands . . .
(Fr. 847 Nauck, scholion to *Plut.* 907)

b. From papyri

Two fragments contain enough material to be useful, and missing bits have been filled in speculatively by, for example, Dodds (1960, pp. 243–44). The two fragments are separated by thirty lines that are lost on the papyrus. Both must fall into the same gap in *Bacchae*, probably the second of the two. What follows is a translation with Dodds' highly speculative supplements:

2a (Probably Cadmus)
. . . bringing Pentheus' furrowed and blood-fouled
limbs, you can be sure, with careful trouble.
Let any mortal who sees this learn the lesson:
It was Zeus who fathered Dionysus the god.

2b (Probably Dionysus)
He whose miserable corpse you hold in your
arms, Agavē, Pentheus, wished to set himself
against your frenzies. But them . . .
             . . . his irreverence . . .

3. Imitations

a. From *Christus Patiens*

Probably sometime between the ninth and thirteenth centuries, a Byzantine writer ("Pseudo-Gregorius") composed a play about the passion of Christ on the framework of *Bacchae*. The author had a complete copy of Euripides' play in front of him and plundered it freely, adapting the lines to suit his purposes. Here is a fairly straight translation of the lines printed in Diggle's edition of Euripides. Line numbers refer to the *Christus Patiens*. Scholars agree that much of this material—though certainly not every word—was taken from *Bacchae*. The words bracketed, following Diggle, are probably not from Euripides.

Agavē (probably fits in the gap after *Bacchae* 1300):

1011 I, a miserable wretch who was once [blessed] . . .[2]

1120 They did not think to put you in a grave.
How did [I bring you down from the tree?]
In what burial mound [may I put] your body?
With what robes [shall I cover] your corpse?

1256 . . . so that [I may draw out] a whole song,
kissing the flesh that I nourished.

1312 How may I, with proper care, take him
to my breast? In what way shall I mourn?

1449 A little consolation for the dead . . .

1466 Come, old man, let us fit the head of this
[thrice-unlucky man] correctly, and put his whole
body in tune, as accurately as possible.
Your dearest face, your young cheeks,

1470 look, with this covering I hide [your head].
And your blood-fouled and furrowed limbs
[and parts]—I [cover] them with new robes.

Dionysus (for the gap after *Bacchae* 1329):

300 You have learned, since you have paid the penalty you
deserved . . .

1360 They were not decent words [the crowd] used
when they said falsely I was born of someone human.
I could not bear merely to suffer these insults.

1663 And so he dies at the hands of those who should least
have killed him, [and he was put in chains and mocked.]

---

2. Dodds (1960) proposes "exultant" to replace the last word.

Such were the things done him by a people [who had   1665
formerly loved him] as a benefactor, now inflamed with malice.
And he suffered these things not [unwillingly],
but what the people³ must suffer—those evils I'll reveal.
They must leave the city and go among foreigners,
willing or [unwilling], be enslaved, and lose their rights,   1670

For that is god's decree: [to run] through every foreign land
to be captives of the spear and suffer many evils.
[The father of all proclaims to all unbelievers:]
they are to leave this city in order to pay the penalty
of their unholy pollution to him they killed in their malice,   1675
never again [to see] their homeland. For it is not holy
[that murderers should remain by the tombs of the dead.]
They will come to many cities, [dragging]
the yoke of slavery in their misfortune.

As for this man, I will declare the sorrowful destiny he will fulfill.   1690

(Addressed to a woman) As murderer, you must leave the city.   1756

b. From Seneca's *Phaedra*

Leinieks, alone among editors, uses the following lines from Seneca's Latin play for his reconstruction of the lament: 1247–50, 1254–70, and 1273 of *Phaedra* (also known as *Hippolytus*). As Theseus laments over the battered body of his son Hippolytus, he tries (and fails) to put pieces of the body back in their proper places. Leinieks takes these lines to be a version of Agavē's lament.

I doubt that the lines that follow are based closely on *Bacchae*. We do not have firm evidence that Agavē did try to reconstruct the body of Pentheus, beyond restoring its head. Furthermore, I do not believe it was Seneca's practice to follow the Greek word for word. Finally, modern critics have considered the scene to be an overblown horror show, devised for the taste of Romans in the bloodthirsty age of Claudius and Nero. Line 1267 is "arguably the worst

---

3. In its late Christian context, this appears to refer to the expulsion of Jews from their homeland by the Romans. We should not conclude, however, that Dionysus means to expel all Thebans from their land, because it is plainly his purpose to establish his religion among them at Thebes, and because his anger is directed specifically at the royal family, and especially at women; contrast line 33 of the play with line 1673 above.

line in Senecan drama."[4] Readers will see that this line has competition from others in the vicinity, but should keep in mind that modern taste is no measure of what ancient audiences would have admired.

1247 Bring here, bring here the remains of the dear body
and put down the burden of his limbs, collected at random.
Is this Hippolytus? I acknowledge my fault:
1250 I took your life.

Embrace his limbs, whatever remains of your son,
1255 wretched man, lean over them and warm them with your breast.
As his father, put the scattered parts of his torn body
in order and restore each straying part
to its place. Here is where his strong right hand should go;
here's where to put his left, that knew how to control
1260 the reins. I recognize features of his left side.
But how much is missing still, that I cannot mourn!
Be strong, trembling hands, for their sad work,
and cheeks, you must be dry and hold your tears,
while a father counts out the pieces of his son
1265 and prepares the corpse. What is this that has no shape,
an ugly thing torn on every side with many wounds?
What part it is of yours I do not know, but it is part of you.
Here, put it here. That's not its proper place, but it is empty.
Is this that face that shone with the fire of stars,
1270 and made enemies avert their eyes? Has beauty sunk so far?

1273 Look, take these. They are your father's last gifts.

---

4. Coffey and Mayer, pp. 18, 195.

EURIPIDES

Iphigenia at Aulis

Translated, with Notes, by Cecelia Eaton Luschnig

Cast of Characters

AGAMEMNON	king of Mycenae, commander of the Greek forces, husband of Clytemnestra, and father of Iphigenia
OLD MAN	loyal retainer of Clytemnestra and Agamemnon
CHORUS	of young married women from Calchis, a city in Euboea separated from Aulis by the strait of Euripus
MENELAUS	king of Sparta, husband of Helen, brother of Agamemnon
MESSENGER 1	
CLYTEMNESTRA	daughter of Tyndareos, wife of Agamemnon, mother of Iphigenia and Orestes
IPHIGENIA	teenage daughter of Clytemnestra and Agamemnon
ACHILLES	warrior, son of Thetis, a sea goddess, and Peleus, king of Phthia
[MESSENGER 2]	messenger in the spurious epilogue

Nonspeaking Roles

ORESTES	infant son of Clytemnestra and Agamemnon

Various extras are required to serve as attendants for Clytemnestra's carriage, servants at Agamemnon's lodging, and soldiers carrying Achilles' armor.

Iphigenia at Aulis was first produced posthumously with *Bacchae* not long after 406 B.C.E. Euripides' plays won first prize in that year's Greater Dionysia.

Iphigenia at Aulis

SCENE: *The setting is the Greek camp at Aulis where contingents from all over Greece have gathered to sail for Troy. The scene building represents Agamemnon's military quarters. It is night shortly before dawn. Agamemnon enters from his lodge and delivers a monologue. He holds a tablet on which he writes, erases (or scrapes), and rewrites. Stage left is used for entrances and exits from and to the far distance, stage right for those to, from, or through the Greek encampment.*

Prologue

(Enter Agamemnon from his lodge.)

AGAMEMNON:
Thestius' daughter Leda had three daughters,
Phoebe, Clytemnestra my wife, and Helen.   50
For *her*, the very wealthiest young men
from all over Greece came as suitors.
They hurled deadly threats of violence

Prologue: Everything that takes place before the entrance of the chorus. The prologue of this play has textual problems, especially with the order of its parts. Does it begin with the monologue, as is most typical of Euripides, or with the dialogue between Agamemnon and his elderly slave, which actually comes first in the manuscript? Are the two parts of the prologue even compatible? See Introduction, on "The State of the Text." I have chosen to begin with Agamemnon's monologue, 49–96. This is followed by the dialogue between the king and his old slave (1–48). At 97, Agamemnon resumes his narrative explanation, after which the two men conclude their dialogue.

50: Clytemnestra is spelled Klutaimēstra in Greek (without the "n"). By naming her along with the relatively obscure Phoebe and saying "my wife," Agamemnon cleverly puts himself outside the suit for Helen's hand and all its consequences.

against each other—whoever failed to get the girl.
55   Her father Tyndareos was faced with an impasse:
to give his daughter or not. How could he best
take the situation in hand? Then this idea came to him:
to hold a sacrifice of burnt offerings, pour libations,
and have the suitors join right hands, be bound
60   by oath, and call down curses on themselves:
whoever wins Tyndareos' daughter as his wife—
they swore to defend his rights if anyone took her
from home, displacing her husband from her bed,
to raise an army and lay waste the seducer's city—
65   Greek and foreign alike—with force of arms.
When they had taken this pledge, old Tyndareos,
sly fox that he was, managed to outwit them all
by giving his daughter the right to pick one of the suitors,
whichever one the sweet breezes of love should waft her way.
70   And she chose—I wish to god she had picked somebody
          else—
my brother Menelaus. Along comes that man from Troy,
the very one—the story goes—who judged the goddesses,
all the way to Sparta, decked out in the gaudiest attire
glittering with gold, a peacock strutting out of Asia.
75   It was love at first sight for the two of them.
Off he went, Helen in tow, to the cattle pastures
on Mount Ida. Menelaus, of course, was out of town.

55: "Impasse"—The word in Greek is *aporia,* which literally means "inability to cross" and is used both literally, concerning the inability to sail, and figuratively, of the various dilemmas in the play.

61–65: The complexity of the oath is partly expressed through word order and redundancy, using no fewer than four expressions of oath-taking.

72: "Who judged the goddesses"—the Judgment of Paris. Legend has it that at the wedding of Achilles' parents, Peleus, a mortal, and the sea goddess Thetis (see 1036–79), Eris, the goddess of discord, threw an apple into the midst of the celebration with the word *kallistēi* ("for the fairest"), causing strife among Hera, Pallas Athena, and Aphrodite, who competed for the title. The Trojan prince Paris was chosen as judge. He chose Aphrodite. Some say he was bribed by being offered the world's most beautiful woman if he chose her. One wonders if bribery was necessary, given the natures and attributes of the other two goddesses.

But like a crazy man he raced all over Greece
calling up the ancient oaths of Tyndareos, insisting
they had to come to the aid of the husband wronged.
At this the Greeks grabbed their weapons and came   80
    running,
armed to the teeth, and so here they are gathered
by the narrow strait of Aulis with ships and shields
and an endless array of chariots and horses.
Next, they chose me to command the expedition
for Menelaus' sake, because I'm his brother, an honor   85
I wish to god someone else had won instead of me.
So the army is mustered and drawn up in battalions
and here we sit mired in our camp at Aulis, unable to sail.
Calchas, the army's prophet, proclaims a way out of the
    impasse:
he says I must sacrifice my own daughter Iphigenia   90
to the goddess Artemis who lives in these parts;
and we'll have clear sailing and overthrow the Phrygians
[if we sacrifice her, but not if we refuse].

78: Literally, "he gadflied" as if bitten by a gadfly (*oistrēsas*) like the tormented Io. See Euripides, *Phoenician Women* 248, with note.

82: Aulis is a hill with a harbor in Boeotia on the Euripus (a narrow strait separating Boeotia from Euboea) just opposite Chalcis, a major port on the island of Euboea.

89: "The army's prophet"—The very same seer is called "seer of evil" by Agamemnon at Homer, *Iliad* 1.106. Did Calchas announce his prophecy to Agamemnon and a few close advisers or to the whole army (see 106–7)? This is important for the upcoming question of Agamemnon's choice.

91: In some versions, but not this one, Artemis, a goddess fond of hunting, has a reason for punishing Agamemnon: he had killed a stag in Artemis' sacred grove (Sophocles, *Electra* 566–72 and Cacoyannis' 1977 film version, *Iphigenia*). In Euripides, the goddess is more arbitrary and perhaps habitually bloodthirsty. See 186, *polythuton* ("full of sacrifices"), an epithet for Artemis' grove.

92: Phrygian is used again and again in this play as another name for Trojan. In Homer the Phryges were allies of the Trojans (*Iliad* 2.862). The term is often derogatory (e.g., at Euripides, *Alcestis* 675).

93: Brackets around lines in the translation indicate sections of doubtful authenticity.

95   No sooner did I hear this than I told Talthybius to dismiss
        the army in a proclamation loud and clear for all to hear,
        because I would never have the heart to kill my daughter.

        (Agamemnon calls to his slave inside the lodge.)

        Old man, come out here
        in front of the lodge.

        (Enter Old Man from the lodge.)

OLD MAN:

                        I'm coming. What are you up to,
        King Agamemnon?

AGAMEMNON:
        Will you hurry?

OLD MAN:

                        I'm coming as fast as I can.
        Old age is sleepless
5   and keeps my eyes open.

AGAMEMNON:
        What star is that crossing the sky?

OLD MAN:
        That's Sirius shooting across
        midway in the sky, near the seven Pleiades.

AGAMEMNON:
        There is no sound of birds,
10   no sound of the sea. The winds are hushed
        through all Euripus.

94–96: Talthybius—Agamemnon's herald in Homer's *Iliad* and in various
tragedies (e.g., Euripides, *Hecuba*, *Orestes*, and *Trojan Women*). It seems
unlikely that Talthybius carried out this command; Menelaus intervened
(97).

1: "Old man, come out here"—This is the beginning of the play in the
manuscript. Beginnings and endings of scrolls (which were the originals of
our texts) were most likely to suffer damage.

11: Euripus—the strait between Boeotia on the mainland and the island of
Euboea. Its turbulent tidal currents (which reverse directions several times
a day) were remarked on by Plato: "all things, like the Euripus, are always
going up and down" (*Phaedo* 90c).

OLD MAN:
  Why are you so agitated, King Agamemnon,
  pacing outside the lodge?
  It is still quiet here in Aulis
  and the sentinels on the ramparts are undisturbed.   15
  Let's go inside.

AGAMEMNON:
              I envy you.
  I envy any man who passes his life
  free of peril, unsung, anonymous.
  For those in high office I feel no envy.

OLD MAN:
  And yet that is where the good life is found.   20

AGAMEMNON:
  Yes, but the good life is treacherous
  and sweet though it is,
  high status brings grief to those who reach it.
  Sometimes a random act of the gods
  will turn your life upside down; sometimes men's   25
  fickle and dissatisfied
  thoughts will rankle.

OLD MAN:
  This is not the kind of thing I admire in a leader.
  Agamemnon, Atreus
  did not father you just for the good times.   30
  You need to take the good with the bad.
  You were born human. Even if you don't like it
  the gods' will shall be done.
  You have lit a lamp
  and are writing a letter,   35
  which even now you hold clenched in your hands;
  you go back and erase the same letters,
  and you seal it, then open it again;

35: That Agamemnon is writing a letter is made even more interesting by
the fact that two people credited with inventing the alphabet, bringing it to
the Greeks, or adding letters to it, Cadmus (the figurehead on the Boeotian
fleet, 257) and Palamedes (one of the warriors, 197), are named in the parodos, in the choral description of the warriors at rest.

now with tears in your eyes,
40   you throw the tablet on the ground,
and you are close to the diminished capacity
we see in madmen.
What is the problem? My king, what is wrong?
Come now, share your story with me.
45   You'll be talking to a good man who is loyal to you.
Tyndareos gave me to your wife
as part of her dowry,
to be a trusted attendant to your bride.

AGAMEMNON:
My brother pulled out every pretext and convinced me
to do an appalling deed. In the hidden folds of a letter
I wrote to my wife, telling her to send my daughter,
100   with the promise that she was to be married to Achilles.
I built up the man's stature and importance;
I claimed that he was not willing to sail with the Greeks
unless a wife from our family should go to his home in
     Phthia.
This is the inducement I held out to my wife,
105   [to get the girl to come by concocting a bogus wedding.]
We are the only ones of the Greeks that know about this,
Calchas, Odysseus, Menelaus, and I. The terrible mistake
I made then, I am now trying to undo by rewriting
this letter, which you saw me just now, old man,
110   under cover of darkness opening and resealing.
But come on, take this letter and go straight
to Argos. What is hidden inside its folded boards
I will spell out for you—everything that's written in it;
for you are loyal to my wife and my household.

(Agamemnon reads the letter.)

115   Daughter of Leda, I am sending you
a second message to tell you . . .

106–7: Kovacs (2003) and others believe that the story of the privately communicated prophecy was added by a later interpolator. The hero of Homer's *Odyssey* is a villain in most of the tragedies in which he appears (e.g., Euripides' *Hecuba* and Sophocles' *Philoctetes*). Sophocles' *Ajax* is an exception.

OLD MAN:
  Explain this more clearly so I can repeat
  things that will match your writing.

AGAMEMNON:
  Not to send your daughter
  to the bay of Euboea,
  waveless Aulis.   120
  At another season we will feast
  our daughter's wedding.

OLD MAN:
  But won't Achilles get angry
  at you and your wife
  if he is deprived of his marriage?   125
  This makes me queasy. Explain what you mean.

AGAMEMNON:
  Achilles is supplying us with his name, not the fact.
  He doesn't know a thing about the marriage or what we are
      up to.
  He has no idea I promised to give   130
  my daughter to him
  as his bride.

OLD MAN:
  You have done something awful, King Agamemnon—
  you claimed you were giving your daughter as a wife to the
      goddess' son,
  but you were actually bringing her as a sacrifice for the   135
      Greeks.

AGAMEMNON:
  Oh god! I was out of my mind.
  I'm on the brink of ruin.
  Come, get a move on.
  Don't give in to old age.

OLD MAN:
                    I am hurrying, your majesty.   140

134: Achilles is the son of Thetis, a sea goddess, one of the Nereids or
daughters of Nereus (who is called *hálios gérōn* ["the old man of the sea"]
in Homer).

AGAMEMNON:
> Do not sit down to rest by a stream in the woods;
> do not give in to sleep.

OLD MAN:
> Don't even suggest such a thing.

AGAMEMNON:
> Keep your eyes open in all directions
145 > when you reach a crossroads so you won't miss
> a carriage passing quickly by
> bringing my daughter here
> to the Greek fleet.

OLD MAN:
> I'll do that.

AGAMEMNON:
>   Outside the gates
150 > if you meet her with the entourage
> drive them back; shake the reins,
> sending them back to their Cyclopean hearths.

OLD MAN:
> Tell me how I will be believed saying this
> to your wife and daughter.

AGAMEMNON:
155 > Preserve the seal on the letter
> that you are carrying. Go on. The brightening dawn
> is already growing light
> and with it comes the fire of the Sun's chariot.
160 > Help me in my troubles.

(Exit Old Man stage left.)

> No human is well off or happy
> to the end;
> no one was ever born without grief.

(Exit Agamemnon into the lodge.)

152: The massive stone architecture in and around Mycenae was said to
have been built by the Cyclopes (one-eyed giants).

(Enter the chorus along the side passages from both directions.)

Parodos

CHORUS:

[Strophe 1]

I have come to the sands along the coast
of Aulis by the sea.   165
I crossed the narrow stream
of Euripus
and left behind Chalcis, my native city,
nurse of the seawaters
of celebrated Arethusa,   170
to see the army of the Achaeans
and the seagoing oars of Achaean
heroes. Our husbands tell us
with a thousand ships
they will be led   175

Parodos: The entrance song of the chorus. Most choral odes are strophic, that is, the chorus sings and dances in matched strophe and antistrophe. There is sometimes an unmatched stanza between pairs, called a mesode, or, at the end of the song, an epode.

170: Arethusa is the name of several fountains and eponymous Nymphs: in Calchis, Ithaca (Homer, *Odyssey* 13.408), and Syracuse. The last is the most famous one: Arethusa, a virgin and devotee of Artemis, was pursued by the river Alpheus and was transformed into a stream. Alpheus caught her and their waters mingle in a spring on the isle of Ortygia in Syracuse.

173: "Heroes"—the word in Greek is *hemitheoi* ("half-gods" or "demi-gods"). Homer speaks of the race of men half-divine (*hemitheoi*) at *Iliad* 12.23.

173: "Our husbands"—evidence that the chorus is made up of young *married* women (in the Greek, this is line 176). See also 543–57, where the chorus sings about the marriage bed and sex in moderation).

174: A thousand ships is the traditional number and is more poetic than the more specific counts given by Homer in his catalogue of ships, *Iliad* 2.492–877, which add up to 1,186; Thucydides (1.10.4) estimates 1,200.

by redheaded Menelaus
and Agamemnon of illustrious lineage,
going after Helen
from the reedy banks of Eurotas,
180   Helen whom Paris the herdsman took,
the gift of Aphrodite,
after Cypris held a contest
by the dewy streams,
vying in beauty with Hera and Pallas.

[Antistrophe 1]

185   And I went through the forest
of Artemis, a forest full of sacrifices, running,
reddening my cheeks
in youthful modesty because I wanted to see
190   the palisade of shields and the tents
of armored Danaans
and the throng of horses.
I saw the two Ajaxes sitting side by side,
the son of Oeleus and the son of Telamon,
crown of Salamis;
195   and Protesilaus

176: Xanthos ("fair-haired": anywhere from flaxen to redheaded) is used
to describe various Achaean warriors in Homer, e.g., Odysseus, Achilles,
Menelaus.

179: Eurotas is the chief river of Laconia and runs through Sparta.

182–84: Cypris—a name for Aphrodite, the Cyprian, from her birth on the
island of Cyprus; Hera—wife of Zeus, queen of the gods; Pallas Athena—
warrior goddess, patron of Athens, major supporter of the Greeks in the
Trojan War.

186: The forest "full of sacrifices" is foreshadowing. We know that Artemis demands a sacrifice: this adds to the likelihood that it will not be called
off. See Aeschylus, *Agamemnon* 134–38.

192–94: The two Ajaxes are Ajax, son of Oeleus of Locris—the lesser
Ajax—and Ajax, the son of Telamon of Salamis—the greater Ajax, considered the second-greatest Greek warrior after Achilles.

195: Protesilaus (his name means "first leaper") was the first of the Greek
warriors to die at Troy.

at the tables set for checkers
with Palamedes, son of Poseidon's son,
diverting themselves
with the game's intricate moves;
and Diomedes enjoying
the pleasure of the discus,   200
and next Meriones, scion
of Ares, a human marvel,
and the man from the mountainous isles,
Laertes' son, and with them Nireus,
handsomest of the Achaeans.   205

[Mesode]

Achilles, swift as the wind,
his nimble feet flashing,
son of Thetis, reared by Chiron—

196: The game of *pessoi,* a board game (such as the one Achilles and Ajax are
pictured playing on numerous ancient Greek vases) using pebbles of different
colors, the object being to hem in and capture the opponent's pebbles.

197: Palamedes, son of Nauplius. He is said to have invented the game of
pessoi (see note on 196), as well as coinage, numbers, weights, and writing
(or at least to have added letters to the alphabet). Odysseus falsely accused
him of treason and caused him to be condemned to death. In Plato's *Apol-
ogy* (41b) Socrates looks forward to meeting him in the other world so they
can discuss their court cases and wrongful convictions. Among our tragic
losses are a *Palamedes* by each of the three great tragedians, Aeschylus,
Sophocles, and Euripides.

199: Diomedes, son of Tydeus, was the youngest but one of the best of the
Greek warriors. Homer, *Iliad* 5 and part of 6 are devoted to his exploits.

201: Meriones—son of Molus for whom descent from Ares is sometimes
claimed. Though not one of the major characters in Homer, he is frequently
mentioned.

204: Laertes' son is Odysseus. Elsewhere he is called derogatorily the son
of Sisyphus (524, 1362).

204: Nireus was king of Syme and commanded three ships at Troy (*Iliad*
2.671–72). Homer adds that he was the handsomest after Achilles, but
lacked stamina (2.673–75).

208: Chiron—the Centaur who educated heroes, including Jason, Diomedes, and Achilles (see 705–10). He gave lessons in music, hunting, eth-
ics, martial arts, and medicine.

210   I saw him too
       along the seashore,
       running a race in armor;
       I watched as he struggled on foot
       against a four-horse team
215   speeding to victory.
       The charioteer Eumelos,
       Pheres' grandson, shouted them on.
       His beautiful horses I saw
       with golden bits in their mouths,
220   lashed by the goad;
       those in the middle yoked,
       spotted with white hair,
       those outside bearing only the trace
       for ease in running the course,
225   chestnuts, with dappled hide below
       on their fetlocks. Beside these
       Peleus' son was running in arms by the rim
230   and wheels of the chariot.

[Strophe 2]

       Then we came to counting the ships,
       an ineffable vista
       that filled
       our women's sight with sweet pleasure.
235   At the right horn
       of the fleet were
       the Myrmidon troops from Phthia

216: Eumelos—son of Alcestis and Admetus, from Pherae in Thessaly.

221–24: The two outside horses were attached by the trace (a strap connecting them to the vehicle) but were not yoked together to make it easier for them to turn corners (England 1891/1979, at 224).

231–302: Many editors believe these lines are a later interpolation, not by Euripides. They differ from Homer's catalogue in *Iliad* 2. I hesitate to call it a "mere catalogue of the forces" (England 1891/1979, at 161–63) and find it thematically significant. Like Homer, Euripides introduces us to the fighting men who will play such a large part in the final decision to kill Iphigenia.

237: The Myrmidons ("ant people") are Achilles' men. Their homeland is Phthia in Phthiotis, an area of Greece north of Boeotia.

with fifty ships;
upon their keels stood Nereid nymphs
figured in gold,   240
the emblem of Achilles' force.

[Antistrophe 2]

Near them an equal number
of Argive ships were lined up.
Over these Mecisteus' son
was commander—he was brought up by Talaus.   245
With him in command was
Capaneus' son Sthenelus.
Harbored next, Theseus' son commanded
sixty Athenian ships;
he had the goddess Pallas set on a winged chariot   250
with solid-hoofed horses,
a good omen to seafarers.

[Strophe 3]

And I saw the naval force of Boeotia,
fifty vessels,
decked out with emblems,   255
on the beaks of the ships:
Cadmus holding a golden serpent.
Earthborn Leïtus

239: Nereids are sea goddesses: Achilles' mother Thetis and her sisters, the fifty
daughters of Nereus, of whom Homer names thirty-three (*Iliad* 18.39–49).

244: Mecisteus' son—Euryalus. In Homer's *Iliad*, Argos is under Diomedes'
command with Sthenelus (247) and Euryalus under him.

248–50: In non-Homeric sources Theseus' sons Acamas and Demophon
are both said to have taken part in the Trojan War. In the *Iliad* Menestheus
is the leader of the Athenian contingent of fifty ships (2.545–53). Pallas
Athena is the patron of Athens.

257: Cadmus of Phoenicia was the founder of Thebes, the major city of
Boeotia. He killed a serpent and sowed its teeth, which produced the Sown
Men or *Spartoi* (see Euripides, *Phoenician Women* 657–75, 818–22, 931–44).

258: In Homer, Leïtus and four others commanded the Boeotians' fifty
ships (*Iliad* 2.494–510). It is in this passage (2.510) that the number of
men—120—on each ship is mentioned.

commanded their navy.
260   From the land of Phocis
and commanding equal Locrian ships
came Oeleus' son, who had left behind
the far-famed city of Thronion.

[Antistrophe 3]

265   From Cyclops-built Mycenae,
the son of Atreus had gathered sailors in
a hundred ships.
With him Adrastus shared command
friend with friend,
270   so that all Hellas might exact revenge
from the wife who abandoned her home
for foreign marriage.
From Pylos I saw the ships
of Nestor the Gerenian,
275   with a four-footed bull, the sign of
Alpheus, his river neighbor.

[Strophe 4]

A twelve-ship force
of Aenians was there, commanded
by their king, Gouneus. Next to these came
280   the dynasts of Elis,
who were called by the people Epeians;
Eurytos was their king,

260–63: In Homer's *Iliad,* the Phocians and Locrians are separate contingents, each with forty ships. For Ajax, son of Oeleus, see 192–94.

268: Adrastus was the Argive king who gathered the forces for the War of the Seven against Thebes and the War of the Epigoni (the sons of the Seven). Polynices married his daughter (see Euripides, *Phoenician Women* 77, 408–25). His presence is curious since he is not usually associated with the Trojan War.

273–76: Nestor, king of Pylos (in Messenia, in the western Peloponnesus), is prominent as a long-winded counselor in the *Iliad* and a survivor of the war who entertains Telemachus in the *Odyssey.* Gerenios is his Homeric epithet, perhaps a place-name meaning "from Gerenia." The Alpheus is the longest river in the Peloponnesus.

and he led the white-oared Taphian army,
whose king was Meges, son of Phyleus,   285
who had left the Echinae, islands
inaccessible to seafarers.

[Antistrophe 4]

Ajax born in Salamis
joined the right horn to the left   290
nearest to which he was moored
with his ships last, twelve agile vessels.
So I heard and saw the seafaring host.   295
If anyone in foreign barks
joins battle with it,
his return home will be lost to him.
Such a navy I beheld there,   300
and with other things I heard at home
I will remember forever the assembled hordes.

First Episode

(Enter Old Man and Menelaus stage left, fighting over the tablet.)

OLD MAN:
Menelaus, what you are trying to do is criminal.
You must not do it.

MENELAUS:
Get away! You are too loyal to your masters.

OLD MAN:
I take that as a great compliment.   305

MENELAUS:
You'll be sorry if you do what you should not.

277–87: Gouneus is named only once in Homer's *Iliad* (2.748), as leader of the Enienes (spelled Aenians in Euripides) and Peraebi. Eurytos, commander of some of the Epeians, is one of the four leaders of Elis listed at *Iliad* 2.615–24.

289: For Ajax of Salamis, see note on 192–94. In Homer he also commands twelve ships (*Iliad* 2.528–29). He was the best of warriors while Achilles held back from battle (*Iliad* 2.768–69).

OLD MAN:
You had no right to open the letter I was carrying.

MENELAUS:
You had no right to bring ruin on all the Greeks.

OLD MAN:
Take your case somewhere else. Let go of the letter.

MENELAUS:
I will not.

OLD MAN:
310   Neither will I.

MENELAUS:
I'll bloody your head with this scepter.

OLD MAN:
It would be glorious to die for my masters.

MENELAUS:
Let go; for a slave you talk too much.

OLD MAN:
Master! I am wronged. This man has snatched
315 your letter from my hand by force.
Agamemnon, he has no sense of right and wrong.

(Enter Agamemnon from his lodge. Old Man exits into the lodge during this conversation.)

AGAMEMNON:
Hey!
What is this ruckus at my door? Why raise an alarm?

MENELAUS:
My word has no more authority than his.

AGAMEMNON:
Why do you fight with him and resort to violence?

MENELAUS:
320 Look at me! So that I can set out my argument.

AGAMEMNON:
I'm Atreus' son. Why should I be afraid to face you?

MENELAUS:
See this letter? A harbinger of disaster.

AGAMEMNON:
I see it. Release it from your hand, at once.

MENELAUS:
No. Not until I show all the Danaans what it contains.

AGAMEMNON:
Have you broken the seal and seen what you should not?   325

MENELAUS:
Yes, to gall you. I have unsealed your secret.

AGAMEMNON:
Where did you intercept it? Oh god! The effrontery!

MENELAUS:
Where I was keeping watch for your daughter
to see when she would come from Argos to the camp.

AGAMEMNON:
Why are you meddling in my affairs? The gall!

MENELAUS:
I had the urge to do it. I'm not your slave.   330

AGAMEMNON:
Isn't this awful? Am I not to manage my own household?

MENELAUS:
Your mind is mercurial—one thing today,
yesterday another, something else tomorrow.

AGAMEMNON:
You talk a good game, but a clever tongue is detestable.

MENELAUS:
Yes, and an unsteady mind is unjust and perfidious
to friends. I'm going to confront you with the truth—   335
don't you go stalking off in a huff. It won't take long.
Have you forgotten when you were on fire
to be leader of the Danaan forces against Troy—
you pretended not to care but you wanted it, all right—
how humble you were, shaking hands with everybody,

340   keeping your doors open to whoever wanted to come in,
        and giving ear to all even if they had nothing to say?
        That was how you tried to bribe your way into office.
        Then when you had reached your goal, you changed;
        you were not much of a friend to your old friends,
345   but unavailable, aloof behind your bolted doors. A man—
        unless he's a villain—should not change his ways
        when he succeeds, but above all should be true to his friends,
        when he is able to benefit them with his own good fortune.
        I bring this up first because this is where I first found you base.
350   Then when you came to Aulis—you and the Panhellenic
            army—
        you were nothing! You were driven wild by your godsent luck,
        held up without a sailing wind. The Greeks were clamoring
        to dismiss the ships and not endure hardship at Aulis for
            nothing.
        You were downcast, miserable because you would not
355   be commander of a thousand ships and bring war to Priam's
            land.
        So you appealed to me: "What shall I do? What way out can I
            find?"
        to keep from being deprived of command and losing your
            renown.
        Then at the sacred rites Calchas told you to sacrifice your
            daughter
        to Artemis and the Greeks would be able to set sail; you were
            delighted
360   and gladly undertook to sacrifice the child. Of your own free
            will,
        not by force—you cannot say that—you told your wife to send
        your daughter here on the pretext of marrying her to Achilles.
        And now you've shifted and I've caught you altering your letter,
        claiming that you will not be your daughter's murderer. Fine:
365   but you know this is the same air that heard your words then.
        Thousands have had the same experience. They are eager
        to rise in the affairs of state but then give up the struggle,
        sometimes because the people are fickle, sometimes
        when they have become incapable of protecting the state.
370   It is unhappy Greece that I am most sorry for;
        we had the chance to do something memorable
        and, now, all because of you and your daughter,

we will let those worthless barbarians laugh at us.
I would never appoint a national leader or troop commander
for his bravado. Intelligence is what a general must have.
Any man can rule the state well if he has his wits about him.   375

CHORUS:
It is terrible when strife comes between brothers
and they fall into familial bickering.

AGAMEMNON:
You are my brother. I can be frank about your faults
but in perspective and without insolence.
A good man always shows respect to others.   380
Tell me, why are you red in the face with rage?
Who wrongs you? What do you need? You want a good wife?
I have none to give you. The one you had you managed
badly. Should I, who did not slip up, pay for your troubles?
My ambition does not rankle you, but you desire to hold   385
your pretty wife in your arms, even if it means throwing
sense and honor to the winds. Base pleasures belong to a bad
    man.
If I got it wrong before and have now changed for the better,
am I deluded? No, it's you. You lost an evil wife and want her
    back,
even though the gods have given you a lucky break.   390
The marriage-mad suitors who swore Tyndareos' oath
were out of their minds: Hope, I think, was what they prayed to,
and what made them do it, not you or your power—
take them, be commander. They are ready for any lunacy.
The mind of god works knowingly and understands
how a person can be entrapped into swearing an oath.   395
In any case I will not kill my child. Your cause will not prosper
at my expense so you can get back the world's worst wife,
while my nights and days will wear me away in tears
for acting against custom and right toward the children I
    fathered.
That, in brief, is what I have to say, clear and easy to   400
    understand.
If you will not be reasonable, I will still control my own affairs.

376–77: When the chorus speaks during an episode, the chorus leader
(*coryphaeus*) speaks alone, representing the group.

CHORUS:
These words are different from what he said,
but I like them better: to spare the children's lives.

MENELAUS:
I have no friends.

AGAMEMNON:
405   Yes, you do, except when you try to ruin them.

MENELAUS:
Will you show that you come from the same father as I?

AGAMEMNON:
I am happy to share in sane action with you, not to be sick
    with you.

MENELAUS:
Friends must share with friends in their suffering.

AGAMEMNON:
Ask my help when doing right, not when hurting me.

MENELAUS:
410   Do you intend to remove your support from the Greek cause?

AGAMEMNON:
Greece, like you, is plagued with a sickness from the gods.

MENELAUS:
Flaunt your scepter while you betray your brother.
I will look to other means wherever I can find them,
and other friends . . .

        (Enter Messenger stage left.)

MESSENGER 1:
                    Hail, king of all the Greeks,
415   Agamemnon, I have come to bring you your daughter,
the one you call Iphigenia in your home.
Her mother has come along, your wife Clytemnestra,

Enter Messenger: This messenger apparently has escorted the women from
Mycenae. They would need a driver and probably several attendants to
protect them on the journey. Many editors think this whole passage
(413–41) is spurious. If genuine, it is natural for him to believe the story
about the wedding.

and your son Orestes—she brought him so you can take
  pleasure
in seeing him after your long absence from home.
Since the journey has been long, they and their mares   420
are refreshing their tender feet beside a fresh spring.
We let the horses loose to graze on a grassy meadow.
I have come ahead to prepare you for their arrival.
The army knows all about it—a swift report passed   425
through their lips—that your daughter is in the camp.
The whole throng came running to see the girl—
everybody admires and celebrates the well-to-do.
They are wondering, "Is it a wedding, or what is going on?   430
Did King Agamemnon miss his daughter and bring her here?"
This is what you would have heard from others:
"Are they initiating the girl to Artemis,
queen of Aulis? Is she to be married?"
Come, then, let's begin the rites for the wedding: 435
crown your head, and you, King Menelaus, get ready
to sing the wedding song. All through the house
let's hear pipes playing and the rhythm of dancing feet.
This day will bring great happiness to your daughter.

AGAMEMNON:
  Thank you. Now go inside the house.   440
  Whatever comes next, it will be well.

    (Exit Messenger into the lodge.)

Oh misery, what can I say? Where to begin?
I have slipped into necessity's noose.
Fate has outsmarted me, proving to be
cleverer by far than my poor schemes.   445
Low birth would be an advantage.
They can weep and say what they wish.
But the highborn must stifle their feelings.
We use pride to guide our lives,
but we are slaves to the masses.   450
I am ashamed to shed tears
and in my misery I am ashamed not to.

433–34: Young Athenian girls were initiated as *arktoi* ("bears") to Artemis
at Brauron. This was one of the rituals that prepared girls for marriage.

I have come into the greatest tragedy of my life.
It comes to this. What will I say to my wife?
455   How will I welcome her? With what expression on my face?
On top of the miseries I already have, she has ruined me
by coming here uninvited. Of course it's right
for her as mother of the bride to accompany her daughter
and to perform for her those intimate acts.
Now she will find me out as a villain.
460   And the poor girl. What about the girl?
It's Hades that soon will take her as his bride.
How sorry I feel for her—she will beg me:
"Father, are you going to kill me? I wish you
and those you love would make a marriage like this."
465   And Orestes will be here wailing baby talk,
and even though he's still an infant, he'll understand.
Damn Helen's marriage—it has ruined me—
and Priam's son Paris, who is to blame for all this.

CHORUS:
I too feel pity. Even a stranger can weep
470   over the tragedies of the royal family.

MENELAUS:
Brother, give me your right hand to touch.

AGAMEMNON:
Here it is. You win, I give in.

MENELAUS:
By Pelops, my father's father and yours,
and by Atreus, my father, I swear
475   that I will speak straight from my heart
with nothing contrived, but just what I feel.
When I saw the tears welling up in your eyes
I felt pity and shed tears for you in my turn;
I now recant my earlier words
480   and no longer feel savage toward you.
I am where you are now. I don't want the sacrifice;
I won't put my own interest first. It is not right
for you to grieve and me to be happy,
for your child to die and mine to live.
485   Really, what do I want? Couldn't I take another

choice bride, if it's marriage I am after?
Will I ruin my brother, something I should never do,
to get Helen back, and take evil in exchange for good?
I was foolish and naive then. I took a hard look
and saw what killing your child would mean.   490
Pity came over me for the poor girl
who was to be sacrificed for my marriage,
and I remembered our common kinship.
What does your daughter have to do with Helen?
Let the army be disbanded and leave Aulis,   495
and you stop filling your eyes with tears,
brother—you are moving me to tears, too.
Whatever part you have in the oracles about the girl,
let me have no part. I yield to you.
I retract the cruel things I said to you.   500
I have undergone a change of heart and turned
to love for my own brother. This is not the way
of a bad man, always to practice what is best.

CHORUS:
Tantalus, son of Zeus, would be proud of what
you have said. You have not disgraced your forebears.   505

AGAMEMNON:
Thank you, Menelaus. I did not think it possible,
but you have laid out an argument worthy of you.
Strife between brothers comes about through resentment
and greed for a greater share. Such a kinship
is bitter to both sides and I despise it. But we have come   510
to a twist of fate that makes it inevitable
to carry out the bloody murder of my daughter.

MENELAUS:
What? Who will compel you to kill your child?

AGAMEMNON:
The whole assembled forces of the Greek army.

MENELAUS:
Not if you send them back to Argos.   515

AGAMEMNON:
I might escape here, but back there I haven't a chance.

MENELAUS:
Why? One should not be in such dread of the mob.

AGAMEMNON:
Calchas will proclaim his oracles to the whole army.

MENELAUS:
Not if you kill him first. That's easy enough.

AGAMEMNON:
520   Prophets, as a profession, are spiteful and ambitious.

MENELAUS:
Good for nothing and useless wherever they are.

AGAMEMNON:
Something occurs to me: aren't you worried?

MENELAUS:
How can I answer until you tell me what it is?

AGAMEMNON:
Sisyphus' spawn knows all about this.

MENELAUS:
525   There is no way Odysseus can hurt the two of us.

AGAMEMNON:
He has a versatile mind and the crowd is with him.

MENELAUS:
He is possessed by ambition, a subversive evil.

AGAMEMNON:
Don't you suppose he will stand up in their midst
and reveal the oracles Calchas proclaimed,
530   how I undertook to carry out the sacrifice
and then reneged? Will he not now seize control
of the army and order the Argives to kill me
and sacrifice the girl? Even if I flee to Argos,
they will come to the very Cyclopean walls,
535   occupy the city, and devastate the land.

520: Prophets and seers do not come off well in tragedy, especially in Euripides. In *Phoenician Women* (954–59), Tiresias himself, depicted as an old hypocrite, suggests that nobody but a fool would practice the seer's craft.

This is the turmoil I suffer in my misery.
What a dilemma I am in by the gods' will.
Take care of one thing, Menelaus—go through the army
and see that Clytemnestra does not find out about this
until I take the child and dispatch her to Hades.   540
That way I can suffer the worst with the least tears
possible. And you, women, keep this a secret.

*(Exit Menelaus stage right. Agamemnon exits into the
lodge.)*

First Stasimon

CHORUS:

[Strophe]

Happy are they
who enter the marriage bed
with virtue and modest love,   545
feeling the stillness
without the raging passions
to which golden-haired Eros
stretches a double bow of desires:
one for a happy fate,   550
one for life's ruin—
I shut it out of my chamber,
fairest Cypris.
May my love be moderate,
my desires pure.   555
May I share in Aphrodite's favors
but fend off her excesses.

[Antistrophe]

Different the natures of men,
different their ways. But the straight course
is always clear.   560
Upbringing that is trained
tends strongly to goodness:
to feel respect is wisdom
and holds a transforming grace,
by intelligence to look   565

into one's duty where repute brings
glory to life that does not grow old.
The hunt for goodness is a splendid thing:
for women it is hidden in love
570   but in men inherent order
will increase ten-thousand-fold
the city's grandeur.

[Epode]

Paris, you came back to where you were raised
as a herder among the white flocks
575   on Ida,
piping alien tunes,
blowing on the Phrygian flute variations
of the piper, Olympus.
Cows, their udders full, browsed nearby
when the judgment of the goddesses made you mad,
580   which dispatched you to Greece,
to the halls of ivory,
and there you stood with Helen's eyes
looking straight at you,
and you filled her with love;
585   with love you too were trembling.
From this, strife brings more strife:
an angry Greece with spears, with ships
comes against Troy's fortress.

Second Episode

*(Clytemnestra, Iphigenia, and extras arrive in a carriage
stage left.)*

CHORUS:
590   Oh, oh, great is the happiness
of the great. The king's daughter,
behold her. Iphigenia, my queen,
and Tyndareos' daughter Clytemnestra,
they are sprung from the mighty

577: Olympus, not to be confused with a mountain of the same name, was
a famous flutist of Phrygia and son of Marsyas, who was said to have invented the double flute.

and are lifted high in fortune. 595
The powerful and wealthy are gods
to those less than blessed.
Let us stand still, daughters of Chalcis,
and help our queen step from the chariot
onto the ground, not precariously 600
but with the gentle strength of our hands,
lest the glorious daughter of Agamemnon,
newly arrived, shy from us
or as strangers we cause alarm
to the Argive visitors. 605

CLYTEMNESTRA:
Your kind and gentle words are a happy omen.
I have a certain hope that I am here to attend
a noble marriage. Help me lift down the things 610
I have brought for my daughter's dowry
and remove them carefully into the house.
And you, my child, leave the carriage.
Set down your tender, elegant feet,
and girls, you take her in your arms 615
and help her out of the conveyance,
and someone give me a steadying hand
so I too can climb down gracefully.
Somebody, stand in front of the harnessed horses;
their eyes shy at anything unfamiliar. 620
This child, Orestes, Agamemnon's son,
take him in your arms. He's just a baby. Little one,
are you asleep, tired out by the horses' gait?
Wake up to celebrate your sister's wedding.
My little prince, your sister is marrying 625
a prince, the godlike son of Nereus' daughter.
Now, dear daughter, stand here by me, Iphigenia,
next to your mother, and show these women
what a fortunate woman I am, with you by my side.
Here he comes—speak to your dear father. 630

(Enter Agamemnon from the lodge.)

IPHIGENIA:
Oh, Mother, don't be angry with me if I run
from your side and throw my arms around Father.

CLYTEMNESTRA:
　　My great pride, King Agamemnon,
　　we are here obedient to your command.

IPHIGENIA:
635　　[And I wish, Father, to run and throw my arms
　　around you after so long a time apart.]
　　I long to see your face. Don't be angry with me.

CLYTEMNESTRA:
　　Of course, my dear, it's only right. Of all my children
　　you have always been the one who loves your father most.

IPHIGENIA:
640　　Oh Father, I am happy to see you after so long.

AGAMEMNON:
　　And I you. We are both of the same mind about that.

IPHIGENIA:
　　Cheer up. It was a good idea to bring me to you, Father.

AGAMEMNON:
　　I don't know what to say, whether to agree or not.

IPHIGENIA:
　　Ah!
　　You look so anxious. A minute ago you were glad to see me.

AGAMEMNON:
645　　As king and commander, I have a great many concerns.

IPHIGENIA:
　　Be with *me* now and put aside your worries.

AGAMEMNON:
　　Right now I am all yours and nowhere else.

IPHIGENIA:
　　Don't scowl so—turn your face to look at me lovingly.

AGAMEMNON:
　　There. I'm as happy as I can be, seeing you, dear.

_639:_ See Euripides' _Electra_, 1102–4, on Electra's preference for her father
over her mother.

IPHIGENIA:
But there are tears welling up in your eyes.   650

AGAMEMNON:
We will be apart for a very long time.

IPHIGENIA:
I don't understand, Father dear, really I don't.

AGAMEMNON:
When you make sense, you make me sadder.

IPHIGENIA:
Then I'll make nonsense if that will cheer you up.

AGAMEMNON:
Oh god! I cannot bear to hold back. You're a good girl.   655

IPHIGENIA:
Stay home, Father, stay with your children.

AGAMEMNON:
I wish I could. It hurts me that I cannot even wish it.

IPHIGENIA:
This war and Menelaus' woes—I wish they would all go away.

AGAMEMNON:
Others will go first, just as I must go away soon.

IPHIGENIA:
You have been away a long time, here in the bay of Aulis.   660

AGAMEMNON:
Even now we are prevented from deploying.

IPHIGENIA:
Where is it that these Phrygians live, Father?

AGAMEMNON:
Where Paris is from, and I wish to god he had never been born.

657: "I cannot even wish it."—Editors are uncomfortable with this expression, but given Agamemnon's inconsistencies and his simultaneous wish
to be general and to disband the army and not to have made his final decision, it makes sense (see Gurd 2005, p. 70). An alternative suggestion would
read, "It hurts me to think of what cannot be."

IPHIGENIA:
You are going far away, Father, when you leave me.

AGAMEMNON:
665   Your plight is the same as your father's.

IPHIGENIA:
Ooh.
If only there were some way I could sail with you.

AGAMEMNON:
You are going on a trip, too; you will forget your father
there.

IPHIGENIA:
Will I go alone or with my mother?

AGAMEMNON:
All alone without your father and mother.

IPHIGENIA:
670   Father, are you sending me to live in another home?

AGAMEMNON:
Enough of this! Girls should not know these things.

IPHIGENIA:
Hurry back from Troy, Father, after you fix things there.

AGAMEMNON:
There is a sacrifice I have to make here first.

IPHIGENIA:
Religious ceremonies—aren't they the priests' business?

AGAMEMNON:
675   You will be there. You will stand by the holy water.

IPHIGENIA:
Will we stand by the altar in a chorus, Father?

AGAMEMNON:
I envy you for not knowing all that I know.
Go inside. Girls should keep out of sight.
Kiss my cheek and give me your hand
680   since for a long time you are going to live far away.
Oh breast and cheeks, oh yellow hair,

what a burden to you the Phrygians' city
and Helen have proven—I must stop this talk.
A tear is welling up in my eye when I hold you.
Go on inside.

(Exit Iphigenia into the lodge.)

       Daughter of Leda, I ask   685
your pardon if I have shown too much feeling
on the eve of giving my daughter to Achilles.
The girl's departure is a happy occasion, but still
it grieves parents when, after all their toil,
they send their children to another man's home.   690

CLYTEMNESTRA:
I am not so insensitive—you should realize
that I feel just the same, so I can't scold you—
when I prepare my daughter for marriage.
But in time custom will diminish our sense of loss.
I know the name of the man to whom you promised   695
our daughter, but I'd like to learn more about his family.

AGAMEMNON:
It starts with Asōpus, who had a daughter Aegina.

CLYTEMNESTRA:
Was her husband one of the gods or a mortal?

AGAMEMNON:
By Zeus she gave birth to Aeacus, headman of Oenone.

CLYTEMNESTRA:
What son of Aeacus came to inherit his house?   700

AGAMEMNON:
Peleus, who married Thetis, daughter of Nereus.

CLYTEMNESTRA:
With the gods' blessing or did he take her by force?

697: Asōpus was a river god. His daughter Aegina was abducted by Zeus. She later married a man named Actor and they had a son Menoetius who later became the father of Achilles' comrade Patroclus.
699: Oenone—the island that came to be called Aegina.

AGAMEMNON:
  Zeus as her guardian betrothed and gave her in marriage.

CLYTEMNESTRA:
  Where did they marry? Beneath the sea's surge?

AGAMEMNON:
705   Where Chiron lives in the sacred dells of Pelion.

CLYTEMNESTRA:
  Where the race of Centaurs is said to dwell?

AGAMEMNON:
  Yes, the gods held the wedding feast of Peleus there.

CLYTEMNESTRA:
  Did Thetis or his father bring up Achilles?

AGAMEMNON:
  Chiron raised him so he would not learn the ways of wicked
    men.

CLYTEMNESTRA:
  Ah.
710   A wise teacher and even wiser those who engaged him.

AGAMEMNON:
  This is the man who will be your daughter's husband.

CLYTEMNESTRA:
  Not to be ashamed of. What Greek city does he live in?

AGAMEMNON:
  Near the river Apidanus, in Phthian territory.

CLYTEMNESTRA:
  Will he take my daughter to live there?

703: In some legends Thetis was brought up by Hera, and out of affection
for her foster mother she rejected the advances of Zeus. In another well-
known story Zeus was warned that any son Thetis bore would be greater
than his father, a prediction particularly troubling to the king of the gods.
He therefore took care to marry her off to a mortal.

705: Pelion—a mountain in Thessaly.

707: For the wedding of Peleus and Thetis, see the third stasimon (1036–
79).

AGAMEMNON:
  That will be his decision once they are married.   715

CLYTEMNESTRA:
  May the gods bless them. What day is the wedding?

AGAMEMNON:
  When the moon is full, an omen of good luck.

CLYTEMNESTRA:
  Have you sacrificed first offerings for your child?

AGAMEMNON:
  I am about to. We are busy with this affair.

CLYTEMNESTRA:
  And then you will feast the marriage the next day?   720

AGAMEMNON:
  After I have made the requisite sacrifice to the gods.

CLYTEMNESTRA:
  Where will we arrange the women's celebration?

AGAMEMNON:
  Here beside the well-built ships of the Argives.

CLYTEMNESTRA:
  You make a virtue of necessity. I pray all goes well.

AGAMEMNON:
  You know, wife, what you should do? Listen to me.   725

CLYTEMNESTRA:
  What is it? It is my custom always to listen to you.

AGAMEMNON:
  It is our job, here where the intended husband is—

CLYTEMNESTRA:
  What do you intend? To usurp my place as mother?

AGAMEMNON:
  To give away your child in the presence of the
    Danaans.

CLYTEMNESTRA:
  Where am I supposed to be at this time?   730

AGAMEMNON:

Go home to Argos and tend to your other daughters.

CLYTEMNESTRA:

And leave my child? Who will hold the wedding torch?

AGAMEMNON:

I will provide the flame that is fitting for her wedding.

CLYTEMNESTRA:

This is not our custom. It should not be treated so lightly.

AGAMEMNON:

735   It is not proper for you to mingle with this mob of armed
men.

CLYTEMNESTRA:

It is proper that as her mother I give my child in marriage.

AGAMEMNON:

It is proper that your girls not be left alone at home.

CLYTEMNESTRA:

They are well protected, guarded in their chambers.

AGAMEMNON:

Obey me.

CLYTEMNESTRA:

          No, in the name of the goddess queen of Argos.
You go. Take care of arrangements outside the house.
740   Inside, it is my job to tend to whatever is fitting
for a young woman getting married.

(Exit Clytemnestra into the lodge.)

AGAMEMNON:

Ah me. I have spent my effort but been thwarted
in my hope, trying to remove my wife from my sight.
I am plotting against those nearest and dearest to me
745   and looking for stratagems, but I am defeated on all fronts.
Still I will go meet with the seer Calchas
to track down what the goddess desires,
unlucky for me and the bane of Greece.

739: The Argive goddess is Hera, also guardian of marriage.

A wise man should keep in his home
a useful and good wife or not keep one at all.   750

(Exit Agamemnon stage right.)

Second Stasimon

CHORUS:

[Strophe]

It is coming to Simois,
to the river's silver-gleaming eddies—
the assemblage of the army of Greeks
on ships, with arms—
to Ilium,
to Apollo's plain at Troy,   755
where I hear Cassandra
shakes her golden locks
entwined with the glossy-leaved green
laurel when the god breathes on her   760
the prophetic compulsion.

[Antistrophe]

They will stand on the towers
and around the walls of Troy,
Trojan men, when with the rowing of well-built ships,
from across the sea, shielded in bronze,   765
Ares, war god, approaches
the channels of Simois
desiring to claim her back from Priam—
Helen, sister of the twin sons of Zeus in the sky—   770

751: Along with the Scamander, the Simois was the major river of Troy.

755: "Apollo's plain"—in Greek *Phoebian*, so called because Phoebus Apollo and Poseidon built the walls of Troy.

756: Cassandra—the doomed prophetess of Troy who foresaw her own and her city's disaster but was destined not to be believed. She was dedicated to Phoebus Apollo as his priestess and seer.

770: The twin sons of Zeus are the Dioscuri, Castor and Polydeuces, brothers of Helen and Clytemnestra, who became stars in the constellation Gemini.

take her back to the land of Greece
won by the war-wearying spears
and shields of the Achaeans.

[Epode]

As it circles Pergamon, the Phrygian city,
around the stone walls,
775 with murderous Ares
tearing the severed heads,
destroying the citadel of Troy
down from its heights,
it will make Priam's daughters
780 and the wife of Priam weep many tears;
Zeus' daughter Helen too
will sit shedding floods of tears
because she left her husband.
To my children and their children
785 may this expectation never come!
The Lydian and Phrygian wives
rich in gold
will stand by their looms
saying to each other,
790 "Who will stretch out his arm to drag me away
in tears by my beautiful hair?
Who will take me as spoils of war
when my homeland lies in ruins?"
Because of you, daughter of the long-necked swan,
795 if the story is true
that Leda really lay with a winged creature
when Zeus was metamorphosed,
or if in the musings of poets
the myths handed these things down
800 to mankind off the mark in vain.

794–97: Helen and Polydeuces are the children of Zeus from when he came
to Leda in the guise of a swan. Clytemnestra and Castor were fathered by
Tyndareos.
798: "The musings of poets"—in Greek, "the Pierian tablets," that is, the
writings of the poets, inspired by the Muses of Pieria.

Third Episode

(Enter Achilles stage right.)

ACHILLES:
Where is the commander of the Achaeans?
Will one of you servants tell him that Peleus' son,
Achilles, is looking for him here at his gate?
Listen to me: not all of us linger here equally   805
on the banks of Euripus; some of us, not yet married,
have left our homes empty to come here
and sit idle on the beach; others, though married,
are childless. Some god has sent this fierce passion
for military adventure to afflict the Greeks.
Like anyone else who wants to speak for himself   810
I have the right to voice my grievance.
After leaving the land of Pharsalus and Peleus
I tarry here because of the light breezes of Euripus,
trying to restrain my Myrmidons. They keep pressing me:
"Achilles, what are we waiting for? How long a time   815
must we fritter away before the fleet heads for Troy?
Do something if you are going to, or lead the army home.
Stop putting up with the delays of the sons of Atreus."

(Enter Clytemnestra from the lodge.)

CLYTEMNESTRA:
Hello, son of the sea goddess, wait. From inside the lodging
I heard what you had to say and have come out to meet you.   820

ACHILLES:
I am struck with awe! Who is this woman I see,
in every way most stunningly beautiful to my eyes?

CLYTEMNESTRA:
No wonder you don't recognize me. We have never met
before. I appreciate your respect for modesty.

ACHILLES:
But who are you? Why have you come into the Greek army,   825
a woman surrounded by armed and dangerous men?

803: This line suggests that there are attendants at the general's head-
quarters, or perhaps he comes with a small entourage of his own.

CLYTEMNESTRA:
    I am Leda's daughter. Clytemnestra
    is my name. King Agamemnon is my husband.

ACHILLES:
    All your words are well said and to the point,
830   but I am not used to conversing with women.

CLYTEMNESTRA:
    Wait. Don't run off. Join your right hand
    in mine, as a blessing to begin the marriage.

ACHILLES:
    What are you saying? Take your hand?! I would shame
    Agamemnon if I were to touch another man's woman.

CLYTEMNESTRA:
835   Of course you may, son of Thetis, the sea goddess,
    Nereus' daughter. You are going to marry my daughter.

ACHILLES:
    What marriage are you talking about? Madam,
    I'm at a loss for words. You must be deluded.

CLYTEMNESTRA:
    This happens to everyone—you feel awkward
840   with new in-laws when your marriage is brought up.

ACHILLES:
    Madam, I never courted your daughter; no word
    about a marriage has come to me from Atreus' sons.

CLYTEMNESTRA:
    What can it mean? You may well wonder at my words
    once again. Yours are quite bewildering to me, too.

ACHILLES:
845   In a situation like this a person can only make a guess.
    Perhaps we have both been victims of a deception.

CLYTEMNESTRA:
    Am I the victim of abuse? I have been soliciting
    a marriage that does not exist. I am so embarrassed.

ACHILLES:
    Someone must be playing tricks on the two of us.
850   But don't pay it any mind. Make nothing of it.

CLYTEMNESTRA:
Good-bye. I can never look you in the face again,
now that I am turned into a liar and put to shame.

ACHILLES:
I have the same to say to you. But it's your husband—
I have come to the house looking for your husband.

(Old Man peers out of the lodge door.)

OLD MAN:
Stranger, wait. Grandson of Aeacus, I mean you,   855
son of the goddess; you too, daughter of Leda.

ACHILLES:
Who are you, peeking out the door and calling anxiously?

OLD MAN:
I'm a slave. My fortune doesn't let me be delicate about it.

ACHILLES:
Not mine. What's mine and what's Agamemnon's are different.

OLD MAN:
I'm from her house. Her father Tyndareos gave me to her.   860

ACHILLES:
Well, we are waiting. Tell us why you are holding us back.

OLD MAN:
Are you two the only ones out there in front of the door?

ACHILLES:
Yes, it's just us. No need for you to hover inside.

OLD MAN:
I pray that Luck and Foresight come to your aid.

ACHILLES:
What you say sounds ominous for our future.   865

CLYTEMNESTRA:
Please, do not delay if you have something to tell me.

OLD MAN:
You know me. I am loyal to you and your children.

CLYTEMNESTRA:
Yes, I know you. You are an old slave of my house.

OLD MAN:
> And King Agamemnon took me as part of your dowry.

CLYTEMNESTRA:
870
> You came to Argos with me and were always mine.

OLD MAN:
> That is so. I am loyal to you but less so to your husband.

CLYTEMNESTRA:
> Disclose now whatever news you have to tell us.

OLD MAN:
> Your daughter—her father is planning to kill her.

CLYTEMNESTRA:
> What? Old man, I don't believe you. It can't be right.

OLD MAN:
875
> He plans to cut the poor girl's pale throat with a sword.

CLYTEMNESTRA:
> Oh my god, it can't be! Has my husband gone mad?

OLD MAN:
> Yes, though he is sane enough except toward you and the girl.

CLYTEMNESTRA:
> What is his reason? What demon of revenge is driving him to it?

OLD MAN:
> Oracles. At least the seer Calchas says so—to let the army go forward.

CLYTEMNESTRA:
880
> Go forward? I am devastated if her father is going to kill her.

OLD MAN:
> Yes, to the Trojans' city, so Menelaus can get Helen back.

CLYTEMNESTRA:
> Iphigenia's life is the price for the return of Helen?

OLD MAN:
> That's it. Her father is going to sacrifice her to Artemis.

CLYTEMNESTRA:
> What about the marriage he used to lure me from home?

OLD MAN:
That was so you would be glad to bring her as Achilles' bride.   885

CLYTEMNESTRA:
My daughter, you have come here to your death—you and your
mother.

OLD MAN:
You both suffer pitifully. Agamemnon has done something
awful.

CLYTEMNESTRA:
I am devastated. I can no longer hold back my tears.

OLD MAN:
To lose a child is tragic. You have reason to weep.

CLYTEMNESTRA:
But, Old Man, how is it that you learned these things?   890

OLD MAN:
I was sent to carry a letter about what had been written
before.

CLYTEMNESTRA:
Forbidding or ordering me to bring the child to be killed?

OLD MAN:
Telling you not to bring her, when your husband was in his
right mind.

CLYTEMNESTRA:
How did it happen that you did not give me the letter?

OLD MAN:
Menelaus, the cause of all our woes, tore it from my hands.   895

CLYTEMNESTRA:
In the name of your mother and father, do you hear this?

ACHILLES:
I do hear your troubles and am upset over my part in them.

CLYTEMNESTRA:
They will kill my child after tricking her with marriage to you.

ACHILLES:
Your husband is to blame and I cannot swallow this lightly.

CLYTEMNESTRA:

900   Modesty will not keep me from falling at your knees,
       a mortal before a goddess' son. What pride have I left?
       Who do I have to care about more than my own child?
       For your mother's sake, please help me, in my helplessness,
       and your wife, as she was called, in vain—but still
905   I put a crown on her head and brought her here to be married
       and now am leading her to slaughter. It will be your shame
       if you do not help. Even if you were not joined in marriage
       you were called dear husband of the tragic maiden.
       By your beard, by your right hand, by your mother, I
910   beg you: your name, instead of being a support to us,
       has ruined me. I have no altar to fly to except your knees.
       There's no friend who smiles on me. You hear what cruel and
            vile
       things Agamemnon does. I have come, as you see, a woman,
       to the military camp, into an unruly mob, ready for mischief
915   but effective to help if they want. If you dare to raise your hand
       to protect us, we are saved, but if not we are surely lost.

CHORUS:

       To give birth is terrifying; still, it has a powerful pull—
       all mortals share in toiling tirelessly for their children.

ACHILLES:

       My spirit rises up with indignation
920   [though it knows how to restrain itself in disaster
       and in prosperity to moderate its exultation.
       Among mortals, men like this have figured out
       how to pass their lives with principle and good sense.
       There is a time when it is pleasant not to reason too much
925   and another when it is useful to have understanding.
       Reared in the home of Chiron, a most respectful man,
       I have learned to have uncomplicated ways.]
       As for Atreus' sons, if they show good leadership

920–27: These might be the sorts of things he learned at Chiron's knee, but
many editors and readers find them too disjointed even for the old-fashioned
and somewhat sententious Achilles of this play. England (1891/1979, at
920–27) calls them "an ill-joined patchwork of 4 *detached couplets*."
928–29: The audience would remember the quarrel between Achilles and
Agamemnon that opens Homer's *Iliad*.

I will obey them, but when they do not, I will not.
Here and in Troy I present myself as a free agent: 930
I will honor Ares with my spear as best I can.
You have suffered abuse from those dearest to you:
as far as youth allows me I shall set things right,
covering myself in compassion as in my armor.
Your daughter was called my wife—she will never   935
be slaughtered by her father. Your husband has
no right to weave his plots on me or what is mine.
It is my name, even if it does not raise the sword,
that will be your daughter's murderer. The blame
belongs to your husband. But my body is no longer clean   940
if through me and marriage to me, the girl,
who has suffered terrible, unendurable things,
will be killed and dishonored so shamelessly.
I would be the worst man of all the Argives.
I would be nothing and Menelaus would count as a man,   945
as if I were the son not of Peleus but of some demon,
if my name commits murder for your husband.
By Nereus, nurtured in the waves of the sea,
father of Thetis, who gave me birth,
Agamemnon the king will not touch your daughter,   950
not as far as to lay the tip of his finger on her dress.
Truly Sipylus, fortress of barbarians,
the land of our generals' birth, will be a city,
but the name of Phthia will be wiped off the earth.   955
To his cost Calchas the seer will begin the ritual
with sacrificial cakes and purifying waters.
What man is really a seer who tells a few things right
and gets everything else wrong? When he fails he is useless.
It is not for the sake of the marriage that I say this.
Thousands of girls are pursuing me for marriage.   960
Not that, but King Agamemnon has insulted me.
He should have asked me for the use of my name
as a bait for the girl. Clytemnestra certainly

952: Mount Sipylus (modern Spil) is in the Lydian region near the Aegean
coast of what is now Turkey. Niobe's rock, looking like a weeping woman,
is still visible. This was the ancestral home of Tantalus, father of Niobe and
her brother Pelops, for whom the Peloponnesus is named. Pelops was the
father of Atreus.

would have been persuaded to give her daughter to me.
965   I would have given my name for Greece if the passage
to Troy was held up by this. I would not have refused
to enhance the common good of my fellow soldiers.
But now I am nothing to the military commanders.
It's a matter of indifference to them if I succeed or not.
970   My sword will soon know—before we even go to Troy—
I will stain it with blood, the color of death,
if anyone deprives me of your daughter.
[Now, allay your fears. I am not a god, but to you
I have appeared as if a great god and so I will be.]

CHORUS:
975   What you have said, son of Peleus, is worthy of you
and of your mother, the sea goddess, revered divinity.

CLYTEMNESTRA:
Ah.
What words can I use to praise you without excess
and still not lose your favor through a shortage of praise?
When good people are praised, they often
980   hate their praisers if they praise too much.
I feel ashamed appealing to your pity, when I am
in distress, since my problems are not your concern.
But, you know, a good man, even if he is unaffected
by their ills, appears noble helping the unfortunate.
985   Pity us. What we have suffered deserves your pity:
first I believed you were to be my son-in-law
and pressed an empty hope. And then, it could happen,
if my child dies she might become an evil omen—
something to be aware of—for a future marriage of yours.
990   Your words are reassuring from start to finish.
If you are so minded my daughter will be saved.
Do you want her to clasp your knees in supplication?
This is unbecoming a young girl, but if you wish
she will come out, keeping her face veiled in modesty.
995   If without her presence I can achieve the same results,

---

959–74: These lines are considered by many critics to be inconsistent with
Achilles' character as portrayed so far; 973–74 are especially disturbing because they seem irrelevant.

let her stay inside the house and protect her modesty.
We must respect decorum as best we can.

ACHILLES:
Do not bring your child into my sight, madam.
We must avoid reproach from the ignorant.
The troops are away from home with nothing to do: 1000
they are subject to shabby and malicious rumors.
All in all, whether or not you supplicate me
it will come to the same: I am facing one contest,
the most serious I have ever faced: to save you from disaster.
I have given my word: you can be sure that I tell   1005
you no lies. If I speak falsely and my words
prove vain, let me die, but not if I can save the girl.

CLYTEMNESTRA:
God bless you for helping the unfortunate.

ACHILLES:
Listen now so the affair will come to a good end.

CLYTEMNESTRA:
No need to tell me; I have no one but you.   1010

ACHILLES:
Let's first try to persuade her father to think better of it.

CLYTEMNESTRA:
He is a coward and lives in fear of the army.

ACHILLES:
Words can sometimes wrestle weaker words and defeat them.

CLYTEMNESTRA:
My hope grows cold. But tell me what I must do.

ACHILLES:
First beseech him not to kill the girl.   1015
If he resists, then you must come to me.
If he agrees to do what you desire, there is no need

997: Clytemnestra's respect for propriety is evident throughout and perhaps is explained by her early history as Agamemnon's abused wife (see 1146–1205).

for my intervention. That will bring you safety
and I will stand in better stead with my friends,
1020   and the army will not blame me if I act with reason
rather than brute force. If things work out well,
all the better for my allies and for you,
even if you have no need of my support.

CLYTEMNESTRA:
What you say makes sense. It must be done your way.
1025   However, if we do not succeed as we hope,
where will we see you again? Where must I go
in my misery to find your hand to protect us from ills?

ACHILLES:
We will keep a lookout for you in case there is need
so no one will see you in a frenzy rushing
1030   through the mob of Greek men. Do not disgrace
your father's home. Tyndareos does not deserve
bad repute—he is a great man throughout Greece.

CLYTEMNESTRA:
Yes, I'll do that. I'm yours to command. I must be your slave.
You are a good man and if gods exist, fortune
1035   will favor you, but if not, what is the point?

*(Exit Achilles stage right. Exit Clytemnestra and Old Man
into the lodge.)*

Third Stasimon

CHORUS:

[Strophe]

What wedding song raised its cry
to the Libyan pipe
and dance-loving lyre
and beneath the reedy panpipes,
1040   when up Pelion
to the feast of the gods,
the fair-haired Muses
beating on the ground
their gold-sandaled footsteps,
1045   came to the wedding of Peleus

with tuneful sounds celebrating
Thetis and Aeacus' son
on the Centaurs' hillsides
through the woods of Pelion.
Dardanus' son, beloved luxury
of Zeus' bed,   1050
poured drinks
into the wine craters' golden bowls,
a Trojan named Ganymede.
Along the white sands
whirling in circles,   1055
the fifty daughters of Nereus
danced at the wedding.

[Antistrophe]

Up through the pines and crowns of greenery
came the sacred horse band of Centaurs
to the gods' feast   1060
and the wine craters of Bacchus.
A great cry went up, "O daughter of Nereus,
the seer Chiron, inspired by the prophetic muse,
promised that you would bear a child,   1065
a great light to Thessaly,
who will come to the land
with Myrmidons, spear and shield in hand,
to burn famous Troy, Priam's city."   1070
Around his body he is covered
and helmeted
by golden armor
Hephaestus-made
gifts from his goddess
mother Thetis.   1075
Then the gods blessed
the marriage of the well-begotten
daughter of Nereus
of the sea and her wedding to Peleus.

[Epode]

But you, girl, the Argives will crown   1080
your beautiful hair like a spotted heifer

coming unblemished
from the rocky caves in the mountains,
making your mortal throat stream blood;
1085   you were not raised to the panpipe
nor with the whistling of herdsmen
but beside your mother
as a bride for your wedding to an Argive.
Where does the face of modesty
1090   or goodness prevail?
Godlessness holds sway now;
goodness is cast aside by mortal men;
lawlessness tramps down the laws;
there is no effort common among men
1095   to avoid the gods' envy.

Exodos

(Enter Clytemnestra from the lodge.)

CLYTEMNESTRA:
I have come outside to look for my husband,
who has been away for a long time.
1100   My poor girl is in tears, crying her eyes out
ever since she learned her father is planning to kill her.
I am speaking of Agamemnon, and here he is, coming
1105   this way. Now he will be caught out abusing his child.

(Enter Agamemnon stage right.)

AGAMEMNON:
Daughter of Leda, it's a good thing I find you outside
the house so I can speak to you without our daughter
hearing things a girl should not hear before her marriage.

CLYTEMNESTRA:
What is it that makes it so convenient to you?

AGAMEMNON:
1110   I want you to send the child out with her father.
The lustral waters are prepared with the sacrificial
      grain
to throw into the cleansing flame, and the heifers
that are to be slaughtered before the wedding
are ready to shed their black blood to Artemis.

CLYTEMNESTRA:

Your words sound fine, but what you are doing? 1115
I do not know how I could say you speak well.
Come outside, my daughter. You know what
your father intends to do. Bring your baby brother
Orestes, wrapped in your robe, my child.
Look, here she is, obedient to you. 1120
The rest I will speak for her and myself.

(Enter Iphigenia, carrying Orestes, from the lodge.)

AGAMEMNON:

Why are you crying, dear? Aren't you glad to see me any more?
Why are you downcast now? Why hide your face in your robe?

CLYTEMNESTRA:

Ah. Where should I start my list of woes?
I could put them all in first place 1125
and all last and anywhere in the middle, too.

AGAMEMNON:

What is it? Why are you both so upset?
I can see it in your troubled expressions.

CLYTEMNESTRA:

Answer me honestly, husband, whatever I ask.

AGAMEMNON:

No need to ask that. I'm ready to be questioned. 1130

CLYTEMNESTRA:

Are you planning to kill your daughter—my daughter?

AGAMEMNON:

Ah! Ugly talk! You have a suspicious mind.

CLYTEMNESTRA:

No more evasions. First answer what I asked.

AGAMEMNON:

If you ask a reasonable question, I'll answer reasonably.

CLYTEMNESTRA:

I have nothing else to ask. Don't you evade the question. 1135

AGAMEMNON:

Fate rules our lives. My luck has turned sour.

CLYTEMNESTRA:
Mine and hers, too. We are all three unlucky.

AGAMEMNON:
Have I done anything that has wronged you?

CLYTEMNESTRA:
You ask me that? You have no feelings.

AGAMEMNON:
1140   I am ruined. My secrets have been betrayed.

CLYTEMNESTRA:
I know everything. I have found out what you are planning
to do to us. Your silence and your self-pity
are your confession. Don't bother to say any more.

AGAMEMNON:
Here, then, I am silent. Why tell any more lies
1145   and add brazen impudence to my misery?

CLYTEMNESTRA:
Listen while I tell my story. I will use
no more distorting riddles and half-truths.
First, then, I will revile you with my first wrongs:
against my will you married me—took me by force,
1150   after killing Tantalus, my former husband,
and tearing my infant son from my breast,
you smashed him on the ground with violent hands,
and the sons of Zeus, my two brothers,
on horseback, weapons flashing, made war on you.
1155   Then Tyndareos, my aged father, saved you
when you came as suppliant and you took me to your bed.
So I was reconciled to you and your house.
You will bear witness that I was a perfect wife,
modest in my love and increasing your house
1160   so that when you were home you were happy
and outside your home you were prosperous.
It's a rare catch for a man to get a wife like that,
though there's no shortage of worthless women.
I bore you this son besides our three daughters.
1165   Now you are about to rob me of one of them.
If anyone asks why you are going to kill her,
what will you say? Must I answer for you?

To recover Helen for Menelaus. A fair price
you will pay in trading your child for an evil woman.
We will buy what is most loathed for the life of our dear girl.   1170
Tell me this: if you go away, leaving me at home
while you remain over there, through your long absence,
what feelings do you think I will nurse in my heart
when I see chairs all through the house empty of her
and the girls' rooms empty? I will sit always alone   1175
in tears, missing her: "Your father killed you, my child,
your own father, himself, no one else, no other's hand;
this is what he left behind for the house to revenge."
It will need only a little pretext for me   1180
and my surviving daughters to welcome you
home the way you deserve to be taken back.
Please, do not, in the gods' name, do not force me
to be evil toward you, and do not be evil yourself.
Is this, then, how it will be? You will sacrifice our child.   1185
What prayers will you say as you cut her throat?
What good will you pray for when you kill your child?
A homecoming as deadly as when you set out from home?
Is it right for me to pray for anything good for you?
Wouldn't we be saying the gods are stupid
if we treat murderers like everyone else? When you come   1190
home to Argos will you embrace your children one by one?
That would be wrong. Will any of your children
even look at you, when you have killed one of them?
Did you reason it out and come to this conclusion, or do only
your scepter and command mean anything to you?   1195
You should have argued logically with the Argives,
"Achaeans, do you wish to sail to the Phrygians' land?
Leave it to chance. Cast lots to see whose daughter must die."
That would be fair, but not to offer your own daughter
as the victim for the Greeks, chosen by her own father.   1200
Or let Menelaus kill Hermione in return for her mother,
who has a stake in this. I have preserved intact
my marriage to you and will be deprived of my daughter.

1182: In Aeschylus' *Agamemnon* (1107–35), the returning king and commander is enticed into his home and killed by his wife in his bath. In Homer
(*Odyssey* 4.534–35; 11.410–11), he is welcomed with a banquet where he
is killed by Aegisthus, Clytemnestra's lover.

1205
But she who transgressed will take her daughter
back to Sparta and live a happy life there.
Answer me if I have gotten any of this wrong.
But if my words ring true, do not kill our daughter,
yours and mine. That would show you to be wise and good.

CHORUS:
Listen to her. It is good to have a part in saving the child,
1210
Agamemnon; there's no one who would contradict this.

IPHIGENIA:
If I had the speech of Orpheus, Father,
and by singing could persuade the rocks to follow me
and charm anyone I wished with my words,
then I would resort to that, but now I will offer
1215
the only wisdom I have—my tears. That is all I can do.
As your suppliant I hold onto your knees
with my body, which my mother bore to you.
Do not kill me before my time. For the light is sweet
to see; do not force me to look at the dark down there.
1220
I was the first to call you father, you to call me child.
I first sat on your knees and we exchanged
sweet gestures of affection. This is what
you would say to me: "Will I see you,
dear sweet child, happy in your husband's home,
1225
living in prosperity that will do me credit?"
And in reply this is what I said, holding onto
your beard, which now again I grasp in my hand:
"How will it be between us? Will I welcome you
in your old age with loving hospitality to my home,
1230
Father, repaying your devoted nurture in my youth?"
I still keep these words in my memory,
but you have forgotten them and want to kill me.
Do not, by Pelops and by your father Atreus, I beg you,
and by my mother here, who bore the pangs of labor
1235
and now bears these second pangs for me. Do not kill me.
What have I to do with the marriage of Paris
and Helen? Why is Paris to be my death, Father?
Look at me. Give me just a glance and a kiss
so I will have this memory of you when I die,
1240
if you will not be convinced by my words.

Brother, you are so little to be my helper
but still join me in tears; beseech your father
not to make your sister die. Even babies have
feeling for the misfortunes of those they love.
Look, Father, he begs you by his very silence.   1245
Respect me and take pity on my short life.
By your beard, we two loving children beg you,
the one a nestling, the other full grown.
Speaking one brief argument I shall defeat them all;
the light here is sweetest for men to see, all that comes   1250
after is nothing. It is mad to pray for death.
To live badly is better than honorably to die.

CHORUS:
   Wretched Helen, because of you and your marriage
   a great struggle looms for Atreus' sons and their children.

AGAMEMNON:
   I am aware of what is to be pitied and what is not,   1255
   and I do love my children. I am not a madman.
   It is terrible for me to do these things, woman,
   and terrible not to—yet still I must do it.
   You see the size of this seafaring army,
   how many Greek commanders, armed in bronze,   1260
   who will be unable to cross to Troy's stronghold
   if I do not sacrifice you, as the seer ordains,
   nor lay low the city's famous foundations.
   Some passion has maddened the army of the Greeks
   to sail with all speed against the barbarians' land   1265
   and to put a stop to the rape of Greek men's wives.
   They will come to Argos and kill my girls
   and you and me, if I break the goddess' commands.
   It is not Menelaus who has enslaved me, my child.
   I have not come here in pursuit of his wishes,   1270
   but it is Greece for whom I must sacrifice you,
   whether I want to or not. We are no match for this.
   My dear child, Greece must be free, as far as in you lies,
   and in me. As Greeks we must not let our women
   be plundered from their homes by force of foreign arms.   1275

   (Exit Agamemnon stage right.)

CLYTEMNESTRA:
> My child, and you, stranger women,
> ah me, for my grief at your death,
> your father is gone—he has abandoned you to die.

IPHIGENIA:
> Ah me, Mother. This same song
1280   of fate has fallen to us both.
> No more for me the light,
> no more the rays of sunlight.
> Woe, woe—
> snowstruck glen of the Phrygians and ridges of Ida
1285   where Priam once cast out a helpless infant—
> took him from his mother for the fate
> of death—Paris, was called after Ida:
1290   he was named Paris of Ida in the Phrygians' town.
> If only Paris, the herder
> raised among the cattle,
> had never lived
> near the clear water,
1295   where run the springs of Nymphs
> and a meadow flourishing
> with green shoots and blossoms
> of roses and hyacinths for goddesses to pick.
1300   There once Pallas came and wily-minded Cypris
> and Hera, with Hermes, Zeus' messenger—
> Cypris delighting in desire,
1305   Pallas in the spear,
> and Hera in the royal bed
> of Zeus the king,
> to be judged in their loathsome contest
> for beauty—but for me, girls, it was death
1310   that brings a name to the men of Greece.

CHORUS:
> Artemis has taken you
> as a first blood sacrifice for Troy.

IPHIGENIA:
> But he who fathered me, his unhappy child,
> Mother, Mother,
> he is gone—he has left me all alone.

Oh my sad fate, I have seen   1315
the bitter, bitter bane of Helen.
I am murdered, I am slain,
by the godless sacrifice of a godless father.
How I wish Aulis had not berthed
the prows of the bronze-beaked ships   1320
in these harbors,
the fleet bound for Troy,
nor Zeus breathed an opposing wind
on Euripus while he sends another,
a favoring breeze to other mortals   1325
to rejoice in their filling sails,
and to some grief, to others constraint,
to some to set sail and others to reach port,
and others to be held back.
Full of sorrow is the race of mortals, full of sorrow.   1330
Men are doomed
to find some misfortune.
Woe, woe.
Great suffering, great sorrows
Tyndareos' daughter caused the Greeks.   1335

CHORUS:
    I pity you for meeting a doom
    you were never meant to meet.

IPHIGENIA:
    Mother, Mother, I see a mob of men coming this way.

CLYTEMNESTRA:
    It's the goddess' son, for whom you were brought here.

IPHIGENIA:
    Open up the house, servants, so I can hide myself.   1340

CLYTEMNESTRA:
    Why are you running away, child?

IPHIGENIA:
                          I'm ashamed to see Achilles.

1316: The word she uses, translated here as "bane of Helen," is the adjective *duselena*, a pun on Helen's name. See note on 1475–76.

CLYTEMNESTRA:
Why is that?

IPHIGENIA:
The failure of my marriage makes me ashamed.

CLYTEMNESTRA:
Stay here. Delicacy plays no part in our present tragedy.
There is no place for prissiness if we can succeed.

(Enter Achilles with soldiers, stage right.)

ACHILLES:
Unhappy woman, daughter of Leda.

CLYTEMNESTRA:
1345   That name fits my fate.

ACHILLES:
Terrible outcries are heard among the Achaeans.

CLYTEMNESTRA:
What is it? Tell me.

ACHILLES:
About your daughter . . .

CLYTEMNESTRA:
What you say makes me shudder.

ACHILLES:
That she must be sacrificed.

CLYTEMNESTRA:
Did no one speak against it?

ACHILLES:
Yes, and I got myself in trouble for it.

CLYTEMNESTRA:
What trouble, stranger?

ACHILLES:
Of being stoned to death.

CLYTEMNESTRA:
1350   Trying to save my daughter?

ACHILLES:
Yes, that was the reason.

CLYTEMNESTRA:

Who would dare to lay hands on you?

ACHILLES:
All the Greeks.

CLYTEMNESTRA:
The army of the Myrmidons—weren't they on your side?

ACHILLES:
They were the first to turn ugly.

CLYTEMNESTRA:

My dear child, we are ruined.

ACHILLES:
They called me a slave to my marriage.

CLYTEMNESTRA:

And what did you say to that?

ACHILLES:
That they must not kill my future bride . . .

CLYTEMNESTRA:

as was right . . .   1355

ACHILLES:
promised to me by her father . . .

CLYTEMNESTRA:

and sent here from Argos.

ACHILLES:
But I was overwhelmed by the outcry.

CLYTEMNESTRA:

A mob can be terrifying.

ACHILLES:
I will still defend you.

CLYTEMNESTRA:
Fight the army by yourself?

ACHILLES:
Do you see these men bearing my armor?

CLYTEMNESTRA:

Bless you for your good intentions.

ACHILLES:
We will beat them.

CLYTEMNESTRA:

1360

Then my child will not be killed.

ACHILLES:
Not with my consent.

CLYTEMNESTRA:

Will someone come to lay hands on her?

ACHILLES:
Ten thousand, with Odysseus in the lead.

CLYTEMNESTRA:

The son of Sisyphus?

ACHILLES:
The very same.

CLYTEMNESTRA:

On his own or is he following orders?

ACHILLES:
He has his orders, but he's glad to do it.

CLYTEMNESTRA:

A cruel choice, to stain his hands with blood.

ACHILLES:
Well, I will hold him back.

CLYTEMNESTRA:

1365

Will he seize her and take her against her will?

ACHILLES:
Yes, and drag her by her yellow hair.

CLYTEMNESTRA:

What must I do, then?

ACHILLES:
Hold onto your daughter.

CLYTEMNESTRA:
And that will keep her from being killed?

ACHILLES:
It will come to this.

IPHIGENIA:
Mother, listen to me.
You are angry at your husband, but what is the use?
There is no way we can fight the inevitable.   1370
We are grateful to the stranger for his desire to help,
but we cannot let him be slandered by the army—you must see
   this—
we gain nothing while he meets an unhappy end.
Listen to what came into my mind as I thought it over.
It is decreed that I am to die and I want to do this   1375
nobly and put out of my mind all that is base.
Look at it with me, Mother, and see how well I speak:
all Greece with all its might now looks to me.
On me depends the crossing of the ships, the Phrygians' fall,
and when we have avenged Helen whom Paris carried off,   1380
we will not allow barbarians to harm our women
anymore, nor steal them from our fertile lands.
All these I will redeem by dying, and my glory
will be blessed, since I will make Greece free.
I should not be too much in love with my life;   1385
you bore me for the common good, not yourself alone.
Ten thousand men are hedged with shields,
ten thousand grasping oars; when their country
suffers wrong they dare to meet the enemy and die
for Greece; will my single life prevent all this?   1390
Would that be right? Would I have a word to say?
We come to this. This man must not go into battle
with all the Greeks and face death for one woman's sake.
One man living is worth ten thousand women's lives.
If the goddess Artemis is determined to take my body,   1395
who am I to oppose her, a mortal against the goddess?
It must not be. I give my body freely for Greece.

1397: Iphigenia claims that she gives herself, becoming the active counter-
part of Helen, who is called the gift of Aphrodite (181).

Sacrifice it. Take Troy. That is my memorial for ages yet to come.
That will be my children, my marriage, and my glory.
1400   It is right for Greeks to rule barbarians, Mother,
not for barbarians to rule Greeks. They are slave, we are free.

CHORUS:
Your words are noble, dear girl, but fate
and the goddess share the same sickness.

ACHILLES:
Daughter of Agamemnon, one of the gods wanted
1405   to make me a happy man, if I were to marry you.
I envy Greece you and you Greece. You have said things
worthy of your country and said them eloquently.
Fighting against a god would only defeat you—
by yielding, you have made a virtue of necessity.
1410   All the more a longing to marry you comes over me
when I see your nature, for you are truly noble.
Look, I still want to help you and take you home as my bride.
Thetis be my witness—it grieves me if I cannot save you
1415   by fighting all the Greeks. Think about it. Death is bad.

IPHIGENIA:
I say these things because I have no more fear.
It is enough that Helen's body will cause
battles and the deaths of men. You, stranger,
do not die for me; do not kill anyone for me.
1420   Allow me if it lies in my power to save Greece.

ACHILLES:
Oh brave spirit, you have made your decision
and left me with nothing more to say about it.
Your mind is noble. A truer word I cannot say.
But still you might have a change of heart
1425   [that you may understand what I have said].
I will go and put these weapons near the altar.
I will not allow you to die and will prevent it.
You might even come to want what I promise
when you see the sword approach your neck.

1421–32: Various parts of this speech have been suggested for deletion as
redundant or contradictory. Line 1425 seems added as an explanation.

I will not permit you to die, then, from rashness,　　　　　　1430
but I will go with these arms to the temple
of the goddess and watch for your coming.

(Exit Achilles stage right.)

IPHIGENIA:
Mother, why are your eyes moist with silent tears?

CLYTEMNESTRA:
As a grieving mother I have cause to be pained at heart.

IPHIGENIA:
Stop, Mother. Don't make me a coward, but be convinced.　　1435

CLYTEMNESTRA:
Tell me. I do not want to cause you grief, my child.

IPHIGENIA:
Then do not cut your hair in grief
nor put on black clothes in mourning.

CLYTEMNESTRA:
Why not, my child, when I have lost you?

IPHIGENIA:
I shall be saved and through me you will have glory.　　　　1440

CLYTEMNESTRA:
What do you mean? Am I not to mourn your life?

IPHIGENIA:
No, since no mound will be raised for me.

CLYTEMNESTRA:
Why not? If you are dead, a mound is customary.

IPHIGENIA:
The altar of the goddess, Zeus' daughter, will be my memorial.

CLYTEMNESTRA:
My child, what you say is brave and I believe you.　　　　　1445

IPHIGENIA:
How lucky I am as the benefactress of Greece.

CLYTEMNESTRA:
What shall I say to your sisters?

IPHIGENIA:
Do not dress them in black clothes.

CLYTEMNESTRA:
What word of love may I bring the girls?

IPHIGENIA:
1450   Tell them good-bye. And raise Orestes to manhood for me.

CLYTEMNESTRA:
Take him in your arms. This is the last time you will see
him.

IPHIGENIA:
Dearest one, you helped me as much as you could.

CLYTEMNESTRA:
Is there any favor I can do for you in Argos?

IPHIGENIA:
Do not hate my father, your husband.

CLYTEMNESTRA:
1455   He will have an agonizing struggle to face.

IPHIGENIA:
It is against his will that he will kill me.

CLYTEMNESTRA:
Not so, but by deceit. A vicious act, unworthy of Atreus.

IPHIGENIA:
Who will come to take me before I am seized by the hair?

CLYTEMNESTRA:
I will go with you—

IPHIGENIA:
1460   No, not you. That is not a good idea—

CLYTEMNESTRA:
and hold onto your robes.

IPHIGENIA:
                    Please, listen to me, Mother.
Stay here. It is better this way for me; for you, too.
Let one of Father's attendants escort me
to the meadow of Artemis where I will be sacrificed.

CLYTEMNESTRA:
  My child, you are gone.

IPHIGENIA:
                    And I will not come back.   1465

CLYTEMNESTRA:
  Will you leave your mother?

IPHIGENIA:
                    Yes, as you see, not worthily.

CLYTEMNESTRA:
  Wait! Stop! Do not leave me.

IPHIGENIA:
                    I will not let you shed tears.
  Young women, celebrate the goddess Artemis,
  daughter of Zeus, in a hymn for my passing.
  Let the solemn blessing go out among the Greeks.
  Someone, begin the ritual, casting grain from the baskets;   1470
  let the fire burn bright with purifying barley.
  Let my father stand on the right of the altar. I go now
  to bring the salvation of victory to the Greeks.

        (Iphigenia begins her slow exit stage right, singing.)

  Lead me away,   1475
  the sacker of Ilium and the Trojans.
  Bring a woven crown
  to put on my hair
  and water for washing.
  Begin the dance whirling about the temple   1480
  and altar of Artemis,
  Artemis the queen,
  the blessed goddess.
  With my sacrificial blood   1485
  I will wash away her oracle.
  Mother, revered Mother, we shed

1475–76: "Sacker of Ilium"—Iphigenia calls herself by the epithet *heleptolis*, literally, "city-destroyer," a term Aeschylus invented for Helen (as a pun on Helen's name at *Agamemnon* 689, as if the first three letters of Helen's name were the same as the root *hel-*, "to destroy").

no tears for you:
1490   they do not suit these rites.
Oh girls,
sing to Artemis along with me,
living across from Calchis,
where the spears are eager for war,
1495   held here in my name
in the narrow anchorage of Aulis.
O earth mother, O ancient Argos
and my Mycenaean home.

CHORUS:
1500   You call on the fortress of Perseus,
labor of Cyclopean hands?

IPHIGENIA:
You reared me to be a light for Hellas.
I do not refuse to die.

CHORUS:
Your glory will not leave you.

IPHIGENIA:
1505   Oh, oh,
day of my wedding torch
and light of Zeus, another and another
age and fate we will live.
Farewell, dear light.

CHORUS:
Oh, oh,
1510   behold her, the sacker
of Ilium and the Trojans,
going away, upon her head a crown;
she casts the lustral waters
on the altar of the goddess
1515   with drops of blood
staining her beautiful neck
at her slaughter. Dewy streams,
ancestral waters await you
and the army of Achaeans eager
1520   to sail to the city of Troy.
Let us celebrate Artemis

queen of gods as for a happy fate.
Oh holy, holy goddess, happy
in human sacrifice,
conduct the army of the Hellenes
into the Phrygians' land   1525
and to the treacherous Trojans.
And grant that by the spear
Agamemnon may put on his head   1530
a most glorious crown for Greece,
glory never to be forgotten.

(The chorus files out stage left with this song.)

[Epilogue]

(Enter Messenger, running, stage right.)

[MESSENGER 2:
   Daughter of Tyndareos, Clytemnestra, come out,
   come out of the house and hear my story.

CLYTEMNESTRA:
   I heard your cry and have come out here
   frightened out of my wits with terror   1535
   that you are here to bring me another,
   new tragedy on top of the one I have suffered.

MESSENGER 2:
                                 About your daughter
   I want to tell you strange and marvelous things.

The chorus files out: Stage left, if they are thought of as returning home, or
if they accompany Iphigenia, they would exit stage right. I prefer the lonely
departure of Iphigenia. Most editors believe the epilogue is spurious. But it
is part of one of the versions and a director might well choose to stage it,
in which case the chorus does not file out until the end of the messenger
scene.

Epilogue (1533–end): For reasons of style, taste, literary structure, and
dramatic convention, this section has been condemned by most critics. It
may have been added to bring this play into line with the earlier *Iphigenia
among the Taurians,* in which Iphigenia survives her sacrifice to serve at the
temple of Artemis in the faraway land of the Taurians.

CLYTEMNESTRA:
Do not delay, but tell them as fast as you can.

MESSENGER 2:
1540 My dear mistress, you will have a clear account
of everything, from beginning to end, unless my memory
fails me and my tongue garbles my story.
When we reached the grove of Zeus' daughter
Artemis and her flowered grasslands,
1545 where the whole Greek army had gathered
with your daughter in tow, at once the crowd
of Achaeans gathered around. When Agamemnon,
our king, saw his daughter walking into the grove
for slaughter, he cried aloud, turned his face away,
1550 and wept, covering his head with his cloak.
And she, standing next to her father, said,
"Father, I am here for you. My body
I give for my fatherland and for the whole
1555 land of Greece to put upon the altar
of the goddess and sacrifice, if that is god's will.
I pray you prosper as far as it depends on me,
meet with the gift of victory, and return home.
Besides this, no one of the Argives touch me—
1560 in silence I will present my throat with a brave heart."
She said this and everyone who heard it was amazed
at the courage and goodness of the girl.
Talthybius standing in their midst—that was his job—
called for respectful silence from the army.
1565 Then onto a gold-studded tray Calchas the seer
placed a sharp knife that he had drawn out
of its case, and he crowned the girl's head.
The son of Peleus, taking the tray, sprinkled
the holy waters in a circle around the altar.
1570 And he said, "Daughter of Zeus, animal killer,
spinning your bright light in the nighttime,
receive this sacrifice that we offer you,
the army of the Greeks and King Agamemnon,
unstained blood from a virgin's throat,
1575 and grant that the sailing of the ships be safe
and that we take the Trojans' land with the spear."
The sons of Atreus and the whole army stood watching.

The priest, taking up the knife, made a prayer
and looked at her throat for the place to strike.
Wave upon wave of grief came into my heart; I stood   1580
with my head down. Then something amazing happened:
everyone clearly heard the sound of the blow, but the girl—
no one could see where in the world she had gone.
The priest cried out, and the whole army reverberated,
seeing a sudden miracle from one of the gods,   1585
which, even though we saw it, was hard to credit.
For there lay panting on the ground a hind
of magnificent size and beauty, a sight to behold,
and the altar of the goddess was stained with blood.
At this Calchas—imagine his joy—said,   1590
"Lords of the united Greek army,
do you see this sacrifice that the goddess
has placed on the altar, a mountain-roaming hind?
She very much prefers this to the girl's life
so that her altar will not be polluted with noble blood.   1595
She has gladly received this and grants us
a fair sailing and incursion into Ilium.
Every sailor, then, take courage from this
and go to the ships, since on this day we must leave
the deep recesses of Aulis and cross over   1600
the Aegean Sea." But when the entire victim
was turned into ashes in Hephaestus' flame,
he prayed for the army's return, as was right.
Agamemnon sent me here to tell you this
and to inform you of the fate she has from the gods.   1605
She has reached undying glory throughout Greece.
I was there and saw the deed and can say that
your daughter has flown away to the gods.
Give up your grief and your anger at your husband.
The works of the gods come unexpected to men;   1610
they preserve those they love. This day has seen
your daughter dead and seeing the light of life.

   (Exit Messenger stage right.)

1611: Less common than the expression "He whom the gods love dies
young."

CHORUS:
How happy I am to have heard the messenger—
he says your child is alive and lives among the gods.

CLYTEMNESTRA:
1615   My child, by which of the gods were you stolen?
How do I address you? How can I be sure that
these words are not a vain consolation
to make me give up my mourning for you?

CHORUS:
Here comes King Agamemnon
1620   to tell you the same story.

(Enter Agamemnon stage right.)

AGAMEMNON:
Woman, we should be happy for our daughter;
she really is in the company of the gods.
You must take this young whelp and go
home. The army is preparing to sail.
1625   Farewell. It will be a long time before I address you
when I come home from Troy. May all go well for you.

(Exit Agamemnon stage right.)

CHORUS:
Son of Atreus, go rejoicing to the Phrygian land
and return rejoicing
with the finest spoils from Troy.]

(Exit the chorus stage left.)

−END−

Select Bibliography

Works on Greek Tragedy and the Greek Theater

Arnott, Peter D. *Public and Performance in the Greek Theatre*. London: Routledge, 1989.

Bieber, Margarete. *The History of the Greek and Roman Theatre*. Princeton, NJ: Princeton University Press, 1961.

Csapo, E., and W. J. Slater. *The Context of Ancient Drama*. Ann Arbor: University of Michigan Press, 1995.

Easterling, P. E., ed. *The Cambridge Companion to Greek Tragedy*. Cambridge: Cambridge University Press, 1997.

Foley, Helene. *Female Acts in Greek Tragedy*. Princeton, NJ: Princeton University Press, 2001.

Garner, Richard. *From Homer to Tragedy: The Art of Allusion in Greek Poetry*. London: Routledge, 1990.

Gregory, Justina, ed. *A Companion to Greek Tragedy*. Malden, MA: Blackwell, 2005.

Loraux, Nicole. *Tragic Ways of Killing a Woman*. Translated by Anthony Forster. Cambridge, MA: Harvard University Press, 1987.

Mastronarde, Donald J. *Contact and Discontinuity: Some Conventions of Speech and Action on the Greek Stage*. Berkeley: University of California Press, 1979.

———. "Actors on High: The Skene Roof, the Crane, and the Gods in Attic Drama," *Classical Antiquity* 9.2 (1990): 247–94.

Pickard-Cambridge, A. W. *The Dramatic Festivals of Athens*. 2nd rev. ed. Oxford: Clarendon, 2003.

Rehm, Rush. *Greek Tragic Theatre*. London: Routledge, 1992.

Segal, Charles. *Interpreting Greek Tragedy: Myth, Poetry, Text*. Ithaca, NY: Cornell University Press, 1986.

Taplin, Oliver. *Greek Tragedy in Action*. Berkeley: University of California Press, 1978.

Walton, J. Michael. *Greek Theatre Practice*. Westport, CT: Greenwood Press, 1980.

———. *The Greek Sense of Theatre*. London: Methuen, 1984.

————. *Greek Living Theatre: A Handbook of Classical Performance and Modern Production*. New York: Greenwood Press, 1987.

Wiles, David. *Greek Theatre Performance*. Cambridge: Cambridge University Press, 2000.

Winkler, John J., and Froma I. Zeitlin, eds. *Nothing to Do with Dionysos?* Princeton, NJ: Princeton University Press, 1990.

Texts, Commentaries, Translations, and Textual Helps

Arrowsmith, William. *The Bacchae*. Vol. 5 of *Euripides,* edited by David Grene and Richmond Lattimore. Chicago: University of Chicago Press, 1959.

Bagg, Robert. *The* Bakkai *of Euripides*. Amherst: University of Massachusetts Press, 1978.

Burian, Peter, and Brian Swann. *Euripides:* The Phoenician Women. Oxford: Oxford University Press, 1981.

Coffey, Michael, and Roland Mayer. *Seneca Phaedra*. Cambridge: Cambridge University Press, 1990.

Craik, Elizabeth. *Euripides:* Phoenician Women. Warminster, UK: Aris and Phillips, 1988.

Cropp, M. J. *Euripides:* Elektra. *With Translation and Commentary*. Warminster, UK: Aris and Phillips, 1988.

Denniston, J. D. *Euripides:* Electra. *With Introduction and Commentary*. Oxford: Oxford University Press, 1939.

Diggle, James. *Euripidis Fabulae*. Vols. 2, 3. Oxford: Clarendon, 1981, 1994.

Dodds, E. R. *Euripides:* Bacchae. 2nd ed. Oxford: Oxford University Press, 1960.

England, E. B. *The* Iphigenia at Aulis *of Euripides*. London: Macmillan, 1891; New York: Arno, 1979.

Esposito, Stephen J. *Euripides'* Bacchae. Newburyport, MA: Focus Publishing/Ron Pullins, 1998.

Fagles, Robert. *Aeschylus:* The Oresteia. New York: Viking Penguin, 1975.

Kirk, Geoffrey S. *The* Bacchae *of Euripides. Translated with an Introduction and Commentary*. Cambridge: Cambridge University Press, 1970, 1979.

Mastronarde, Donald J. *Euripides:* Phoenissae. *Edited with Introduction and Commentary*. Cambridge: Cambridge University Press, 1994.

Meineck, Peter. *Aeschylus:* Oresteia. Indianapolis: Hackett, 1998.

Meineck, Peter, Cecelia Eaton Luschnig, and Paul Woodruff. *The Electra Plays*. Indianapolis: Hackett, 2009.

Meineck, Peter, and Paul Woodruff. *Sophocles: Theban Plays*. Indianapolis: Hackett, 2003.

Murray, Gilbert. *Euripides: Bacchae*. New York: Longmans Green, 1900.

———. *Euripidis Fabulae*. Vols. 2, 3. Oxford: Clarendon Press, 1913.

Paley, F. A. *Euripides. With an English Commentary*. Vol. 2. London: Whittaker, 1874.

Roisman, H. M., and C. A. E. Luschnig. *Euripides' Electra*. Norman: University of Oklahoma Press, 2011.

Roux, Jeanne. *Euripide: Les Bacchantes*. 2 vols. Paris: Les Belles Lettres, 1970.

Schwartz, Eduard. *Scholia in Euripidem*. Berlin: Reimer, 1887; Berlin: Walter de Gruyter, 1966.

Seaford, Richard. *Euripides' Bacchae. With an Introduction, Translation and Commentary*. Warminster, UK: Aris and Phillips, 1996.

Williams, C. K. *The Bacchae of Euripides: A New Version*. New York: Farrar, Strauss and Giroux, 1990.

Woodruff, Paul. *Euripides: Bacchae. Translated, with an Introduction and Notes*. Indianapolis: Hackett, 1998.

Studies

Altena, Herman. "Text and Performance: On Significant Actions in Euripides' *Phoenissae*." In Cropp et al., *Euripides and Tragic Theatre* (1999–2000), 303–23.

Arnott, W. G. "Double the Vision: A Reading of Euripides' *Electra*." *Greece & Rome* 28 (1981): 179–92.

Arrowsmith, William. "A Greek Theater of Ideas." *Arion* 2, no. 3 (1963): 32–56.

Arthur, Marilyn. "The Choral Odes of the *Bacchae* of Euripides." *Yale Classical Studies* 22 (1972): 145–79.

———. "The Curse of Civilization: The Choral Odes of the *Phoenissae*." *Harvard Studies in Classical Philology* 81 (1977): 163–85.

Baldry, H. C. "The Dramatization of the Theban Legend." *Greece & Rome* 3 (1956): 24–37.

Barlow, Shirley A. *The Imagery of Euripides*. Bristol, UK: Bristol Classical Press, 1986.

Burgess, Dana. "The Authenticity of the Teichoscopia of Euripides' *Phoenissae*." *Classical Journal* 83 (1978): 103–13.

Burkert, Walter. *Greek Religion.* Translated by John Raffian. Cambridge, MA: Harvard University Press, 1985.

Conacher, D. J. *Euripidean Drama: Myth, Theme, and Structure.* Toronto: University of Toronto Press, 1967.

Cribiore, Raffaella. "The Grammarian's Choice: The Popularity of Euripides' *Phoenissae* in Hellenistic and Roman Education." In *Education in Greek and Roman Antiquity,* edited by Yun Lee Too, 241–60. Leiden, Netherlands: Brill, 2001.

Cropp, Martin, Kevin Lee, and David Sansone. *Euripides and Tragic Theatre in the Late Fifth Century. Illinois Classical Studies* 24–25 (1999–2000). Champaign, IL: Stipes.

de Jong, I. J. F. "Three Off-Stage Characters in Euripides." *Mnemosyne,* 4th ser., 43 (1990): 1–21.

Demand, Nancy. *Thebes in the Fifth Century.* London: Routledge and Kegan Paul, 1982.

Dodds, E. R. *The Greeks and the Irrational.* Berkeley: University of California Press, 1951.

Fisher, Raymond K. "The 'Palace Miracles' in Euripides' *Bacchae." American Journal of Philology* 113 (1992): 179–88.

Foley, Helene P. "The Masque of Dionysus." *Transactions of the American Philological Association* 110 (1980): 107–33.

———. *Ritual Irony.* Ithaca, NY: Cornell University Press, 1985.

Gellie, George. "Tragedy and Euripides' *Electra." Bulletin of the Institute of Classical Studies* 28 (1981): 1–12.

Gibert, J. "Change of Mind in Greek Tragedy." *Hypomnemata* 108 (1995): 31–54.

Goff, Barbara E. "The Shields of *Phoenissae." Greek, Roman, and Byzantine Studies* 29 (1988): 135–52.

———. "The Sign of the Fall: The Scars of Orestes and Odysseus." *Classical Antiquity* 10 (1991): 259–67.

Gregory, Justina. "Comic Elements in Euripides." In Cropp et al., *Euripides and Tragic Theatre* (1999–2000), 59–74.

———. Introduction to Meineck et al., *The Electra Plays* (2009), vi–xxxii.

Gurd, Sean Alexander. *Iphigenias at Aulis: Textual Multiplicity, Radical Philology.* Ithaca, NY: Cornell University Press, 2005.

Halporn, J. W. "The Skeptical Electra." *Harvard Studies in Classical Philology* 87 (1983): 101–18.

Hammond, N. G. L. "Spectacle and Parody in Euripides' *Electra." Greek, Roman, and Byzantine Studies* 25 (1984): 373–87.

Hartigan, K. V. *Ambiguity and Self-Deception: The Apollo and Artemis Plays of Euripides.* Frankfurt am Main: Peter Lang, 1991.

Henrichs, Albert. "Male Intruders among the Maenads: The So-Called Male Celebrant." In *Mnemai: Classical Studies in Memory of Karl K. Hulley,* edited by Harold D. Evjen, 69–92. Chico: California Scholars Press, 1984.

———. "The Last of the Detractors: Friedrich Nietzsche's Condemnation of Euripides." *Greek, Roman, and Byzantine Studies* 27 (1986): 369–97.

———. "Between Country and City: Cultic Dimensions of Dionysus in Athens and Attica." In *Cabinet of Muses: Essays on Classical and Comparative Literature in Honor of Thomas G. Rosenmeyer,* edited by M. Griffith and D. J. Mastronarde, 257–77. Atlanta: Scholars Press, 1990.

———. "He Has a God in Him: Human and Divine in the Modern Perception of Dionysus." In *Masks of Dionysus,* edited by Thomas H. Carpenter and Christopher A. Faraone, 13–43. Ithaca, NY: Cornell University Press, 1993.

Jones, John. *On Aristotle and Greek Tragedy.* Oxford: Oxford University Press, 1962.

Jouan, F. *Euripide et les légendes des chants Cypriens: Des origines de la guerre de Troie à l'Iliade.* Paris: Les Belles Lettres, 1966, 2009.

King, K. C. "The Force of Tradition: The Achilles Ode in Euripides' *Electra.*" *Transactions and Proceedings of the American Philological Association* 110 (1980): 195–212.

Kitto, H. D. F. "The Final Scenes of the *Phoenissae.*" *Classical Review* 53 (1939): 104–11.

Knox, B. M. W. "Second Thoughts in Greek Tragedy." *Greek, Roman, and Byzantine Studies* 7 (1966): 213–32. Reprinted in *Word and Action* (1979), 231–49.

———. "Euripides' *Iphigenia in Aulide* 1–164 (in that order)." *Yale Classical Studies* 22 (1972): 239–61. Reprinted in *Word and Action* (1979), 275–94.

———. "Euripidean Comedy." In *Word and Action: Essays on the Ancient Theater,* 250–75. Baltimore: Johns Hopkins University Press, 1979.

Kovacs, David. "Toward a Reconstruction of *Iphigenia Aulidensis.*" *Journal of Hellenic Studies* 123 (2003): 77–103.

Kubo, M. "The Norm of Myth: Euripides' *Electra.*" *Harvard Studies in Classical Philology* 71 (1966): 15–31.

Leinieks, Valdis. *The City of Dionysos: A Study of Euripides' Bakchai.* Stuttgart: Teubner, 1996.

Lloyd, M. "Realism and Character in Euripides' *Electra*." *Phoenix* 40 (1986): 1–19.

Luschnig, C. A. E. "Time and Memory in Euripides' *Iphigenia at Aulis*." *Ramus* 11 (1982): 99–104.

———. *Tragic Aporia: A Study of Euripides'* Iphigenia at Aulis. Berwick, Australia: Aureal, 1988.

———. *The Gorgon's Severed Head: Studies of* Alcestis, Electra, *and* Phoenissae. Leiden: Brill, 1995.

Marshall, C. W. "Theatrical Reference in Euripides' *Electra*." In Cropp et al., *Euripides and Tragic Theatre* (1999–2000), 325–41.

Mastronarde, Donald J., and Jan Maarten Bremer. *The Textual Tradition of Euripides'* Phoinissai. University of California Classical Studies 27. Berkeley: University of California Press, 1982.

Mellert-Hoffmann, G. *Untersuchungen zur 'Iphigenie in Aulis des Euripides.'* Heidelberg: Carl Winter, 1969.

Meltzer, Gary S. *Euripides and the Poetics of Nostalgia.* Cambridge: Cambridge University Press, 2006.

Meredith, H. O. "The End of the *Phoenissae*." *Classical Review* 51 (1937): 97–103.

Michelakis, Pantelis. *Euripides:* Iphigenia at Aulis. London: Duckworth, 2006.

Michelini, Ann Norris. *Euripides and the Tragic Tradition.* Madison: University of Wisconsin Press, 1987.

———. "The Expansion of Myth in Late Euripides: *Iphigenia at Aulis*." In Cropp et al., *Euripides and Tragic Theatre* (1999–2000), 41–59.

Morwood, J. H. W. "The Pattern of the Euripides *Electra*." *American Journal of Philology* 102 (1981): 362–70.

Murray, Gilbert. *Euripides and His Age.* London: Home University Library, 1913; Oxford: Oxford University Press, 1965.

Nussbaum, Martha. Introduction to Williams, *The* Bacchae *of Euripides* (1990), vii–xlvii.

O'Brien, M. J. "Orestes and the Gorgon: Euripides' *Electra*." *American Journal of Philology* 85 (1964): 13–39.

O'Connor-Visser. *Aspects of Human Sacrifice in the Tragedies of Euripides.* Amsterdam: B. R. Gruner, 1987.

Oranje, Hans. *Euripides'* Bacchae: The Play and Its Audience. Leiden, Netherlands: Brill, 1984.

Page, Denys. *Actors' Interpolations in Greek Tragedy.* Oxford: Clarendon, 1934.

Papadopoulou, Thalia. *Euripides:* Phoenician Women. London: Duckworth, 2008.

Podlecki, Anthony J. "Some Themes in Euripides' *Phoenissae.*" *Transactions of the American Philological Association* 93 (1962): 355–73.

Prag, A. J. N. W. *The Oresteia: Iconographic and Narrative Tradition.* Chicago: Bolchazy Carducci, 1985.

Rabinowitz, Nancy Sorkin. "The Strategy of Inconsistency in Euripides' *Iphigenia at Aulis.*" *Classical Bulletin* 59 (1983): 21–26.

———. *Anxiety Veiled: Euripides and the Traffic in Women.* Ithaca: Cornell University Press, 1993.

Rawson, Elizabeth, "Family and Fatherland in Euripides' *Phoenissae.*" *Greek, Roman, and Byzantine Studies* 11 (1970): 109–27.

Ronnet, G. "Réflexions sur la date des deux *Électre.*" *Revue des études greques* 83 (1970): 309–32.

Rosenmeyer, Thomas G. *The Masks of Tragedy: Essays on Six Greek Dramas.* Austin: University of Texas Press, 1963; New York: Gordian, 1971.

Rosivach, V. J. "The 'Golden Lamb' Ode in Euripides' *Electra.*" *Classical Philology* 73 (1978): 189–99.

Sale, William. *Existentialism and Euripides: Sickness, Tragedy, and Divinity in the* Medea, *the* Hippolytus *and the* Bacchae. Berwick, Australia: Aureal, 1977.

Sansone, D. "Iphigenia Changes Her Mind." *Illinois Classical Studies* 16 (1991): 161–72.

Schlegel, A. W. "Comparison between the *Choephoroe* of Aeschylus, the *Electra* of Sophocles and That of Euripides." Lecture 9 in *A Course of Lectures on Dramatic Art and Literature* (1833). Translated by J. Black and edited by A. J. W. Morrison. London: N. G. Bohn, 1946.

Seaford, Richard. *Reciprocity and Ritual: Homer and Tragedy in the Developing City-State.* Oxford: Clarendon, 1994.

———. *Dionysos.* New York: Routledge, 2006.

Segal, Charles P. *Dionysiac Poetics and Euripides'* Bacchae. Princeton, NJ: Princeton University Press, 1982; expanded ed. 1997.

———. "Tragedy, Corporeality, and the Texture of Language: Matricide in the Three Electra Plays." *Classical World* 79 (1985): 7–23.

———. *Interpreting Greek Tragedy: Myth, Poetry, Text.* Ithaca: Cornell University Press, 1986.

Seidensticker, Bernd. "Comic Elements in Euripides' *Bacchae.*" *American Journal of Philology* 99 (1978): 303–20.

Siegel, H. "Self-Delusion and Volte-Face of Iphigenia in Euripides' *Iphigenia at Aulis.*" *Hermes* 108 (1980): 300–321.

Solmsen, F. "Electra and Orestes: Three Recognitions in Greek Tragedy." In *Kleine Schriften* 3, 32–63. Hildesheim, Germany: G. Olms, 1982.

Originally appeared in *Mededelingen der Koninklijke Nederlandse Akademie van Wetenschappen* 30, no. 2 (1967): 31–62.

Sorum, C. E. "Myth, Choice, and Meaning in Euripides' *Iphigenia at Aulis*." *American Journal of Philology* 113 (1992): 527–42.

Tarkow, T. "The Scar of Orestes." *Rheinische Museum* 124 (1981): 143–53.

Thury, E. M. "Euripides' *Electra*: An Analysis through Character Development." *Rheinische Museum* 128 (1985): 5–22.

Vellacott, Philip. *Ironic Drama: A Study of Euripides' Method and Meaning.* Cambridge: Cambridge University Press, 1975.

Verrall, A. W. *Euripides the Rationalist.* Cambridge: Cambridge University Press, 1895.

——. *The Bacchants of Euripides and Other Essays.* Cambridge: Cambridge University Press, 1910.

Walsh, G. B. "The First Stasimon of Euripides' *Electra*." *Yale Classical Studies* 25 (1977): 277–89.

Webster, T. B. L. "Three Plays by Euripides." In *The Classical Tradition: Literary and Historical Studies in Honor of Harry Caplan,* edited by Luitpold Wallach, 83–97. Ithaca, NY: Cornell University Press, 1966.

——. "Euripides: Traditionalist and Innovator." In *The Poetic Tradition: Essays on Greek, Latin, and English Poetry,* edited by D. C. Allen and H. T. Rowell, 27–43. Baltimore: Johns Hopkins University Press, 1968.

Willink, C. "Some Problems of Text and Interpretation in the *Bacchae*." *Classical Review,* N.S. 16 (1966): 27–50, 220–42.

——. "The Prologue of *Iphigenia at Aulis*." *Classical Quarterly* 21 (1971): 343–64.

Winnington-Ingram, R. P. *Euripides and Dionysus: An Interpretation of the Bacchae.* Cambridge: Cambridge University Press, 1948; Bristol, UK: Bristol Classical Press, 1998.

Woodruff, Paul. "Justice in Translation: Rendering Ancient Greek Tragedy." In Gregory, *Companion to Greek Tragedy* (2005), 490–504.

——. *The Necessity of Theater: The Art of Watching and Being Watched.* New York: Oxford University Press, 2008.

Zeitlin, Froma I. "The Argive Festival of Hera and Euripides' *Electra*." *Transactions and Proceedings of the American Philological Association* 101 (1970): 645–69.

——. "Thebes: Theater of Self and Society in Athenian Drama." In Winkler and Zeitlin, *Nothing to Do with Dionysos?* (1990), 130–67.

Zuntz, G. *The Political Plays of Euripides.* Manchester, UK: University of Manchester Press, 1955.